Cambridge Imperial and Post-Colonial Studies

The Cambridge Imperial and Post-Colonial Studies series is a well-established collection of over 100 volumes focussing on empires in world history and on the societies and cultures that emerged from, and challenged, colonial rule. The collection includes transnational, comparative and connective studies, as well as works addressing the ways in which particular regions or nations interact with global forces. In its formative years, the series focused on the British Empire and Commonwealth, but there is now no imperial system, period of human history or part of the world that lies outside of its compass. While we particularly welcome the first monographs of young researchers, we also seek major studies by more senior scholars, and welcome collections of essays with a strong thematic focus that help to set new research agendas. As well as history, the series includes work on politics, economics, culture, archaeology, literature, science, art, medicine, and war. Our aim is to collect the most exciting new scholarship on world history and to make this available to a broad scholarly readership in a timely manner.

More information about this series at
http://www.palgrave.com/gp/series/13937

Haruki Inagaki

The Rule of Law and Emergency in Colonial India

Judicial Politics in the Early Nineteenth Century

palgrave
macmillan

Haruki Inagaki
Aoyama Gakuin University
Tokyo, Japan

ISSN 2635-1633 ISSN 2635-1641 (electronic)
Cambridge Imperial and Post-Colonial Studies
ISBN 978-3-030-73665-1 ISBN 978-3-030-73663-7 (eBook)
https://doi.org/10.1007/978-3-030-73663-7

This Palgrave Macmillan imprint is published by the registered company Springer Nature Switzerland AG.
The registered company address is: Gewerbestrasse 11, 6330 Cham, Switzerland

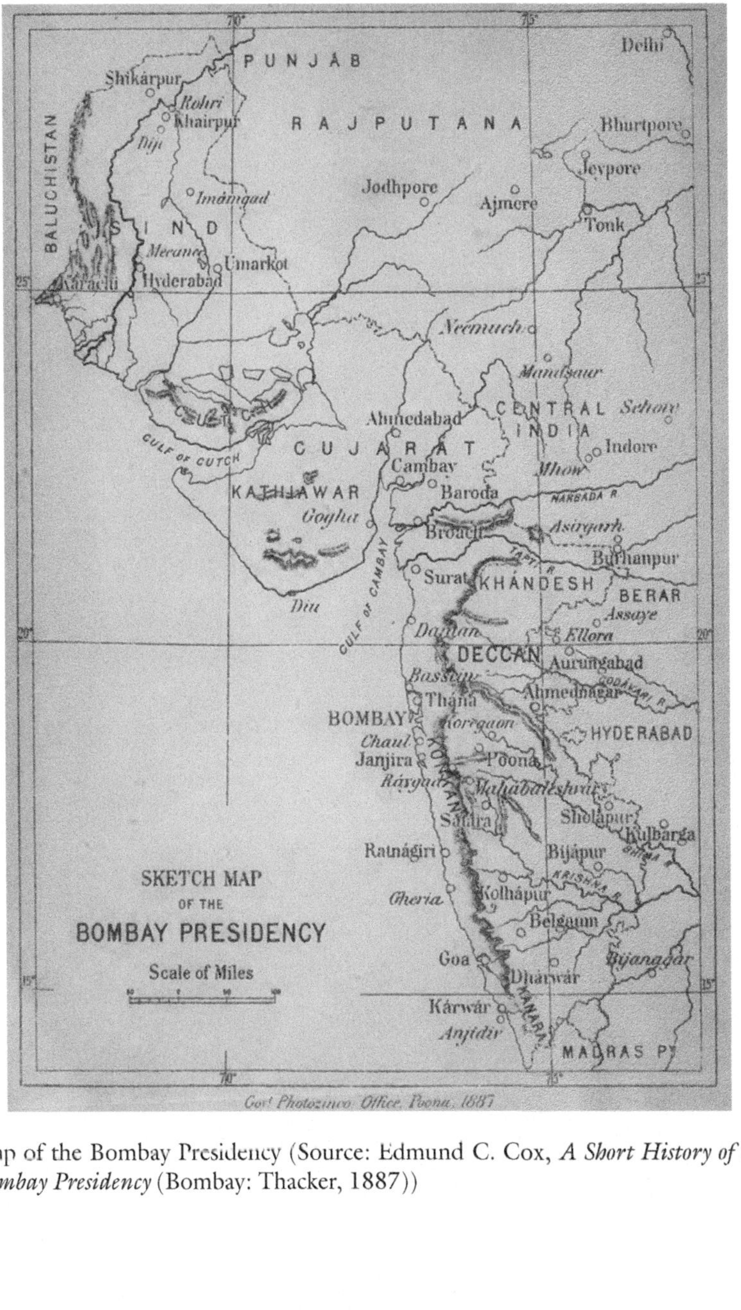

Map of the Bombay Presidency (Source: Edmund C. Cox, *A Short History of the Bombay Presidency* (Bombay: Thacker, 1887))

To Akiko, Saki and Lisa

Acknowledgements

This work is supported by the following scholarships and research grants: JSPS Kakenhi (17H06986 (2017–19), 20K13217 (2020–23)), Japan Student Services Organisation (2012–2015), King's College London (2014, 2015), Royal Historical Society (2015), Suntory Foundation (2017) and Resona Foundation (2017–2018).

My special thanks go to librarians, archivists and staff members of the libraries and archives in the United Kingdom, India and Japan. To Jon Wilson, Margot Finn, the late David Washbrook and anonymous reviewers, whose comments were invaluable to develop ideas discussed in this book. To Sugiko Nishikawa, Kazuhiko Kondo and Hiroki Shin for their continuous support and encouragement. To colleagues and students at Tokyo Metropolitan University and Aoyama Gakuin University for their stimulating conversation.

To my family Akiko, Saki and Lisa for their love. They always kept me happy and made me smile, which was the power to endure the hardships of this COVID-19 pandemic and bring this book into being. It is to them that this book is dedicated.

Praise for *The Rule of Law and Emergency in Colonial India*

"Inagaki's methodical study demonstrates how the Company's disputes and eventual subjugation of the independent King's Court in Bombay embedded the logic of state necessity and perpetual emergency into the governing fabric of the British colonial regime. In so doing, it offers a compelling and important new insight into how colonial rule privileged security and political order over the rule of law."

—Mark Condos, Lecturer, *King's College London, UK*

"Britain's empire did not arrive fully formed in India. Haruki Inagaki's superbly-researched, well-argued book traces its emergence in a proliferating set of arguments between different groups of British officers, who variously fought with and co-opted Indian elites. It traces the debates which raged amongst British officers about the character of Britain's presence in India during the early nineteenth century, in doing so unravelling the fractured, debated character of the imperial enterprise itself. British India's Imperial constitution was, he argues, forged within the opposition between radically different logics of power. Inagaki's book offers a compelling account of the real life of empire in motion. A vital contribution to the burgeoning field of imperial legal history, it speaks well beyond narrow thematic categories, and is vital reading for anyone interested in the history of empire more broadly and the Indian subcontinent."

—Jon Wilson, Professor, *King's College London, UK*

Contents

List of Tables

CHAPTER 1

Law and Emergency: Two Logics of Colonial Governance

For the British East India Company (EIC) in the early nineteenth century, a top priority was the reform of judicial administration. This is not because its own court of law was inefficient (though it was), but because the EIC was greatly annoyed with another judiciary that lay outside its control. This court, the King's Court, assumed not only legal but political authority independent from the EIC. The court was used to challenge the EIC by the Indian inhabitants of presidency towns of Calcutta, Madras and Bombay and those who lived in the vast inner provinces (the mofussil). The EIC's officials considered this practice dangerous to the very existence of the empire in India. The British rule in the newly conquered territories was always highly unstable, relying heavily on local rulers. The very existence of the King's Court was conceived as a threat to the EIC's position as the sovereign of the subcontinent. The EIC prioritised the post-war settlements after successive wars of conquest, but the King's Court was becoming a rallying point for discontented Indians.

The crisis reached a climax in a legal dispute in Bombay in 1828. The King's Court of Bombay issued a writ of habeas corpus to a nobleman of the former Maratha empire. This was an outright subversion of the Bombay government's policy of conciliating local rulers to securely govern the newly conquered territories. The government ordered the court to halt the proceedings. This led to an open collision between the two British authorities that was to persist for more than two years. John

H. Inagaki, *The Rule of Law and Emergency in Colonial India*, Cambridge Imperial and Post-Colonial Studies,
https://doi.org/10.1007/978-3-030-73663-7_1

Malcolm, the Governor of Bombay at that time, considered the situation so dire that he feared that the empire was on the brink of collapse:

> Our physical power in this country (as European nation) is nothing. We stand solely upon that of opinion and above all that which attached to a belief of our complete union amongst ourselves & our consequent means of prompt combination to crush any opposition of unsupported princes or divided tribes & nations. .... If an impression is once given that we are divided, as it must be if a collision of British authorities is apparent to the natives of our provinces, the latter ignorant and incapable of comprehending our system of law, its forms and its fictions will see nothing in the clashing of the warrants and writs of the Supreme Court with the rules and orders of the local government, but a struggle for power of the extent of which they are uninformed but which will be alike magnified by the fears of those who look for our support and the hopes of those who anticipate our downfall. In the progress of such impressions, I repeat my opinion that there is more danger than in the defeat of our armies or the loss of provinces. Such misfortune may be recovered, but the charm of opinion and above all that which rests upon the supposed union and concord of the different branches of our rule, if once broken will never be redeemed.[1]

This sense of danger emanated from the government officials' basic assumptions about colonial governance, which was diametrically opposed to that of the lawyers. The different perspectives—what I refer to as 'the logic of emergency' and 'the logic of law'—were derived from different conceptions of politics, society and law in India. The government's logic of emergency insisted that the executive should retain the power of extra-legal intervention in judicial affairs because India was always in a constant state of emergency. This was due to the EIC officials' security concerns along the internal and external frontiers, which were porous, fluid and unstable due to complex processes of acquisition and settlement, resulting in a mosaic of territories in which the lands directly ruled by British officials were intersected with those indirectly ruled by hereditary armed gentry (called the chiefs and sardars) and those of the independent princely states.

The King's Court's logic of law held that the colonial government should be constrained by the independent judiciary as obtained in Britain. The key to this legal attitude was the judges' construction of the rights of the British subjects in India, which was to be achieved through the Indian subjects' uses of the court and various legal devices developed in Britain such as the writ of habeas corpus. This basic difference of perspective made it difficult for both the government officials and the King's Court judges to conciliate with each other. The conflict between the government officials and the lawyers was significant in the making of British despotism in India. Despotism signified an amalgamation of powers in the hand of the executive. It was an opposite state of the rule of law, which was characterised by a separation of powers between different branches of the state and especially by the independent judiciary's check upon the executive's rule of men.

The 1828 Bombay crisis was a watershed moment in the emergence of British despotism in India—and this is why I focus on Bombay instead of Calcutta or Madras in the following narrative. Governor Malcolm's sense of danger was shared by the Supreme Government in Calcutta and the home authorities in London (the Court of Directors and the Board of Control). When the EIC's charter was renewed in 1834, they tried to subjugate the King' Court to the EIC by vesting the Governor-General in Calcutta an all-India legislative power as the head of a Legislative Council. This meant that the British parliament exempted the colonial government in India from the rule of law. It was during this debate that Thomas Babington Macaulay made his famous vindication of Britain's 'enlightened and paternal despotism' in India.[2] Although the Indians continued to use British legal institutions after the passage of this legislation, the Bombay crisis marked a turning point in British colonial governance. This book analyses the historical circumstances that led to the restriction of the rule of law and the expansion of despotism in colonial India.

The Judicial Structure of British India in the Early Nineteenth Century

Before starting to consider the typology and historical significance of these concepts, it is necessary to understand the basic judicial structure of Bombay in the 1820s. The King's Court (the Mayor's Court 1726–1798, the Recorder's Court 1798–1824, the Supreme Court 1824–1862) was situated in Bombay city. It was run by a Chief Justice, two Puisne Judges, 20–30 European officers and numerous Indian clerks, writers and servants (630 in number in 1827).[34] The King's Court was characterised by its multiple jurisdictions. The court functioned as the common law court, the equity court, the ecclesiastical court and the admiralty court. It also constituted the small cause court and the court of enquiry. The court exercised jurisdiction over all criminal cases of the Company's servants and all other British subjects as a court of Oyer and Terminer and Gaol Delivery. The jurisdictions of the King's Court and the Company's Court were demarcated geographically and personally. The King's Court had jurisdiction over the British in both the city and the mofussil. The Indians in the city, and those employed by the Europeans or by the Company in any part, were also amenable to the court. The King's Court applied English common and statute laws. It also applied Hindu or Muslim private laws when the defendant was a Hindu or a Muslim inhabitant. The number of cases tried in the Supreme Court seems to have been small.[5] The cost of making suits in the court could be expensive especially in cases of equity.[6] In addition to the ordinary writs, the judges of the King's Court also issued prerogative writs at their discretion.[7] A case could be appealed to the Privy Council in Britain.

Barristers and attorneys were the key figures in Bombay's judicial politics. Before 1834, they needed to acquire a licence from the Court of Directors to enter and practice as a lawyer in India. The barristers came from Inns of Court in London, while there was no qualification for attorneys. Their number was small, though the late 1820s were marked by the increase of the number of attorneys, probably the reflection of the expanding prospect of business in the mofussil (Table 1.1).

The government appointed its law officers among them. The Company's Solicitor was recruited from the attorneys. The barristers were commissioned the Advocate General (called the Company's Standing Counsel till 1806) to represent the Company when it was civilly sued or to file criminal information in the King's Court. Most of the barristers led by Advocate Generals George Norton and G. C. Irwin were firmly in support of the government. Barrister James Morley was the important exception, who constantly annoyed the government. He was the only barrister who had

Table 1.1 The number of barristers and attorneys in Bombay in the 1820s

	1817	1818	1819	1820	1821	1822	1823	1824
Barrister	3	4	5	5	5	5	6	6
Attorney	6	7	7	7	7	6	6	6
	1825	1826	1827	1828	1829	1830	1831	1832
Barrister	7	7	8	8	9	9	8	8
Attorney	10	14	16	15	14	15	11	11

Source: *East India Register and Directory*

not been called to the Inns of Court. On the other hand, the attorneys of the court were often in support of the King's Court. Most famous among them were Frederick Ayrton, Thomas W. Browne and William Fenwick. The conflict became clear when the barristers submitted a memorial criticising the Recorder in 1823, and the Recorder suspended them from appearing in the court.[8] The conflict between the government and barristers, on the one hand, and the King's Court and its attorneys, on the other, formed part of the basic political structure in Bombay in the 1820s.[9]

Another key person was the sheriff.[10] The sheriff summoned the grand and the petty juries from the British inhabitants in the presidency. The writ of the court was executed by the sheriff and his officers such as bailiffs. On a complaint of anyone against a person in the court's jurisdiction, the court issued a summons to appear at a given time and place. In default of appearance, the court issued a warrant to the sheriff to bring the defendant before the court. The defendant was to be detained in custody unless bail might be allowed. Then, after the judgement was given, the defendant was imprisoned until the judgement was fulfilled.[11] The sheriff's execution of the writs caused deep concern among the government officials, as we shall see in Chap. 3.

It is also necessary to look at the structure of the EIC's judiciary or 'the Company's Court' in the 1820s, in which the distinction between the executive and the judiciary was blurred. In the Konkan and Gujarat (called the Old Provinces),[12] the EIC introduced a separate judiciary to exercise civil and criminal jurisdiction over the Indians in the mofussil, though Collectors retained jurisdiction over the matters of revenue. The Judges were the Company's civil servants. They applied 'Regulations' legislated by the Governor-in-Council instead of English law. It also applied Hindu or Muslim civil laws in cases involving Hindus or Muslims as the defendant. The structure of the Company's Court was three-tiered. The traditional arbitration court called the panchayat was at the bottom of the mofussil justice. The second tier was the district (*zilla*) court presided by the European Judges. The zilla court was composed of a judge, a senior assistant judge, a junior assistant judge, a register, an assistant register, Sadr Ameens and Native Commissioners. There were six zillas in the presidency between 1818 and 1826: Surat, Broach (incorporated in Surat and Kaira in 1827), Kaira (Eastern Zilla North of the Myhee), Ahmedabad (Western Zilla North of the Myhee), Northern Konkan and Southern Konkan. Each establishment of the zilla court held 500–2500 Indian servants, which was generally larger than the Collectors' office.[13] The final tribunal in Bombay were the Sadr Diwani Adalat (civil) and the Sadr Foujdari Adalat (criminal) run by three or more judges, a register, assistant registers and Hindu and Muslim law officers.[14] The court of circuit to try serious crimes was held at each Sadr stations by one of Sadr Judges in rotation.[15] An appeal was allowed from there to the Privy Council in London.

The Deccan had a different system. The rule of law in terms of the separation of the judiciary from the executive was not introduced in the Deccan after the conquest in 1818. The Commissioner, Collectors and their subordinate Indian officers all combined the executive, judicial and magisterial duties. The Bombay government tried to retain the Maratha system of justice intact as far as possible. Governor Elphinstone ordered that all civil cases were to be referred to the panchayat, whose decision was final unless there was gross error or corruption. But, as James Jaffe shows, it soon became clear that its procedures were dilatory, its members were difficult to find, and it was plagued by bribery and corruption.[16] The role of the panchayat was being replaced by more regular works of Indian subordinate judges and magistrates. In the rural areas, the Mamlatdars (Indian revenue officers) oversaw minor civil and criminal cases. In urban areas, civil magistrates called Amins and Munsifs tried similar small cases. Collectors tried serious crimes aided by Hindu law officers (shastris) and appeal cases from Indian subordinate judges. The Deccan Commissioner supervised all of this judicial apparatus. He received appeals from the Collectors' courts and solely in charge of the claims against the sardars.[17] But the judicial work put pressure on the Collectors' revenue business, and the government needed to think about introducing a separate judiciary. Accordingly, the Zilla Judges of Ahmednagar (including Khandesh) and Poona (including Sholapur) were appointed in 1825, and the Commissioner was abolished in 1826.[18] In this situation, as we shall see, the government officials in the Deccan felt deep anxiety about the King's Court's assertion of complete separation between the judiciary and the executive.

Despotism and the Rule of Law

Many scholars have argued that British colonialism in India became more despotic in the early nineteenth century. They have characterised this process as a transformation from plural, hybrid and networked colonial politics centred on maritime coastal cities to a bureaucratic, militarist and sovereign territorial domination based on colonial knowledge. This was a moment of 'proconsular despotism', 'garrison-state militarism', 'dominance without hegemony', 'despotism of law', 'domination of strangers' or the end of the idea of 'ancient Mughal constitution'.[19] Recent histories of ideas note that an earlier attitude of enlightenment universalism was replaced by utilitarian liberal authoritarianism that denied the rights of the colonial subjects.[20] A central focus of this discussion on despotism has been the nature of rule of law in the colony. While the colonial judiciary did reduce the coerciveness of the colonial state in certain contexts,[21] the preponderance of evidence of everyday violence indicates that the colonial state's regime of violence curtailed the political and personal liberties of Indian subjects based on reason of state.[22] David Washbrook succinctly summarises this as follows:

> Here, as in the colonial Empire more generally, the idea of a rule of law became fatally confused with that of a rule by law under which 'civil society', while perhaps directed by general legal principles, is denied any part itself in formulating those principles; while the state may make law for its subjects, it posits itself as above that law and as unaccountable to it. British-Indian law became less a tool of liberty than an instrument of despotism.[23]

How can we understand this transition? Legal historians have provided crucial insight into this problem by pointing out a parallel change from hybrid and multi-centred legal pluralism to a more state-centred sovereign form of justice in the early nineteenth century.[24] They have also argued that the background to this transition lay in a dialectic between two discourses of colonial rule. The colonial government's discourse prioritised the security of the empire through conquest of territories and subjugation of colonial population. This was opposed by the discourse of imperial legal protection demanding the rule of law and criticising the government's arbitrary exercise of violence.[25] The dialogue between the two discourses was most marked when the colonial state experienced states of emergency such as wars and rebellions. Legal scholar Nasser Hussain has examined the martial law and suspension of habeas corpus in British colonies (particularly India and Jamaica) and argued that the state of emergency was not outside the rule of law but constitutive of it.[26] Later historians have confirmed that colonial authorities tended to institutionalise the state of exception in times of conquest and to embed the reason of state in ordinary law.[27] The typical example was the colonial governments' dealing with 'thuggees' and 'criminal tribes' in Northern India, Punjab and the

North-Western Provinces as they legislated draconian and (if enacted in Britain) unconstitutional measures such as the Frontier Crimes Regulations despite opposition from the colonial judiciary.[28] To retain the power of discretionary intervention in times of counter-insurgency, it was vital for the colonial government to be unshackled from the judiciary.[29] These studies suggest that the transition to despotic legal pluralism was an outcome of the colonial governments' opposition to the rights-based approach of the colonial judiciary in times of emergency.

But I would emphasise the banality of emergency. Certainly, the tribal raids and rebellions motivated the government authorities to elevate the rule of men over the rule of law. But the colonial state's antipathy to law was not limited to overtly exceptional situations. As Ranajit Guha suggests, the colonial state was always obsessed with the maintenance of political order and prioritised it over the improvement of social, economic and cultural institutions.[30] This was because the everyday use of legal recourse by the Indians did influence the development of colonial politics.[31] Local people's active appropriation of available legal forums and authorities was a common feature of precolonial India.[32] Reflecting the diffused and shared nature of sovereignty, civil and criminal justice was characterised by its high pluralism.[33] This continued to be so under British rule. The British court was popular because the Indian litigants were quite familiar with its procedures and processes.[34] The court was used by local princes and zamindars (landed gentry) to settle family conflicts, which constituted an inalienable aspect of local politics.[35] Since the law was central to the rule of property in the colony, the colonial state's engagement in revenue extraction and market policing resulted in the judicialization of politics over property matters.[36] For the same reason, the social policy of the colonial government necessarily involved complex and protracted negotiations with Indian groups, particularly in the realms of family, property, charity and caste.[37] These legal practices affected the institutional development of the colonial judiciary, the identities of the colonised and the conception of the law itself.[38] The EIC's political legitimacy was no less secure in these legal disputes, and, as Lauren Benton and Arthur Mitchell Fraas suggest, the colonial government's aspiration to control the situation led them to construct a more exclusionary colonial order.[39] The government's emergency measures percolated through to the civil administration even in times of peace.

The social histories of law referenced here do not directly address the issues of emergency and the rule of law, but I contend that the political emergency and the legal agency should be analysed within the same analytical framework because, as the chapters in this book will demonstrate, contemporary witnesses were conscious of the political implications of the colonial subjects' everyday legal practices. We need to probe the connections between the Indians' use of law in social and economic spheres and the state-level institutional changes that resulted from this. We must seek the driving force of the transition to plural despotism in the realm of popular culture of law and the legal agency of indigenous people, along with the colonial government's antipathy to the law in times of emergency. Bearing these points in mind, this book addresses the following questions. What was the driving force of the despotic regime change in India? How can we characterise these changes from an everyday legal perspective? What actors were involved in the process of change? How did practices of Indians affect the process? What kind of ideas did these Indians have about the function of law in the colonies? How did British judges and lawyers respond to the Indian practices? How did the government officials react? What were their ideological and pragmatic assumptions and priorities? What do these analyses imply about the nature of British colonial rule in India?

Early nineteenth-century Bombay is an ideal subject for this investigation. The city's King's Court was an institutional embodiment of legal pluralism. This allows us to examine colonial judicial politics from the perspective of interactions between agency and structural change. The jurisdiction of the King's Court was limited in the presidency town of Bombay, and the inner provinces (mofussil) were under the jurisdiction of the Company's Court. But the King's Court sometimes insisted on their extended jurisdiction in the mofussil, hence conflicting with the EIC's judicial authority. The Indians actively used the King's Court to challenge the government and, by doing so, buttressed the court's legitimacy. The jurisdictional jockeying between the King's Court and the local government was common in the early nineteenth century in Bengal, Madras and the Prince of Wales Island (Penang).[40] But, even if the structure of conflict was already manifested in Bengal in the eighteenth century, I suggest that the conflict in Bombay in the 1820s catalysed despotic government in India because it induced both the ministers and the EIC's directors in London to subjugate the independent judiciary to the colonial executive through imperial legislation.

The central argument of this book is that the Indian practice of appropriating the jurisdictional conflict led the government to construct a unitary and hierarchical judicial structure, wherein the government retained the power of political intervention in judicial affairs in states of emergency.

The background was the political, economic and social crisis in the newly conquered territories in the 1820s. The main concern of the government was the raids and rebellions of the so-called wild tribes in the hills and their collaboration with the Indian princes and sardars in the plains. The government tried to deal with this through a form of indirect rule relying on Indian local chiefs and sardars in the mofussil. But the King's Court obstructed the policy by subjugating these chiefs and sardars to the court's warrants and writs, hence weakening their honour and respectability in the courtroom that was commonly deemed as an arena of demystification of kingly authority.[41] Moreover, the King's Court endangered the EIC's political authority in the mofussil by overturning the decisions of the Company's Court and by trying and punishing Governors and other EIC officials. The government believed that the King's Court should be subordinated to the EIC and a unitary judicial structure should be devised. This tension exploded in two cases of habeas corpus in 1828 and resulted in official recognition of the EIC's despotism in the 1834 charter renewal. By examining this process, I contend that the driving force of the transition from hybrid to government-centred colonialism in early nineteenth-century Western India was the legal agency of the colonial subjects and the government's anxiety about sovereignty in the aftermath of the conquest. Against the backdrop of this post-conquest insecurity, the ordinary uses of law and law courts by the Indians were construed as politically dangerous. I argue that the Bombay case represented the pattern of judicial politics in nineteenth-century India, where the British government was involved in the incessant process of conquest, settlement and strengthening of the logic of emergency. The need to cope with the crises at the frontiers of the empire put the colonial government under constant pressure to defend its power to resort to emergency measures in the face of the judiciary's cry for the rule of law, which made the overall tenor of the British domination more despotic and emergency-oriented.

The Logic of Law and the Logic of Emergency: A Typology

The Bombay controversy highlighted the conflict between the King's Court's logic of law and the government's logic of emergency. I argue that the conceptualisation of these politico-legal principles better explains the processes of transition from the multi-centred justice system in the eighteenth century to a more state-centred legal regime in the nineteenth century. This book will establish the following typology.

The government employed the logic of 'emergency', 'state necessity' or 'reason of state' in its contest with the King's Court. It was a logic of 'danger' and 'self-preservation', enabling the government to act freely in times of emergency without constraints by the judiciary. The officials were concerned about the crises on the spot. For the officials, India was *always* in a state of crisis. They believed that they were constantly jeopardised, not only by the Indian rebels but also by sepoys, disobedient 'native' servants, revenue defaulters and even by European settlers and lawyers.[42] The officials' anxiety reflected their understanding that political boundaries in India were invariably blurred. For instance, there were no clear lines of demarcation between war, rebellion and raid in the frontier, since the gathering of the raiders was often the first step for larger rebellions that would, in turn, invite the intervention of foreign princes. There was not even a clear distinction between territories under the direct control of the EIC and those controlled by Indian rulers including the princely states: the British territories were riddled with the internal frontiers, in which armed rural bosses enjoyed the same de facto independence as foreign rajas, exerting control in defiance of the EIC's revenue officers.[43] The boundary between the inner provinces (the mofussil) and the presidency towns was fuzzy in terms of the danger of robberies, riots and rebellions.[44]

In such a situation, government officials were concerned about its sovereignty in Carl Schmitt's sense: sovereignty 'not as the monopoly to coerce or to rule, but as the monopoly to decide'.[45] They assumed that the boundaries in society should be solely determined by the government. Political matters, such as concluding treaties with Indian princes or introducing a separate judiciary in the post-war settlement, were to be determined by the government through reference to 'state policy'. The courts were not supposed to have any say in such issues. The government did not entirely deny the role of law—the separate judiciary was necessary to absolve Collectors from judicial business and to ensure efficient revenue collection. The political liberty of the Indians was to be utterly denied, but their personal liberty might or might not be allowed by the government in reference to necessities.[46] What was problematic was that the government's political decisions were hindered by the judges' power to hear and rule on politically important cases.

Because of this, government officials disliked the common law's technicalities of procedures and precedents, which were the source of the judges' power to control the court. Naturally, they resorted to the other major source of law: legislation.[47] Mountstuart Elphinstone, the Governor of Bombay, was a Benthamite in this sense. He read Bentham well and implemented a major codification project (commonly called the Elphinstone Code) in 1827, compiling a comprehensive set of regulations with constitutional, civil, criminal, revenue and military branches—Bombay's Pannomion.[48] The code was endorsed and expanded by the next Governor John Malcolm. By this means, the Bombay government attempted to limit the role of judges to the simple application of the code, hence asserting executive superiority over the King's Court without overtly denying the importance of rule of law in colonial governance. The government's deployment of the logic of state necessity was a Hobbesian moment in Indian history: the King's Court's view of law as the means of protecting rights was overridden (or at least stamped) by the government's positivist view of law as the command of the sovereign.[49] This reflected a similar development in Britain. A remarkable development in the metropolitan legal world in the eighteenth century was the rise of legislative positivism and the parallel decline of judge-made law.[50] Its theoretical background was complex and sometimes self-contradictory,[51] but the practical effect was the decline of the power of the judiciary in the face of the executive and the legislative and the diminution of popular participation in legal processes, or the shift 'from consent to command'.[52] Parallel to this was a larger process of transition of British political culture from a mixed constitution to a parliamentary government.[53] But it should be emphasised that the government officials' sense of crisis and their solutions were generated from their engagement with the local conditions in the Indian society and their administrative experiences rather than by any enlightened understanding of Hobbes or Bentham.

The government's logic of emergency was confronted by the King's Court's logic of law. The latter required the government to be 'lawful', 'regular' and 'constitutional'. It was based on the court's exercise of ordinary jurisdiction and the logic of constitutional check and balance informed by the British idea of a mixed constitution. First, the King's Court assumed the power of trying the EIC as ordinary defendants in ordinary civil cases. The court's fundamental assumption was that Indian society was under a civilian, not military, rule in which the municipal court could exercise jurisdiction. The judges did not deny the existence of state necessity and emergency in which they did not have jurisdiction, but they argued that such a situation was extremely rare and that it was the court, not the government, that should decide whether a situation was an emergency or not. As a corollary, while they admitted that there might be limitations on political liberty for Indian subjects, personal liberty should always be protected by the regular court. The government's liability was advocated by relying on such precedents as Lord Mansfield's decision that the colonial Governor's illegal actions could be sued in the English courts of law in *Fabrigas* v. *Mostyn* (1773).[54]

This rigid dichotomy between the civil and the military state of society was based on the judges' clear distinction between pre-conquest 'Indian' India and post-conquest British India. Their position was that, once territories were conquered, the state of war was terminated, and the court of law's juridical sovereignty was established. Their notion of the law did not allow anomalous legal spaces between war and peace. By assuming this abrupt transformation from war to peace and from Indian to British India, the judges could argue that the laws of England, in tandem with customs and usages, were immediately applicable to the newly conquered territories. They asserted that the Indian society in conquered provinces was an orderly society in which the regular courts of law should dominate. This stood in marked contrast to the government officials' view of the frontiers as emergency zones where the government retained the power of extra-legal interventions.

In addition to the 'ordinary' jurisdiction, the King's Court also claimed its 'extraordinary' power to check the government. This was based on the assumption that the royal charter conferred the judges with the same power and authority of the Court of the King's Bench in Britain. It was exercised by issuing the king's prerogative writs of *habeas corpus*, *mandamus*, *certiorari*, *prohibition* or *procedendo*.[55] By this means, the King's Court reviewed and overturned the government's (and the Company's Court's) decisions. The prerogative powers of the King's Court were vindicated by referring to precedents and legal authorities in the English common law tradition. It included the opinion of Edward Coke's formulation that the king's non-remedial writs could run in its overseas territories in *Calvin's Case* (1608) and in his *Institutes of the Lawes of England* (1628–44).[56] This was supplemented by later authorities such as Mansfield advocating the English High Court's power to issue prerogative writs to king's subjects, whether in Britain or aboard, in *R. v. Cowle* (1759)[57] or Lord Eldon approving the power of the chancery court to issue habeas corpus in *Crowley's Case* (1818),[58] together with the Indian judgements endorsing the English court's jurisdiction over the Indian princes such as *R. v. Monisse* (1810).[59]

The judges' chief weapon against the government was their judicial discretion in controlling the procedures in the court. As Michael Lobban shows, British lawyers in the eighteenth century conceived the common law primarily as a system of remedies based on reasoning rather than a set of rules based on theory, asserting the central importance of legal procedures that enabled them to deny the validity of pleas or reject evidence.[60] Their control of the case was also secured by the fact that the doctrine of *stare decisis* (the absolute necessity to obey the precedent) was not established until the mid-nineteenth century.[61] But grave political conflicts were generated when this political independence of lawyers was applied in the colony, where the imperative of the executive should be paramount. So deep was the divide between the two logics that the conflict between the King's Court and the government transcended the boundary of Bombay and provoked an imperial dispute about the law and politics in British colonial governance.

Looking at colonial politics as a dialectic between these two logics allows us to understand the contested dynamics of the rise of British territorial sovereignty in India. The colonial government suppressed rather than promoted the rule of law because it was preoccupied with political exigencies caused by minor and mobile sovereigns in the frontier. The government saw the court's independence as a major hindrance to its frontier governance and impelled the imperial legislation to institutionalise the reason of state and the logic of emergency. The discourse about these logics concretised the sense of crisis on the spot and influenced the contours of the modern political and legal arguments in the metropole. During this process, the British empire became more despotic.

Chapters

This book makes the argument in seven chapters. To deal with the problem of the King's Court as broadly as possible, I will examine both the presidency towns and the mofussil, the civil and the criminal justices, and the states of normalcy and emergency. Chapter 2 explains the early history of the King's Court in eighteenth-century Bombay and examines the working of the court as a platform for 'reform public' in the 1820s. The chapter also deals with two legal cases in the King's Court where the government was sued by Indian merchants. In these cases, the King's Court displayed a civilian view of Indian society in which the law and the court held a paramount power, rebutting the government's militarist perspective of state necessity in times of emergency.

Chapter 3 examines the King's Court's problems in the mofussil. Although its jurisdiction was limited to the presidency towns, the court nonetheless instigated various problems for the government in the mofussil. The summons of the Company's district officials hindered their day-to-day business. The sheriff's execution of the writs caused disturbances in the mofussil. Most problematic was the King's Court's interference in the Company's revenue administration, since the revenue defaulters often approached the King's Court to overturn the decree of the Company's Court. Government officials strongly censured the King's Court, not only because it disrupted their revenue collection but also because negative rulings undermined the Company's sovereignty embodied in its revenue administration.

Chapters 4 examines the Bombay government's security concerns in the mofussil caused by the jurisdictional expansion of the King's Court. This chapter discusses the government's policy towards local military rulers (chiefs and sardars), focusing on issues of policing in the mofussil. The 1820s was a period of raids and rebellions caused by alliances between the 'wild tribes' in the hills and the sardars and princes in the plains. To deal with this, the government vested the chiefs and sardars with police authority and upheld their social influence by exempting them from the Company's Court. But this strategy was obstructed by the King's Court in two ways. First, the chiefs and sardars were subjected to the process of the King's Court through summonses and attachments of persons and properties. The Indian magnates complained that this was injurious to their respectability, while the government became concerned about the impact on security in the mofussil. Second, to make matters worse, the independent princes of Kolhapur, Satara and Baroda began to rely on the authority of the King's Court to extract political concessions from the government. In this way, the government's paramountcy over these internal and external allies was jeopardised by the court.

Chapter 5 examines the habeas corpus cases in 1828–1829, which were the culmination of the developments discussed in previous chapters. These cases exploded into open conflict between the government and the court. The government sent a letter to the King's Court to halt the proceedings, while the judges petitioned the Privy Council in Britain about the government's political interference. This event exacerbated the government's unease about the King's Court's encroachment on sovereignty in the mofussil. In the dispute, both the judges and the government officials fully developed their logics of law and emergency.

Chapter 6 discusses the wider impact of the Bombay cases on the subsequent structure of Indian governance. The Bombay government urged the Supreme Government in Calcutta and the home authorities in London to reform the judicial order so the judiciary would be subject to the executive. The Bombay government's concerns were shared by higher officials in Calcutta and Madras, who had experienced similar conflicts with the King's Court. As a solution, they proposed the establishment of a Legislative Council in the East India Company's new charter in 1834. This was a watershed moment. The King's Court's power of judicial check was officially curtailed, while the EIC's government was vested with exclusive and supreme authority in determining the political affairs.

Chapter 7 first examines the relationship between the executive and the judiciary after the 1834 charter renewal to show that Indians' forum shopping and the consequent jurisdictional jockeying continued after the institutional change. It then summarises the findings of this book and concludes by suggesting some directions for further investigation into the empire, law and emergency themes.

The main primary sources of this study are government records (judicial, general/public, revenue and political departments) in the India Office Records of the British Library. These are supplemented by the department files in the Maharashtra State Archives.[62] I have also drawn on periodicals and newspapers including *Bombay Gazette*, *Bombay Courier*, *Oriental Herald* and *Asiatic Journal* and governmental and parliamentary publications such as *Selections of the Records of the Bombay Government*, *British Parliamentary Papers* and *Parliamentary Debates*.

Notes

1. British Library [BL], India Office Records [IOR] L/PJ/3/918, Bombay Judicial Letter [BJL], Bombay Government [Gov.] to Court of Directors [CoD], 27 Sep. 1828, John Malcolm, minute, 24 Aug. 1828.
2. Parl. Debs. (series 3) vol. 19, col. 533 (10 July 1833), T. B. Macaulay, speech.
3. *Parliamentary Papers* [PP] 1830 (633), 257. The list of major officers was printed in *Bombay Calendar and Almanac* (Bombay) and *East India Registers* (London).

4. We could not know the number for the 1820s without access to the High Court Record in the Maharashtra State Archives. The government record did not contain the information.
5. The yearly average number of cases filed in the plea side of the court in the 1830s was 24.4. PP 1847 (14), 278. A far more frequently used was the small cause court. In the 4 years between 1824 and 1827, the court took a total of 5465 cases, with an annual average of 1366. PP 1829 (205), 3.
6. See, for instance, PP 1830 (646), 81–82, 138–40, E. H. East, evidence, 9 and 23 Mar. 1830.
7. Cf. William Hook Morley, *An Analytical Digest of All the Reported Cases Decided in the Supreme Courts of Judicature in India, in the Courts of the Hon. East India Company, and on Appeal from India, by Her Majesty in Council. With an Introduction, Notes ... and an Appendix*, 2 vols. (London, 1849–50), 1:363–97, 'Jurisdiction'.
8. Barristers criticised the Recorder's management of the small cause court, in which attorneys were allowed to act as barristers and the parties could plead their cause by themselves to reduce court costs. The barristers criticised that this was the infringement of their right and doubted the legality of the court itself. They submitted a memorial to the court containing some insinuation on the 'most unworthy motives' of the Recorder not to abolish the court. The court unanimously suspended five barristers (i.e. all barristers in Bombay except James Morley) who signed the memorial for six months. *Asiatic Journal*, new series, 16 (1835), 5–8.
9. Attorneys in Calcutta were similarly involved in conflicts with the government. Tarit Kumar Mukherji, 'Aldermen and Attorneys: Mayor's Court, Calcutta', in A. J. R. Russell-Wood, ed., *Local Government in European Overseas Empires 1450–1800* (1950; Aldershot: Routledge, 1999).
10. The sheriff was appointed yearly by the Governor and Council. Morley, *Digest*, 2:648–49, Supreme Court Charter, s. 20.
11. M. P. Jain, *Outlines of Indian Legal and Constitutional History*, 6th edition (New Delhi: LexisNexis, 2006), 37. Cf. J. H. Baker, *An Introduction to English Legal History*, 4th edition (London: Butterworths, 2007), chapter 4: 'The Forms of Action'.
12. Salsette and Karanja in Thana, Konkan, were conquered in 1774. The rest of the territories in the Konkan were ceded by the Peshwa in 1817. Gujarat was conquered in the Second Maratha War (1803–1805).
13. Usually the number of Indians employed in Collectors' establishments did not exceed 1000. See PP 1830 (633), 252–59.
14. Until 1821, the Governor and Members of the Council were the final tribunal of civil and criminal appeal cases. In that year, Governor Mountstuart Elphinstone introduced a separate judiciary to relieve the burden of the executive. Orby Mootham, *The East India Company's Sadar Courts*

1801–1834 (Bombay: N. M. Tripathi, 1983), 120. The Sadr Adalat was moved from Bombay to Surat in 1821 and relocated from Surat to Bombay in 1828.

15. It was held quarterly in Surat and half-yearly in other zillas.
16. The cases decided in the panchayat comprised less than 5% of the total cases in 1819–1827. Its status was eventually downgraded to an investigatory body assisting the judges. James Jaffe, *Ironies of Colonial Governance: Law, Custom and Justice in Colonial India* (Cambridge: Cambridge University Press, 2015), 57, table 2-2.
17. For the judicial system in the Deccan, see *Poona Gazetteer*, 3:19–24; Jaffe, *Ironies of Colonial Governance*, chapters 1–3; Kenneth Ballhatchet, *Social Policy and Social Change in Western India 1817–1830* (London: Oxford University Press, 1957), 193–213.
18. Part of the Southern Maratha Country were included in the Regulation area in 1830 and called the Zilla of Dharwar.
19. C. A. Bayly, *Imperial Meridian: The British Empire and the World 1780–1830* (London: Longman, 1989); Douglas M. Peers, *Between Mars and Mammon: Colonial Armies and the Garrison State in India 1819–1835* (London: Tauris, 1995); Ranajit Guha, *Dominance Without Hegemony: History and Power in Colonial India* (Cambridge, MA, Harvard University Press, 1997); Radhika Singha, *A Despotism of Law: Crime and Justice in Early Colonial India* (Oxford: Oxford University Press, 1998); Robert Travers, *Ideology and Empire in Eighteenth-Century India: The British in Bengal* (Cambridge: Cambridge University Press, 2007); Jon E. Wilson, *The Domination of Strangers: Modern Governance in Eastern India 1780–1835* (Basingstoke: Palgrave Macmillan, 2008); Philip J. Stern, 'Rethinking Institutional Transformations in the Making of Modern Empire: The East India Company in Madras', *Journal of Colonialism and Colonial History* 9, no. 2 (2008); James Lees, *Bureaucratic Culture in Early Colonial India: District Officials, Armed Forces, and Personal Interest Under the East India Company, 1760–1830* (Abingdon, Oxon: Routledge, 2020).
20. Uday Singh Mehta, *Liberalism and Empire: A Study in Nineteenth-Century British Liberal Thought* (Chicago, IL: University of Chicago Press, 1999); Jennifer Pitts, *A Turn to Empire: The Rise of Imperial Liberalism in Britain and France* (Princeton, NJ: Princeton University Press, 2005); Peter Robb, *Liberalism, Modernity and the Nation* (Oxford: Oxford University Press, 2007); Andrew Sartori, 'The British Empire and Its Liberal Mission', *Journal of Modern History* 78, no. 3 (2006), 623–42; Karuna Mantena, *Alibis of Empire: Henry Maine and the Ends of Liberal Imperialism* (Princeton, NJ: Princeton University Press, 2010); Catherine Hall, *Macaulay and Son: Architects of Imperial Britain* (New Haven, CT: Yale University Pres, 2012).

21. Peter Robb, *Peasants, Political Economy, and Law* (Oxford: Oxford University Press, 2007); Martin J. Wiener, *An Empire on Trial: Race, Murder and Justice under British Rule 1870–1935* (Cambridge: Cambridge University Press, 2009).
22. Johan Geertsema, 'Exception, Bare Life and Colonialism', in Victor V. Ramraj, ed., *Emergencies and the Limits of Legality* (Cambridge: Cambridge University Press, 2008), 337–59; Elizabeth Kolsky, *Colonial Justice in Britain: White Violence and the Rule of Law* (Cambridge: Cambridge University Press, 2010); Partha Chatterjee, *The Black Hole of Empire: History of a Global Practice of Power* (Princeton, NJ: Princeton University Press, 2012), 193–95; Samera Esmeir, *Juridical Humanity: A Colonial History* (Stanford, CA: Stanford University Press, 2012); Jonathan Saha, *Law, Disorder and the Colonial State: Corruption in Burma c.1900* (Basingstoke: Palgrave Macmillan, 2013); Stephen Legg and Diana Heath, eds., *South Asian Governmentalities: Michael Foucault and the Question of Postcolonial Orderings* (Cambridge: Cambridge University Press, 2018).
23. D. A. Washbrook, 'India 1818–1860: The Two Faces of Colonialism', in Andrew Porter ed., *The Oxford History of the British Empire Volume III: The Nineteenth Century* (Oxford: Oxford University Press, 1999), 407.
24. Lauren Benton, *Law and Colonial Cultures: Legal Regimes in World History 1400–1900* (Cambridge: Cambridge University Press, 2002); Lisa Ford, *Settler Sovereignty: Jurisdiction and Indigenous People in America and Australia 1788–1836* (Cambridge, MA: Harvard University Press, 2010); Arthur Mitchell Fraas, 'They Have Travailed into a Wrong Latitude': The Laws of England, Indian Settlements and the British Imperial Constitution 1726–1773' (PhD diss., Duke University, 2011); Gagan D. S. Sood, 'Sovereign Justice in Precolonial Maritime Asia: The Case of Mayor's Court of Bombay 1726–1798', *Itinerario* 37, 2 (2013), 46–72; Lauren Benton and Richard J. Ross, eds., *Legal Pluralism and Empires 1500–1850* (New York: New York University Press, 2013).
25. Mithi Mukherjee, *India in the Shadows of Empire: A Legend and Political History 1774–1950* (Oxford: Oxford University Press, 2009), chapters 1–2; C. A. Bayly, *Recovering Liberties: Indian Thought in the Age of Liberalism and Empire* (Cambridge: Cambridge University Press, 2012), 135–37; Julia Stephens, 'The Phantom Wahhabi: The Liberalism and the Muslim Fanatic in Mid-Victorian India', *Modern Asian Studies* 47, no.1 (2013), 22–52; Alan Lester and Fae Dussart, *Colonization and the Origins of Humanitarian Governance: Protecting Aborigines Across the Nineteenth-Century British Empire* (Cambridge: Cambridge University Press, 2014); Kirsten McKenzie, *Imperial Underworld: An Escaped Convict and the Transformation of the British Colonial Order* (Cambridge: Cambridge University Press, 2016); Lauren Benton and Lisa Ford, *Rage for Order: The British Empire and the Origins of International Law 1800–1850*

(Cambridge, MA: Harvard University Press, 2016); Lauren Benton, Adam Clulow, and Bain Attwood, eds., *Protection and Empire: A Global History* (New York, NY: Cambridge University Press, 2017).

26. Nasser Hussain, *The Jurisprudence of Emergency: Colonialism and the Rule of Law* (Ann Arbor: University of Michigan Press, 2003).
27. Lauren Benton, *A Search for Sovereignty: Law and Geography in European Empires 1400–1900* (Cambridge: Cambridge University Press, 2010); Thomas Poole, *Reason of State: Law, Prerogative and Empire* (Cambridge: Cambridge University Press, 2015); Samera Esmeir, 'On the Coloniality of Modern Law', *Critical Analysis of Law* 2, no. 1 (2015), 19–41; Mark Condos, *The Insecurity State: Punjab and the Making of Colonial Power in British India* (Cambridge: Cambridge University Press, 2017); David Gilmartin, Pamela Price, and Arild Engelsen Ruud, eds., *South Asian Sovereignty: The Conundrum of Worldly Power* (Abington: Routledge, 2020).
28. Kim A. Wagner, *Thuggee: Banditry and the British in Early Nineteenth-Century India* (Basingstoke: Palgrave Macmillan, 2007), 200; Tim Lloyd, 'Thuggee, Marginality and the State Effect in Colonial India circa 1770–1840', *Indian Economic and Social History Review* 45, no. 2, (2008), 201–37; Condos, *Insecurity State*; Elizabeth Kolsky, 'The Colonial Rule of Law and the Legal Regime of Exception: Frontier "Fanaticism" and State Violence in British India', *American Historical Review* 120, no. 4 (2015), 1218–46.
29. Bhavani Raman, 'Law in Times of Counter-Insurgency', in Aparna Balachandran, Rashmi Pant, and Bhavani Raman, eds., *Iterations of Law: Legal Histories from India* (New Delhi, Oxford University Press, 2018).
30. Guha, *Dominance Without Hegemony.*
31. See also, Mitra Sharafi, 'South Asian Legal History', *Annual Review of Law and Social Science* 11 (2015), 309–36.
32. Farhat Hasan, *State and Locality in Mughal India: Power Relations in Western India c. 1572–1730* (Cambridge: Cambridge University Press, 2004), especially chapters 5–6; Sumit Guha, 'Wrongs and Rights in the Maratha Country: Antiquity, Custom and Power in Eighteenth-Century India', in Michael R. Anderson and Sumit Guha, eds., *Changing Concepts of Law and Justice in South Asia* (Delhi: Oxford University Press, 1997), 14–29.
33. V. T. Gune, *The Judicial System of the Marathas* (Poona: Deccan College Post-Graduate and Research Institute, 1953); Sumit Guha, 'An India Penal Régime: Maharashtra in the Eighteenth Century', *Past and Present* 147 (1995): 101–26; Nandini Chatterjee, *Negotiating Mughal Law: A Family of Landlords Across Three Indian Empires* (Cambridge: Cambridge University Press: 2020).

34. Pamela G. Price, 'The "Popularity" of the Imperial Courts of Law: Three Views of the Anglo-Indian Legal Encounter', in W. J. Mommsen and J. A. De Moor, eds., *European Expansion and Law: The Encounter of European and Indigenous Law in 19th- and 20th-Century Africa and Asia* (Oxford: Oxford University Press, 1992), 179–200; Asiya Siddiqi, *Bombay's People 1860–98: Insolvents in the City* (New Delhi: Oxford University Press, 2017).
35. Pamela Price, *Kingship and Political Practice in Colonial India* (Cambridge: Cambridge University Press, 1996); Norbert Peabody, *Hindu Kinship and Polity in Precolonial India* (Cambridge: Cambridge University Press, 2006); Pamela Price, *The Writings of Pamela Price: State, Politics, and Cultures in Modern South India: Honour, Authority, and Morality* (New Delhi: Orient Black Swan, 2012); Faisal Chaudhry, 'A Rule of Proprietary Right for British India: From Revenue Settlement to Tenant Right in the Age of Classical Legal Thought', *Modern Asian Studies* 50, no. 1 (2015): 345–85.
36. D. A. Washbrook, 'Law, State and Agrarian Society in Colonial India', *Modern Asian Studies* 15, no. 3 (1981): 649–721; Nicholas B. Dirks, 'From Little King to Landlord: Property, Law, and the Gift under the Madras Permanent Settlement', *Comparative Studies in Society and History* 28 (1986): 307–33; David Washbrook, 'Economic Depression and the Making of "Traditional" Society in Colonial India 1820–1855', *Transactions of the Royal Historical Society*, Sixth Series, 3 (1993): 237–63; Niles Brimnes, 'Beyond Colonial Law: Indigenous Litigation and the Contestation of Property in the Mayor's Court in Late Eighteenth-Century Madras', *Modern Asian Studies* 37, no. 3 (2003): 513–50; Ritu Birla, *Stages of Capital: Law, Culture and Market Governance in Late Colonial India* (Durham, NC: Duke University Press, 2009); Tirthankar Roy, 'Indigo and Law in Colonial India', *Economic History Review* 64, S1 (2011): 60–75.
37. Indrani Chatterjee, *Gender, Slavery and Law in Colonial India* (Delhi: Oxford University Press, 1998); Durba Ghosh, *Sex and the Family in Colonial India* (Cambridge: Cambridge University Press, 2006); Mytheli Sreenivas, *Wives, Widows and Concubines: The Conjugal Family Ideal in Colonial India* (Bloonmington, IN: Indiana University Press, 2008); Birla, *Stages of Capital*; Rachel L. Sturman, *The Government of Social Life in Colonial India: Liberalism, Religious Law and Women's Rights* (Cambridge: Cambridge University Press, 2012); Eleanor Newbigin, *The Hindu Family and the Emergence of Modern India: Law, Citizenship and Community* (Cambridge: Cambridge University Press, 2013).

38. For Indian judiciary, see, Mahua Sarkar, *Justice in a Gothic Edifice: The Calcutta High Court and Colonial Rule in Bengal* (Calcutta: Firma KLM Private, 1997); Abhinav Chandrachud, *An Independent, Colonial Judiciary: A History of the Bombay High Court During the British Raj 1862–1947* (Oxford: Oxford University Press, 2015); Jaffe, *Ironies of Colonial Governance*. For identity, see Mattison Mines, 'Courts of Laws and Styles of Self in Eighteenth-Century Madras: From Hybrid to Colonial Self', *Modern Asian Studies* 35, no. 1 (2001): 33–74; Chandra Mallampalli, *Race, Religion and Law in Colonial India: Trials of an Interracial Family* (Cambridge: Cambridge University Press, 2011); Mitra Sharafi, *Law and Identity in Colonial South Asia: Parsi Legal Culture 1772–1947* (Cambridge: Cambridge University Press, 2014); Rohit De, *A People's Constitution: The Everyday Life of Law in the Indian Republic* (Princeton, NJ: Princeton University Press, 2018). For the conception of law and everyday legal practice, see, Taylor C. Sherman, *State Violence and Punishment in India* (Abington: Routledge, 2010); Sandra den Otter, 'Law, Authority and Colonial Rule', in Douglas M. Peers and Nandini Gooptu, eds., *India and the British Empire* (Oxford: Oxford University Press, 2012); Saha, *Law, Disorder and the Colonial State;* Nandini Chatterjee and Lakshmi Subramanian, 'Law and the Spaces of Empire: Introduction to the Special Issue', *Journal of Colonialism and Colonial History* 15, no. 1 (2014).
39. Benton, *Law and Colonial Cultures*; Fraas, 'They Have Travailed into a Wrong Latitude'.
40. For Calcutta, see Travers, *Ideology and Empire*, chapter 5; Mukherjee, *India in the Shadows of Empire*, chapters 1–2. For Madras, see Brimnes, 'Beyond Colonial Law'; Mines, 'Courts of Laws and Styles of Self'. For the Prince of Wales Island, see Nurfadzilah Yahaya, *Fluid Jurisdictions: Colonial Law and Arabs in Southeast Asia* (Ithaka, NY: Cornell University Press, 2020). For other relevant cases, see M. B. Hooker, 'The East India Company and the Crown 1773–1858', in C. H. Alexandrowicz, ed., *Grotian Society Paper 1968: Studies in the History of the Law of Nations* (The Hague: Martinus Nijhoff, 1970).
41. For the effect of legal conflict on the kings' and indigenous elites' symbolic capital of prestige, honour and reputation in precolonial and colonial India, see Price, *Kingship and Political Practice*, 75; Peabody, *Hindu Kinship and Polity*; Price, *The Writings of Pamela Price*.
42. For the historiography of the 'weak' British empire stressing fear and anxiety of the administrators on the spot, see Jon Wilson, *India Conquered: Britain's Raj and the Chaos of Empire* (London: Simon and Schuster, 2016); Condos, *Insecurity State*; Harald Fischer-Tiné, ed., *Anxieties, Fear and Panic in Colonial Settings: Empires on the Verge of a Nervous Breakdown* (Basingstoke: Palgrave Macmillan, 2016).

43. Cf. Robert Eric Frykenberg, *Guntur District 1788-1848: A History of Local Influence and Central Authority in South India* (Oxford: Oxford University Press, 1965); David Washbrook, *The Emergence of Provincial Politics: The Madras Presidency 1870–1920* (Cambridge: Cambridge University Press, 1976).
44. On the urban dangers, see C. A. Bayly, *Rulers, Townsmen and Bazaars: North India in the Age of British Expansion 1770–1870* (Oxford: Oxford University Press, 1997), chapter 8.
45. Carl Schmitt, *Political Theology: Four Chapters on the Concept of Sovereignty*, trans. George Schwab (Chicago, IL: University of Chicago Press, 2005) , 13.
46. For selective admission and denial of rights in the sphere of social life, see Sturman, *The Government of Social Life*.
47. William Cornish, et al., eds., *Oxford History of the Laws of England: Volume XI 1820–1914* (Oxford: Oxford University Press, 2010), 41–71.
48. For Bentham's conception of legislation, see David Lieberman, *The Province of Legislation Determined: Legal Theory in Eighteenth-Century Britain* (Cambridge: Cambridge University Press, 1989), 269–90. For Elphinstone and Bentham, see Ballhatchet, *Social Policy*, 34–36.
49. Michael Lobban, *The Common Law and English Jurisprudence 1760–1850* (Oxford: Oxford University Press, 1991), 4; Brian Z. Tamanaha, *On the Rule of Law: History, Politics, Theory* (Cambridge: Cambridge University Press, 2004), 57; Mukherjee, *India in the Shadows of Empire*, 55–71.
50. The metropolitan legal world was coloured by jurisdictional conflicts between, for example, the king's bench and the chancery in the sixteenth and seventeenth centuries. Baker, *An Introduction*, 39–41, 108–9.
51. Lieberman, *The Province of Legislation Determined*; Tamanaha, *On the Rule of Law*; David Dyzenhaus, *The Constitution of Law: Legality in a Time of Emergency* (Cambridge: Cambridge University Press, 2006).
52. David Lemmings, *Law and Government in England During the Long Eighteenth Century: From Consent to Command* (Basingstoke: Palgrave Macmillan, 2011).
53. Angus Hawkins, *Victorian Political Culture: 'Habits of Heart and Mind'* (Oxford: Oxford University Press, 2015).
54. 82 Howell's State Trial 20.
55. For the prerogative writs, see Paul D. Halliday, *Habeas Corpus: From England to Empire* (Cambridge, MA: Belknap Press of Harvard University Press, 2010), 64–95; Baker, *An Introduction*, 143–51.

56. For Calvin's case, see, Daniel J. Hulsebosch, *Constituting Empire: New York and the Transformation of Constitutionalism in the Atlantic World 1664–1830* (Chapel Hill, NC: University of North Carolina Press, 2005), 20–32.
57. 2 Burr 835.
58. 2 Swanst 1, 36 ER 514.
59. 5 Ind. D 216.
60. Lobban, *The Common Law*, 1–16, 61–98.
61. Cornish, et al., eds., *Oxford History of the Laws of England: Volume XI*, 48–52.
62. The High Court Records in the Maharashtra State Archives (Recorder's Court Diary and Supreme Court Diary), which contain the proceedings of everyday business in the courts, could not be consulted. They are not catalogued and currently not accessible to the researchers.

CHAPTER 2

Reform Public and the King's Court in Bombay City

The King's Court of Bombay in the Eighteenth Century

The King's Courts in India emerged out of the necessity of commerce at the presidency towns. The Company needed an independent court in which the Company could sue and be sued for its commercial transactions.[1] The servants of the EIC could derive benefit from such a court of law in their commercial transactions as private country traders.[2] The royal charter of 1726 empowered the Company to establish new courts of law with civil jurisdiction in Calcutta, Madras and Bombay, and accordingly, the Company established the Mayor's Courts in the presidency towns.[3] This was a court of record, comprising a mayor and nine aldermen.[4] It had civil jurisdiction of all cases in Bombay city, including the cases between Indians. The court was used by both European and Indian merchants in their business transactions. Indian business communities of all descriptions—Hindus, Muslims and, especially, the Parsis—proved adept at using the court in their business of money-lending or long-distance trade with Bengal or China. They accessed the court to recover debts, retain their assets, restore reputation and prevent divisions of business property. They also used legal procedures simply to harass rivals, even though the court's orders, such as submitting account books or depositing a large bail, were potentially harmful to their creditworthiness.[5] A significant factor was the

H. Inagaki, *The Rule of Law and Emergency in Colonial India*, Cambridge Imperial and Post-Colonial Studies,
https://doi.org/10.1007/978-3-030-73663-7_2

insecurity of coastal trade due to pirate raids by northern and southern coastal chieftains, which increased cases of insurance and 'respondentia' (loans for cargoes that were paid only when the goods arrived safely).[6]

The conflict between the court and the government was exacerbated in the late eighteenth century. The amateur merchant-judges of the Mayor's Court could not deal with legally intricate issues, the sheer quantity of which was increased by the growth of population and trade of the presidency towns of Bombay and Madras. The Madras government petitioned the Court of Directors for professional judges in 1791, and the British parliament enacted an Act (37 Geo. 3, c.142) enabling the crown to establish a new court of law in the presidency towns. Accordingly, the Recorder's Courts at Bombay and Madras were established in 1798 by a royal charter. This court was also composed of a mayor and three aldermen but presided over by a Recorder who was a professional barrister with five or more years of experience. The court was vested with civil, criminal, ecclesiastical and admiralty (but not revenue) jurisdictions over all the inhabitants in the presidency towns and the Europeans in the mofussil, save for the Governor and the Council.[7] It was not long before the court also started insisting on its role as a constitutional check against the Company.

The battle between the government and the Recorder's Court was part of a wider conflict between the executive and the judiciary over the King's Court's jurisdiction in the mofussil, in which the ideas of the rule of law and emergency became conspicuously incongruous with each other. As Philip Stern argues, the Company had developed an idea that oriental despotism rather than British rule of law was an appropriate mode of justice in India even in the seventeenth and early eighteenth centuries chiefly in its battle with maritime interlopers.[8] The territorial acquisition of the Company after the grant of *diwani* in Bengal in 1765 significantly strengthened this tendency. The divergence in these two concepts of justice first manifested in Bengal. The Supreme Court of Calcutta was established in 1774 and immediately began to interfere in the Company's governance in the mofussil. The Supreme Court took cognizance of Indians' complaints against the Nawab Nizam of Bengal and his servants. It also entertained complaints against the Company's revenue officers and issued writs of habeas corpus to liberate those who were confined for non-payment of revenue. The conflict in Calcutta exploded in the so-called Patna case of 1779, in which the Supreme Court overturned the decree of the Company's Court and ruled in favour of a widow of a zamindar who had filed a suit against the Company's Muslim law officers.

The Patna case was followed by a more open conflict in a banker's case against the zamindar of Cossijurah, in which the Supreme Court ruled in favour of the banker, issued writs of capias and sequestration against the zamindar and sent a small force to execute the writ. In response, the government also sent soldiers who prevented the legal decision from being enforced. These conflicts exposed the problem of the Supreme Court's interference in the mofussil. As the result, the Act of Settlement in 1781 (21 Geo. 3, c. 70) was enacted to provide that the Supreme Court did not have jurisdiction over the revenue affairs, over the zamindars and the revenue farmers, and over the official duties of the Company's servants.[9] The Bengal conflicts were imported to Britain by Edmund Burke at his impeachment trial of Warren Hastings. Burke attacked Hastings by vindicating the Indian law, property and nobility—just as he did in his defence of the British constitution in the aftermath of the French Revolution—while Hastings defended his acts in India as acts of state necessity.[10]

The conflict in Bombay reflected the Company's unstable relationship with private merchants. The vibrant commercial community in Western India tended to criticise the government when they felt the need to do so. In the eighteenth century, the EIC's policies were dominated by the interest of these European merchants engaging in the country trade and their Indian counterparts controlling all the commercial activities of the EIC in the subcontinent based on the network of hundis. For example, the commercial interests of the cotton merchants were the chief motive for the EIC's acquisition of cotton fields in Gujarat and Baroda after the Second Maratha War in 1803–1805.[11] In the Mayor's Court, the merchant-judges represented the commercial interests and asserted their independence from the government, leading to a series of conflicts.[12] The King's Court represented the voices of merchants who, in turn, asserted their autonomy from the government.[13] Besides, the King's Court jeopardised the EIC's political authority by enforcing English court procedures in cases relating to religion and caste, which was against the EIC's judicial policy.[14] The conflicts that ensued eventually resulted in the Charter of 1753, which weakened the Mayor's Court by giving the Governor and Council the power to nominate the mayor and aldermen and removing the court's jurisdiction over cases between Indians.[15]

The conflict was exacerbated by the government's acquisition of territories in the mofussil in the early nineteenth century. The acquisition of inner territories, first in Gujarat in 1803–1805 and then in the Deccan in 1817–1818, meant that the government could expect land revenues that would be the basis of financial autonomy and independence from the merchants. These were the events that spurred Bombay's transformation from 'city state to capital city'.[16] This change was accompanied by an important prohibition imposed on the EIC officials in 1806 from trading in their private capacity.[17] This altered the relationship between the government and the court. Thereafter, the EIC servants were to deal with the King's Court only in their official capacity and therefore unable to derive any benefit from the court as private merchants. As territorial administration became the main duty of the EIC, they needed to deal with Indian magnates in villages, hills and mountains in the mofussil, as well as the British and Indian merchants in the presidency town.[18] A new pattern of politics was emerging in the presidency. In addition to commercial conflicts between the government and the private merchants, disputes between the government and the King's Court over political and legal affairs in the mofussil became the basic framework of politics until 1834.

Reform Public, Press, Police and the King's Court in the 1820s

In the 1820s, the presidency towns of Calcutta, Madras and Bombay were becoming the centre of the reform public. Respectable Indian residents delivered their voice to the government on a wide variety of topics ranging from its conduct of war to everyday commercial and religious issues through the press, public meetings and petitions.[19] In the realm of politics, they relied on the language of English liberty and demanded a liberal political system based on the freedom of the press and the trial by jury.[20] This reformism was most marked in Calcutta, but that in Bombay was no less remarkable. The city developed its own cosmopolitan and reformist atmosphere. It was based on the mixture of Hindu, Muslim, Parsi and Portuguese Christian merchants and their diaspora, as well as the inheritance of Brahmanical bureaucratic and statistical skills of the Maratha empire.[21] Its public sphere was buttressed by the graduates of the Elphinstone College, originally established as the Bombay Native Education Society in 1824, and was coloured by the enlightened discussions in the Bombay Literary Society (later the Bombay Branch of the Royal Asiatic Society).[22] The *Bombay Courier* (1790–) and the *Bombay Gazette* (1791–) were the two major English newspapers with advertisements, news on the arrival and departure of ships, political and social correspondence, and the proceedings of the court of law. The first Gujarati weekly newspaper *Bombay Samachar* was established in 1822 by the city's first vernacular printing press established in 1812 by Parsi printer Fardunji Marzban. Its Marathi counterpart, *Bombay Darpan*, started operating in 1832.[23]

The demand for reform caused friction between the merchants and the government, with the King's Court playing a crucial role. The judges, who frequently allied with the merchants and criticised the government, were important agents of this reform culture. They led, for example, the movement to allow Indians to participate in the grand jury.[24] Their intervention was based on the charter's provisions. They were empowered to supervise and control the justices of the peace (the JPs) in Bombay city and, more significantly, to veto the Governor's legislation of rules, ordinances and regulations effective in the presidency town as the Governor needed to register the rules in the King's Court.[25] Because of these formal provisions, and because the judges were active in asserting their role as the constitutional check against the government's despotism in the presidency town, the politics in Bombay city became a major arena of the conflict between the executive and the judiciary.

Two major actors in the following narrative are Governor Mountstuart Elphinstone and Chief Justice Edward West. West was the Recorder of Bombay (1823) and the first Chief Justice of the Bombay Supreme Court (1823–28). While he is well known as a political economist who formulated the principle of diminishing returns at about the same time as David Ricardo, his Indian career has not been adequately explored, with his evaluation divided between those who supported his reformist outlook and those who criticised his opposition to the government.[26] Governor Elphinstone was a child of the Scottish enlightenment and best known as the writer of the authentic travel narrative of the Kingdom of Kabul in Afghanistan. He was also a disciple of Madras Governor Thomas Munro and one of the major practitioners of the Munro school of paternalist colonial administrators.[27] The animosity between the judge and the Governor is still regarded as an outcome of their personal dislike and mutual misunderstanding. This was true to some extent since West was not a member of the Bombay Literary Society established by Elphinstone, and they almost engaged in a duel.

But their conflict was structural as well as personal. At the core of this rivalry were the different perspectives on the judicial administration in the colony: the Governor stressed the need for discretion; the judge demanded adherence to rules and procedures. This schism was displayed in 1823 when the Chief Justice held a special court to publicly reprehend William Erskine, Elphinstone's protégé, for fraud and extortion. Erskine was judged guilty and dismissed from the offices of the Master in Inquiry and the Clerk of the Small Cause Court.[28] This issue became the subject of a press war between the court and the government. The government claimed that 'informalities in pleading or in technical forms' were necessary in India. By contrast, West defended legality rather than discretion, emphasising that the King's Court was the protector of the Indians from extortion, fraud and oppression.[29] The court's criticism was based on the assumption that liberties (for both Indian and British subjects) should be protected in the same manner as obtained in Britain, while the government took a more particularistic attitude in asserting that the executive power of discretionary intervention should be prioritised in the colonial administration. The court's power to deny registration of the town regulations was problematic for the government because the administrators dealt with the issue of town management in the same manner as mofussil governance, stressing the importance of security over civil liberties.

The court also criticised the government's restriction of the freedom of the press. In 1825, the government tried to introduce press regulation in Bombay city and ended up in a dispute with the King's Court. The issue started with Governor-General John Adam's notorious licencing regulation for Calcutta in 1823.[30] The Court of Directors ordered the Bombay government to pass a similar regulation, explaining that it was aimed at preventing newspapers 'to bring the Government of this country … into hatred and contempt, and to disturb the peace, harmony, and good order of society'.[31] Governor Elphinstone supported this measure, describing that 'some of the natives at the Residencies now read our papers, have papers of their own, talk of liberty and Whigs and Tories' and, especially, the sepoys were 'ready to trample on [the government] if they see it despised by their superiors'.[32] The Bombay government submitted Rule, Ordinance and Regulation I of 1826 to the Supreme Court for registration,[33] but the judges refused to do so. Instead, they criticised the government's attempt to generalise the legislation in Calcutta which they thought was initially intended to deal with a particular problem in that city. Judge West noted that there was not a similarly urgent situation in Bombay which justified the enactment in Calcutta. Charles Chambers, the Puisne Judge, also denied the existence of state necessity, arguing that to introduce the measure at a 'time of perfect tranquillity' and 'not as a remedy for any existing or imminent evil but as a general and permanent act of legislation' was 'most prejudicial to the independence and good spirit of the community'.[34] In other words, they criticised the government's intention to normalise the emergency measure in times of peace. The government's logic of emergency was rejected by the court's defence of civil liberties.

The King's Court's judges also criticised the government's administration of the police in the city. The history of policing in Bombay city was from the start defined by the conflict between the government and the court. In 1808–1811, one of such criticisms by James Mackintosh, the Recorder, led to the reform of the legal system through the introduction of the Court of Petty Sessions consisted of Stipendiary Magistrates (Rule, Ordinance and Regulation I of 1812).[35] Similarly, the police reform provided Edward West with a chance to criticise Elphinstone's administration. In 1825, in a long charge to the grand jury, frequently quoting Mackintosh, West declared that policing in Bombay was 'a system of discretion, and never a system of law'. Like Mackintosh, West singled out the arbitrary use of banishment and flogging which he said was not 'reasonable and moderate' as stipulated in the law. Particularly problematic was the fact that prisoners were denied the chance to petition the King's Court for a writ of habeas corpus. He also followed Mackintosh in criticising the single magistrate's trying, flogging and banishing of felons and concluded that 'the whole system of the police was illegal, it must be entirely eradicated, and a new system must be adopted'.[36]

The grand jury, whose foreman Charles Norris was the government's secretary, denied the need for reform based on the logic of expediency. Norris argued that, on the ground of 'expediency alone, and not the legality of the Police Regulations' and 'considering the peculiar circumstances of Bombay ... any reduction of power of the police magistrates ... would be attended with the greatest danger, and would add much to the increase of crime'.[37] He added that the removal of aliens and the punishment of flogging should be continued with the same frequency and severity, holding that the examples of flogging mentioned in West's charge were moderate in every respect 'however it might shock the feelings of a gentleman unaccustomed to such sights'.[38] From the logic of state necessity, the Members of the Governor's Council were also strongly against West's police charge, arguing that summary conviction and punishment was 'not only salutary, but also absolutely necessary in many cases for the peace, controul, security and convenience of the community'[39] and accusing West of trying to 'disseminate an impression that the duties of the police and all punishments were discharged and inflicted by an arbitrary agent, unchecked and uncontrolled'.[40] The government communicated to the Supreme Court that any 'radical' reform was unnecessary, explaining that the problem was rather a want of energy than the excessiveness or illegality of the police.[41]

What the grand jury and the government were concerned about was the city's vagrant and alien population, which was calculated as 20,000 out of a total of 160,000 in 1826.[42] The city was troubled by the banjaras, fakirs and gosains, whose 'fanaticism' often disturbed the bazaars.[43] Francis Warden, Member of the Council, even said that to deport vagrants without regular means of subsistence was contrary to the laws of England but 'justified by the laws of expediency'.[44] The government had to take action to make sure that the city's Indian population was on their side. In 1826, the Indian inhabitants in Bombay city petitioned the government to strengthen the police to deal with frequent robberies, pointing out that the effects of wars in adjacent countries had led to an increase of refugees in Bombay. They added that robbers avoided punishment by employing attorneys and barristers.[45]

The conflict between West and Elphinstone continued. In 1826 the government proposed a new police regulation to suppress robberies more efficiently.[46] West responded that deteriorating order was not due to police regulations but inefficiency of the government's police magistrates.[47] The government reiterated that the present mode of summary conviction and punishment was necessary in Bombay, but the judges did not listen.[48] Frustrated, Elphinstone decided to terminate the correspondence and proposed a new regulation allowing the police to try felons, which was illegal in Britain as the government's Advocate General pointed out.[49] However, Elphinstone insisted that, if it was not admitted in England, its expediency should be articulated in the preamble of the new regulation, which was accordingly sent to the Supreme Court for registration.[50] West, however, rejected it.[51] After repeating his points, he concluded that he would never admit a system vesting the police with 'the extraordinary powers'.[52] The Chief Justice's criticism of the police was also reported in Calcutta,[53] and soon reached Britain, where London radicals criticised the Bombay government's arbitrary and inhuman administration of the police.[54] Such collaboration between the judges in Bombay and the radicals in London is a recurrent feature of our story. In subsequent years, criticism of policing became a standard point in the King's Court's attack on the government. In 1828, for example, Puisne Judge John Peter Grant, the central figure of the case of Moro Ragonath (the focus of Chap. 5), gave his charge to the grand jury on the issue of police. He criticised illegal summary convictions and harsh punishments by the Company's magistrates, asserting that the system was not administered 'in the spirit of the law of England'.[55]

In their support for Bombay's reform public, the judges expressed their civilian view of law and society, which sharply contrasted with the government's political and militarist outlook. They claimed that the urban administration should be managed through legal procedures stipulated in the law and answerable to the judiciary, not through the discretion of the government officials. Through these causes, they asserted the court's function as the constitutional check against the government.

Civil Trials of War and Emergency

The judges also reviewed and criticised the government's administration in their everyday business in the court. This dimension of the quotidian nature of reform culture was best captured by Indian merchants' use of the court to protect their property. One such user was a renowned Parsi merchant Cursetjee Manockjee. The other was a Hindu merchant called Amerchund Bedreechund. Both of them used the King's Court to protest against the Bombay government's confiscation of goods in times of war. As I have already discussed these cases elsewhere in detail,[56] here I will encapsulate the essence to show that the government constrained the King's Court's civil jurisdiction so that it would not hinder the government's military manoeuvre in times of crisis and emergency.

In 1803, amid the Second Maratha War (1802–1805), Arthur Wellesley (later the Duke of Wellington) sent a request to the Bombay government for rice for his Madras army, then stationed at Poona. Initially not knowing this, Manockjee as a government contractor sold rice at a discounted market rate rather than a higher contract rate. But he then realised that the rice was supplied to the army. He demanded compensation in 1804. This was the start of the famous 'rice case' that continued for more than 25 years. He sent several petitions to the government demanding the principal sum of Rs 148,000. After this attempt failed, he instituted a suit in the Recorder's Court in 1820. In 1823, Judge Edward West decided in favour of Manockjee. West articulated that the government unjustly and shamefully treated Manockjee. He formulated that the court was a constitutional check against the government's oppression of the Indians. The government officials were alarmed as the suit indicated that the King's Court could review the government's military operation in wartime and could command compensation retrospectively. The government appealed to the Privy Council, the final tribunal of colonial legal cases, and reiterated that the terms of the contract could not be applied to 'an extraordinary and accidental supply of rice' to the Madras army. While Manockjee was supported by London radicals such as James Silk Buckingham, the Privy Council overturned the decision of the Supreme Court.[57]

The second case was related to the capture of a Peshwa's treasurer during the Third Maratha War (1817–1818). The King's Court also functioned as a constitutional check against the government, assuming that the rule of law should be achieved in India as practised in Britain. The case originated in 1817 when Captain Henry Dundas Robertson captured the Peshwa's treasurer Narroba Outia's treasure in his house at Poona as war booty. Narroba claimed it was his private property and demanded compensation in the Recorder's Court in 1822. He died soon afterwards, and his trustee, Amerchund Bedreechund, continued his suit in the Supreme Court in 1826. His barrister James Morley pointed out that thousands of those who were under the EIC's injustice would come to complain about their torts for which the EIC's servants were liable. Chief Justice Edward West and Puisne Judge Charles Chambers endorsed Morley's view and decided in favour of Bedreechund in 1826. West emphasised the government's tyrannical nature by quoting Lord Mansfield's judgement in *Fabrigas v. Mostyn* that 'to maintain here that every Governor, in every place, can act absolutely; that he may spoil, plunder, affect their bodies and their liberty, and is accountable to nobody, is a doctrine not to be maintained'.[58] Crucially, the judges refuted the government's militarist logic of emergency by arguing that it was the King's Court, not the government, that could decide whether the state of emergency existed or not. This assumption alarmed the government, as did the court's order that military and confidential papers should be produced as evidence. Worst of all, the court summoned Indian rulers exempted from the EIC's judicial procedures such as the Raja of Satara, the Raja of Vinchorekur and Chintaman Rao Patwardhan. These Indian rulers complained that the summonses damaged their respectability. This was, as we shall see in the next chapter, contradictory to the EIC's policy of conciliating local bosses to realise a stable indirect rule. Elphinstone criticised that this 'exercise of sovereignty' by the court was causing 'a good deal of the ferment in the Deckan'.[59] The government appealed to the Privy Council and, despite fully supported by the London radicals accusing the government's 'despotic violence', the decision of the King's Court was again overturned.[60]

Conclusion

This chapter discussed the conflict between the King's Court and the EIC in relation to Bombay's urban reform culture, particularly focusing on the controversies over the police reform, the press regulation and the trover cases for property protection. It was a staple of the King's Court judges to criticise the government for its arbitrary and despotic urban governance. The two cases of Indian merchants challenging the EIC's higher officials exhibited the same pattern: the government's garrison-state militarism was criticised by the court's commercial and liberal constitutionalism. The contrasting visions of Indian society became a focus of debate in the courtroom, with the government's military conception of society challenged by the King's Court's civilian perspective. At issue was not whether a case was decided for or against the government, but that the government's political and military authority might be denied by the judges vested with procedural discretion in the court in a time of emergency. This anxiety over the sovereign control of political affairs was most marked in the troubles caused by the King's Court in the newly conquered provinces of the Deccan, Konkan and Gujarat, as we shall see in the following chapters.

Notes

1. *Parliamentary Papers* [PP] 1831 (320E), 112–13, Calcutta Supreme Court [Cal. SC] to Bengal Government [Ben. Gov.], 13 Sep. 1830 (no. 26), enclosure 2.
2. Cf. Lakshmi Subramanian, 'Seths and Sahibs: Negotiated Relationships Between Indigenous Capital and the East India Company', in H. V. Bowen, Elizabeth Mancke, and John G. Reid, eds., *Britain's Oceanic Empire:*

Atlantic and Indian Ocean Worlds c. 1550–1850 (Cambridge: Cambridge University Press, 2012), 311–39.

3. A case could be appealed to the Governor in Council and then to the King in Council. At this time, the criminal jurisdiction was vested with the Governor and Council who constituted the Court of Oyer and Terminer and Gaol Delivery. M. P. Jain, *Outlines of Indian Legal and Constitutional History*, 6th edition (New Delhi: LexisNexis, 2006), chapter 6.
4. Two of them could be foreign subjects. S. M. Edwardes, ed., *Gazetteer of Bombay City and Island* [*City Gazetteer*], 3 vols. (Bombay: Gazetteer Department, Government of Maharashtra, 1909), 2:213.
5. Sheila Smith, 'Fortune and Failure: The Survival of Family Firm in Eighteenth-Century India', *Business History* 35, no. 4 (1993), 44–65. See also Niles Brimnes, 'Beyond Colonial Law: Indigenous Litigation and the Contestation of Property in the Mayor's Court in Late Eighteenth-Century Madras', *Modern Asian Studies* 37, no. 3 (2003): 513–50.
6. Subramanian, 'Seths and Sahib'.
7. *City Gazetteer*, 2:213–29; Jain, *Outlines*, 102–3.
8. Philip J. Stern, *The Company-State: Corporate Sovereignty and the Early Modern Foundations of the British Empire in India* (New York: Oxford University Press, 2011).
9. Robert Travers, *Ideology and Empire in Eighteenth-Century India: The British in Bengal* (Cambridge: Cambridge University Press, 2007), chapter 5; Jain, *Outlines*, chapter 8; A. C. Banerjee, *English law in India* (New Delhi: Abhinav Publications, 1984), chapter 1; Chittaranjan Sinha, *The Indian Civil Judiciary in Making 1800–1833* (New Delhi, 1971), 162–69.
10. P. J. Marshall, *The Impeachment of Warren Hastings* (London: Oxford University Press, 1965); Nicholas B. Dirks, *The Scandal of Empire: India and the Creation of Imperial Britain* (Cambridge, MA: Harvard University Press, 2006); Mukherjee, *India in the Shadows of Empire*, chapter 1; Frederick G. Whelan, 'Burke on India', in David Dwan and Christopher Insole, eds., *Cambridge Companion to Edmund Burke* (Cambridge: Cambridge University Press, 2012), 172–76; Daniel O'Neill, *Edmund Burke and the Conservative Logic of Empire* (Berkeley, CA: University of California Press, 2016), 110–23.
11. Holden Furber, *John Company at Work: A Study of European Expansion in India in the Late Eighteenth Century* (Cambridge, MA: Harvard University Press, 1948), 191–224; Pamela Nightingale, *Trade and Empire in Western India, 1784–1806* (Cambridge: Cambridge University Press, 1970), chapters 6–7; Lakshmi Subramanian, *Indigenous Capital and Imperial Expansion: Bombay, Surat and the West Coast* (Delhi: Oxford University Press, 1996), 253–73, 297–8, 315n172.

12. *City Gazetteer*, 2:215–9; Lakshmi Subramanian, 'A Trial in Transition: Courts, Merchants and Identities in Western India circa 1800', *Indian Economic and Social History Review* 41, no. 3 (2004): 269–92.
13. Gagan D. S. Sood, 'Sovereign Justice in Precolonial Maritime Asia: The Case of Mayor's Court of Bombay 1726–1798', *Itinerario* 37, no. 2 (2013): 46–72.
14. For instance, in 1730, a Hindu woman, who converted to Christianity and whose son fled to a relative, sued the relative in the court. The relative complained to the Governor. The Governor warned the court that it could not take cognizance of affairs of religion and caste, but the court strongly protested that it could. Jain, *Outlines*, 40. The Hindu sensitivity was also injured by the so-called cow-oath, by which all Hindu witnesses were made to take hold of a cow's tail and swear to tell the truth in the court. *City Gazetteer*, 2:216–17.
15. Jain, *Outlines*, 43.
16. Jim Masselos, 'Changing Definitions of Bombay: City State to Capital City', in Indu Banga, ed., *Ports and Their Hinterlands in India (1700–1950)* (New Delhi: Manohar, 1992), 273–316.
17. Though we should not overemphasise this. Even in the early nineteenth century, the Governorship of Jonathan Duncan (1795–1811) was still characterised by its concession to the private merchants. Pamela Nightingale, 'Duncan, Jonathan (*bap.* 1756, *d.* 1811)', *Oxford Dictionary of National Biography [ODNB]*; online edition, 21 May 2009 [https://doi.org/10.1093/ref:odnb/8224, accessed 24 Feb. 2021].
18. The domination of merchants was further curtailed by economic depression in the early nineteenth century, which could not rise until the cotton and opium trade started to boost Bombay's economy in the 1830s. Meera Kosambi, 'Commerce, Conquest and the Colonial City: Role of Locational Factors in Rise of Bombay', *Economic and Political Weekly* 20, no. 1 (1985): 32–37; Claude Markovits, 'Bombay as a Business Centre in the Colonial Period: A Comparison with Calcutta', in Sujata Patel and Alice Thorner, eds., *Bombay: Metaphor for Modern India* (New Delhi: Oxford University Press, 1995), 26–46; V. D. Divekar, 'Regional Economy 1757–1857: Western India', in Dharna Kumar, ed., *Cambridge Economic History of India, Volume 2 c.1757–c1970* (Cambridge: Cambridge University Press, 1983), 332–52.
19. P. J. Marshall, 'The Whites of British India, 1780–1830: A Failed Colonial Society?', *International History Review* 12, no. 1 (1990), 26–44; C. A. Bayly, *Indian Society and the Making of the British Empire* (Cambridge, 1998), 68–76; Joseph Hardwick, 'Vestry Politics and the Emergence of a Reform "Public" in Calcutta 1813–36', *Historical Research* 84, no. 223 (2011),

87–108; C. A. Bayly, *Recovering Liberties: Indian Thought in the Age of Liberalism and Empire* (Cambridge: Cambridge University Press, 2012), chapters 1–4; Partha Chatterjee, *The Black Hole of Empire: History of a Global Practice of Power* (Princeton, NJ: Princeton University Press, 2012), chapters 4–7.
20. Jon Wilson, 'The Silence of Empire: Imperialism and India', in David Craig and James Thompson, eds., *Languages of Politics in Nineteenth-Century Britain* (Basingstoke: Palgrave Macmillan, 2013), 228–29.
21. C. A. Bayly, 'Bombay's "Intertwined Modernities" 1780–1880', in Michael S. Dodson and Brian A. Hatcher, eds., *Trans-Colonial Modernities in South Asia* (London: Routledge, 2012), 231–48.
22. Christine Dobbin, *Urban Leadership in Western India: Politics and Community in Bombay City 1840–1885* (Oxford: Oxford University Press, 1972), chapters 1–2.
23. Anant Kakba Priolkar, *The Printing Press in India: Its Beginnings and Early Development* (Bombay: Marathi Samshodhana Mandala, 1958), 72, 78–79.
24. Lynn Zastoupil, *Rammohan Roy and the Making of Victorian Britain* (Basingstoke: Palgrave Macmillan, 2010), 117; Bayly, *Recovering Liberties*, 61–71.
25. Jain, *Outlines*, 66, 68.
26. Maxine L. Berg, 'West, Sir Edward (bap. 1782, d. 1828)', *ODNB*, online edition, 23 Sep. 2004 [https://doi.org/10.1093/ref:odnb/29079, accessed 24 Feb. 2021]; Frederic Dawtrey Drewitt, *Bombay in the Days of George IV: Memoirs of Sir Edward West, with Hitherto Unpublished Documents*, 2nd edition (London: Longmans, 1935).
27. Ballhatchet, *Social Policy*; Shah Hahmoud Hanifi, ed., *Mountstuart Elphinstone in South Asia: Pioneer of British Colonial Rule* (London: Hurst, 2019).
28. *Oriental Herald*, 18 (1828), 137–51.
29. *Asiatic Journal*, 25 (1828), 452–61, the quotation at 454.
30. Cf. Chatterjee, *The Black Hole of Empire*, chapter 4.
31. British Library [BL], India Office Records [IOR] F/4/1241/40865, 7–10, Bombay Public/General Letter, CoD to Gov., 30 Dec. 1825.
32. T. E. Colebrooke, *Life of the Honourable Mountstuart Elphinstone*, 2 vols. (London: Murray, 1884), 2:165, M. Elphinstone to E. Strachey, 17 Nov. 1824.
33. The proposed ROR I of 1826 was printed in *Oriental Herald*, 12 (1827), 211. See also *Asiatic Journal*, 23 (1827), 309–11.
34. *Oriental Herald*, 12 (1827), 212–15.
35. Haruki Inagaki, 'Policing the Market: Metropolitan Ideas and Local Contexts in Police Reform in Early Nineteenth-Century Bombay City', in

Hiroki Shin, Shinobu Majima and Yusuke Tanaka, eds., *Moving Around: People, Things and Practices in Consumer Culture* (Tokyo: Forum for History of Consumer Culture, 2015), 171–76.

36. *Oriental Herald*, 9 (1826), 410–24.
37. Ibid., 424–25, the answer to the charge, 17 Oct. 1825.
38. Ibid.
39. BL, IOR F/4/1336/52921, 159–81, the quotation at 170, Bombay Public/General Consultations [BGC] 4 Jan. 1826, no. 1, R. T. Goodwin, minute, 10 Nov. 1825.
40. As the author of the government report of 1811, Warden was critical of Mackintosh's Rule, Ordinance and Regulations I of 1812. Ibid., 269–70, 283–90, BGC 4 Jan. 1826, no. 11, Francis Warden, minute, 19 Dec. 1825.
41. Ibid., 398–99, 401–3, BGC 4 Jan. 1826, no. 20, Gov. to Bombay Supreme Court [SC], 2 Jan. 1826.
42. Amar Farooqui, 'Urban Development in a Colonial Situation: Early Nineteenth Century Bombay', *Economic and Political Weekly* 31, no. 40 (1996), 2750–51.
43. [James Gray], *Life in Bombay, and the Neighbouring Out-Stations* (London: Bentley, 1852), 141–43. See also, Nitin Sinha, 'Mobility, Control and Criminality in Early Colonial India 1760s–1850s', *Indian Economic and Social History Review* 45, no. 1 (2008), 1–33.
44. BL, IOR F/4/1336/52921, 294–5, 297, BGC 4 Jan. 1826, no. 11, Warden, minute, 19 Dec. 1825.
45. Ibid., 424–33, BGC 15 Mar. 1826, no. 9, Hormasjee Bomanjee, Dundass Hwyewandass and inhabitants of Bombay to Gov., 15 Feb. 1826.
46. BL, IOR P/346/28, BGC 7 June 1826, no. 91, Gov. to SC, 14 Apr. 1826.
47. Ibid., no. 88, E. West to M. Elphinstone, 23 Mar. 1826; Ibid., no. 93, SC to Gov., 18 Mar. 1826; Ibid., no. 95, SC to Gov., 23 Mar. 1826.
48. Ibid., no. 97, Gov. to SC, 14 Apr. 1826; Ibid., no. 99, SC to Gov., 13 Apr. 1826; Ibid., no. 100, M. Elphinstone, minute, n.d.
49. Ibid., no. 113, Gov. to G. Norton, 8 May 1826; BL, IOR P/346/29, BGC 5 Aug. 1826, no. 113, G. Norton to Gov., 28 July 1826.
50. BL, IOR P/346/28, BGC 14 June 1826, no. 23, Gov. to G. Norton, 8 June 1826; BL, IOR P/346/30, BGC 27 Sep. 1826, no. 36, Gov. to SC, 26 Sep. 1826.
51. *Oriental Herald*, 14 (1827), 515–33.
52. Ibid., 532–33.
53. *Oriental Herald*, 9 (1826), 362–65.

54. In the East India House, the radical peer Leicester-Stanhope raised a motion accusing the police regulations. *Oriental Herald*, 10 (1826), 169–83.
55. Drewitt, *Bombay in the Days of George IV*, 291–93.
56. Haruki Inagaki, 'Law, Agency and Emergency in British Imperial Politics: Conflict between the Government and the King's Court in Bombay in the 1820s', *East Asian Journal of British History*, 5 (2016): 207–24.
57. Ibid., 211–17.
58. *Oriental Herald*, 14 (1827), 22–23, quoted in ibid., 219.
59. BL, IOR P/386/19, Bombay Political Consultations 21 Feb 1827, no. 77, M. Elphinstone, minute, 23 Jan. 1827, quoted in ibid., 221.
60. Ibid., 217–22.

CHAPTER 3

Summonses, Writs and Revenue Defaulters in the Mofussil

Introduction

The government officials in Bombay were concerned about pernicious effects of British legal institutions on the traditional social order of India. They believed that the British law was repugnant to the feeling of the Indians and would disturb tranquillity in the mofussil. In this spirit, Elphinstone, in his circular of 1819, ordered that the system of panchayat 'must be exempt from all new forms of interference and regulation on our part'.

> Such forms would throw over this institution that mystery which enables litigious people to employ courts of justice as engines of intimidation against their neighbours, and which renders necessary a class of lawyers, who amongst the natives are the great fomenters of disputes.[1]

It was vital for the Bombay officials to control this 'litigiousness' of the Indian people. Historians have found that the introduction of the British court in the mofussil had a socio-economic levelling effect and that, more importantly, this was not a one-way process of British exploitation. They have revealed that the agrarian policy of the colonial state was constantly appropriated, negotiated, modified and subverted by Indians of various description such as landlords, usurers and peasants.[2] This was also true in

H. Inagaki, *The Rule of Law and Emergency in Colonial India*, Cambridge Imperial and Post-Colonial Studies,
https://doi.org/10.1007/978-3-030-73663-7_3

western India, although the post-conquest period of the early nineteenth century is significantly under-researched.[3] This chapter focuses on the agency of the Indians using the law courts and how this affected the transition from the precolonial to the colonial agrarian order. I will argue that the Indians' use of the King's Court was as important as that of the Company's Court in determining the character of the EIC's agrarian policy and Indian responses in the newly conquered territories.

The practice of colonial law was closely linked to the political structures of the colonial state, and the judiciary never achieved autonomy from the executive. In precolonial India, revenue collection was the key indicator of political power. The enforcement of revenue collection or the voluntary tribute to superiors (called nuzzerana) reflected the assertion and admission of sovereignty of various chiefs in the mofussil and the denial of its payment the expression of sedition and rebellion.[4] This was the reason why Elphinstone issued a proclamation immediately after the conquest of the Deccan in 1818 prohibiting all persons from 'paying revenue to Bajee Row or his adherents'.[5] Since the concept of good government was underpinned by the justness of revenue collection, the government could not freely increase the amount of revenue. Elphinstone's comment is suggestive: 'The most extensive exercise of discretion passes unquestioned if authorised by a statute and exerted in a specific form; but the smallest act of authority becomes suspected if there is anything informal in the proceedings'.[6] The legitimacy of discretion was only retained by complying with the regular process of law. But, as this chapter shows, such emphasis on regularity put pressure on the government officials on the ground because they needed to adapt to the Indian ways to conduct business. Complicated networks of Indian customs forced them to improvise their everyday practices on the spot, and the formality of the European style law courts sometimes severely restricted their discretionary responses to unpredictable events.

The British courts of law were popular among Indians who wanted to access them for various purposes, particularly debt recovery suits.[7] This was partly because the British judges' lack of local knowledge enabled the litigants to manipulate the result of the case.[8] Deccan Commissioner William Chaplin commented that 'all who have bad causes prefer the Udalut'.[9] More significant, though, was the fact that the formal, egalitarian and mechanical procedures of the British courts enabled the creditors to recover debts more easily.[10] Local creditors such as Indian bankers, merchants and moneylenders used the more regular process of the Adalat to sue their debtors living in villages, hills and mountains.[11] The number of cases increased significantly in the late 1820s.[12] Significantly, the Company's Court was used by Collectors of the EIC for the same purpose. Although they were given revenue jurisdiction and could directly attach properties of revenue defaulters, more commonly they sued the defaulters in the Company's Court to put them on the same footing as a private party, hence facilitating collection of the interest as well as the principal of the debt as obtained in an ordinary civil suit.[13]

Socio-economic factors also promoted the use of the Company's Court in Bombay in the 1820s. As Sumit Guha demonstrates, the agricultural depression caused prices to fall dramatically at the beginning of British rule in the Deccan until the 1850s.[14] Collector St John Thackeray remarked that the scarcity of grain increased the grain trade along with related lawsuits.[15] Second, the ryots in the mofussil were inextricably caught in a web of public and private debts.[16] Chaplin described the situation as in 'the hellish torments of Sisyphus'.[17] The village debts were an important cause of litigation.[18] The village headmen contracted the advance of taccavi loan for the purchase of the seed, grain and cattle and, before the instalment of their first earnings, also contracted loans with the savakars who paid the revenue to the government. The savakars were also called on to pay many forced contributions (puttees). The extent of debts was difficult to estimate but 'would probably be found to exceed the means of the country to discharge them'.[19] As the government banned the charge of extra assessment for repayment and any private use of coercion (tuggaza), the only means to recover these debts was the Company's Court. These factors promoted the use of the Company's Court. But the popularity of the EIC's court entailed the accompanying rise of the King's Court in the mofussil and the government officials' difficulty in dealing with it.

Sheriff's Writs and Disturbances in the Mofussil

The exercise of jurisdiction by the King's Court in the mofussil obstructed ordinary business of government officials in several ways. Summonses were the first problem, since it was costly and time-consuming for witnesses and jurors to answer. In the 1820s, it took 2 days to travel to Bombay from Thana (Northern Konkan), 10 days from Poona (Deccan), 20 to 21 days from Surat (Gujarat) and 38 days from Dharwar (Southern Konkan). The journey cost Rs 10 per day.[20] The court would summon the EIC's judges to a criminal case and demanded that they produce documents within a week. The King's Court also summoned Magistrates (i.e. Collectors) to give testimony on cases where they had committed criminals. Non-attendance was fined usually as much as Rs 1000. The officials had to obtain permission from the government as they were prohibited to leave their station without doing so.[21] The court also summoned Indian officials such as the mufti (Islamic law scholar) as witnesses.[22] Sometimes the principal and deputy officers in the same department were summoned to the same sessions.[23] Sometimes all the high officials in a district were summoned and the local administration was paralysed.[24] The court could also issue commissions to take evidence to the officials in the mofussil.[25]

Officials in Bombay city were also troubled by summonses to the grand and petty juries. The sheriff of Bombay could summon the inhabitants of Bombay city as grand jurors because the King's Court was the court of Oyer and Terminer and Gaol Delivery.[26] Attendance on juries was mandatory, and, if residents ignored the summons, they would be fined or imprisoned for contempt of court.[27] Officials disliked jury duty. A member of the government even suggested allowing summary convictions in felonies because the summonses were so onerous.[28] The business of the EIC's judiciary was also hindered when the judges of the Sadr Adalats were summoned.[29] In one instance, a humiliating situation occurred when the testimony of a Member of the Governor's Council was heard in the witness box instead of by the bench.[30] The President of the Board of Control worried about the situation because ceremonial demonstration of authority was important for the stability of rule.[31] The Governor of Madras, Thomas Munro, commented that the judge was in a state of 'legal madness'.[32]

The other troublesome issue was the sheriff's execution of writs issued by the King's Court in the mofussil. When a decree was issued in a civil case, the sheriff appointed bailiffs and sent them to the mofussil to execute the writ. As in England, they were vested with discretionary power to resort to any means to execute it. They usually approached the EIC's Magistrates for assistance as all British subjects were mandated to support such requests. But, fearing violence, the government's officers sometimes refused to do so, hence drawing criticism from the judges of the King's Court. Indeed, sometimes the inhabitants in the mofussil resisted the attachment, especially when they were a third-part debtor or when they simply doubted the validity of the writ. In 1823 in Rajapur, the Southern

Konkan, for example, the execution of writ was violently disrupted by over 200 Brahmans and Bhatias with the support of the local kamavisdar.[33]

The government officials were critical of the sheriff's execution of writ for several other reasons as well. First, the sheriff often skipped selling the attached property at public auction and directly collected money from the third-party debtors to distribute to the creditors. The Bombay government's Advocate General resented that this 'most illegal practice' was prevalent in the mofussil.[34] Second, as the government officials were not protected by the indemnity bond, they might incur personal losses if the process was wrong.[35] Another big problem was false writs. It was easy to pretend to be the bailiffs. A Magistrate of the Southern Konkan reported that no inhabitants in the district could judge whether a writ was genuine because they could not read English.[36] Another and no less problematic issue was conspiracy and collusion between the plaintiff and the defendant. H. D. Robertson, the Collector, Magistrate and Judge of Poona, was involved in a typical situation in 1820 when he was asked to assist the sheriff's officers. He discovered that the defendants in Poona had colluded with the plaintiff in Bombay to snatch property from a person in Poona with whom they had a dispute. The situation highlighted the deep enmity between the local people in the countryside who despised these 'imprudent folks' from Bombay city and the bailiffs who shouted 'Here all you Bramins make gentlemen believe anything. But the case is very different in our Bombay'.[37] Robertson arrested the sheriff's officers for disturbing the peace of the region. But he was in turn prosecuted by the sheriff in the Recorder's Court. The case caused considerable concern among officials.[38]

During the event, Robertson and his superior William Chaplin, the Deccan Commissioner, objected to the King's Court's exercise of jurisdiction in the mofussil. Robertson justified his arrest of the sheriff's officers by saying that they acted 'without legal authority'.[39] He later insisted that the Indians should not be subjected to 'a power, the nature or extent of which had not been explained to them'. It was unjust because, while sheriff's officers could seize anyone's property, those whose property was taken could only obtain redress by going to Bombay and filing a ruinously expensive suit against the officers.[40] Chaplin likewise urged the government to take some measures to 'prevent the permanent establishment of the English Code with all its appurtenances, in a conquered territory, whose inhabitants, religion, laws, moral habits, customs and prejudices are totally repugnant to ... our British institutions'.[41] The government could not intervene in the court's legal proceedings, however. The Company's Solicitor, W. A. Morgan, explained to Elphinstone that Robertson was liable to the Recorder's Court's attachment for impeding the execution of the writ and that he was also liable to a civil action for damages for his 'illegal interference'. The third-party debtor in Poona should have resorted to the King's Court for redress by suing the sheriff. The inconvenience of the suit in Bombay was 'imaginary': he only needed to write to an agent in Bombay to make the suit—even coming to Bombay by himself was no great hardship. In sum, he should not have sought redress outside the King's Court. Eventually, Robertson was judged guilty of contempt and ordered to pay Rs 387 for damages. The judge, W. D. Evans, concluded that any Magistrate would incur the penalty if he took a similar line.[42] Indeed, a comparable case occurred in 1826 when a British officer in Poona refused to assist the sheriff's officer's execution of a writ.[43] But, the government could not maintain this legalist position when the King's Court's jurisdiction in the mofussil started to have detrimental effects on the EIC's revenue collection.

Revenue Defaulters' 'Abuse' of the King's Court

When Collectors and Magistrates were concerned about the danger of the sheriff's writs, the judges of the Company's Court were facing a threat to their judicial authority from Indians' forum shopping: Indians used the King's Court to overturn the decree of the Company's Court, including the decision of the panchayat.[44] In 1823, for example, the Judge of the Northern Konkan, E. H. Baillie, reported that the King's Court had attached a property publicly auctioned in the zilla court and sold it to an inhabitant of Bombay. Baillie cautioned that this would give the impression that the King's Court could nullify a decree of the zilla court without the consent of the government and that the property was insecure even if it was guaranteed under the deed of the zilla court. He pointed out that, if similar cases were allowed in the future, every property was to be placed outside the jurisdiction of the zilla court, even if the said property was situated within the Company's territory, since its owner could effectively lift the zilla court's jurisdiction by applying to the King's Court. Baillie emphasised that it was of 'great importance' that 'the natives should look up to and place the greatest confidence in their legally constituted courts of justice … and to consider that their acts can alone be set aside by the Government, to whom an appeal is always open'.[45]

Forum shopping was facilitated by several factors. One was the 'extremely tardy' process of the Adalat. An Assistant Judge in the mofussil explained that, before the Company's Court could execute its judgement for a plaintiff in the form of public auction, a creditor via the King's Court had sufficient time to commence his action, receive judgement, obtain a writ of execution (fieri facias) and recover the amount of the debt.[46] Another factor was expensive court costs to make a countersuit against the sheriff's officers in the King's Court. In 1825, John A. Dunlop, the Collector of Ahmednagar, reported that a petitioner's property was sold for his brother's debt, although their partnership had been dissolved for two years. Dunlop thought this unjust, but he said that the petitioner was too poor to prosecute the bailiffs in the King's Court and begged the government to pay his expenses.[47] The third factor was Indians' access to lawyers in Bombay city. They were well informed about the pro-government and anti-government attorneys. Those making suits against the government often employed Frederick Ayrton, Thomas W. Browne and William Fenwick. On the other hand, when they were making countersuits against the sheriff and his officers, they employed such attorneys as William A. Morgan and his brother Edward C. Morgan, both the Company's Solicitors in Bombay.

Against this backdrop, revenue defaulters' forum shopping through the King's Court became a serious political problem. As explained before, Collectors usually instituted civil suits against defaulters in the Company's Court to recover debt with interest. This process had one disadvantage: it allowed the debtors to resort to the King's Court to overturn the decree of the Company's Court obtained by Collectors. Many examples of revenue debtors' evasion using the King's Court were recorded in the Company's revenue proceedings. In one of such cases, for example, in the Northern Konkan in 1825, a defaulter called Shaik Ahmed Kubbe in Thana applied the Collector to go to another town in the Northern Konkan to apprehend his security. On his way back to Thana, he visited one Hassein in Bombay city. Kubbe stayed there for four days, was arrested upon a writ of the Supreme Court taken out against him by Hassein and was lodged in the Bombay gaol. The Collector was convinced of collusion between Kubbe and Hassein, but the government could do nothing but blame the peon who took Kubbe to Bombay.[48] It is remarkable that how little power the government had to deal with this kind of revenue evasion.[49]

For the district officials, the crucial issue was the EIC's judicial authority rather than lost revenue. This was well illustrated by the following case.

One Kassem Hoosseen Wohoray was involved in four cases of revenue arrears in the Sadr Diwani Adalat as the security of the prosecuted. He was arrested under the Company's Court's decree in Bombay but was released the next day from the gaol and taken into custody by officers of the deputy sheriff. He was said to be guarded by armed men to prevent further seizure by the Adalat. The Northern Konkan Collector criticised the sheriff and the deputy sheriff and insisted on filing a suit against them.[50] The Northern Konkan Judge expressed his concern that 'if suffered to pass unnoticed and unpunished, it will be the means of lowering the court in the eyes of the natives, and bringing its authority in disrepute'.[51] The Advocate General agreed that it was 'a flagrant contempt of the Adawlut Court' created by 'a conspiracy among the friends of the prisoner to abuse the process of the Supreme Court by a sham suit' but added that their indictment was difficult as it was 'almost impossible that such circumstances can be detected so clearly as to be brought home to the parties'.[52] These cases demonstrate the government's inability to take effective measures against the revenue defaulters' forum shopping.

Native Agents and Revenue Farmers

The government's officials were concerned about detrimental effect of the King's Court on the political authority of high-ranking Indians. The inhabitants of the mofussil either came to Bombay or sent agents to the city to file complaints in the King's Court against the chiefs and sardars. Their suits were chiefly aimed at debt recovery. Chaplin reported that the sardars were 'in general much embarrassed by their creditors, notwithstanding that every possible consideration is extended to them in respect of their debts'.[53] In 1822, for instance, Gunput Row Patwardhan of Shedball, one of the most powerful sardars in the Deccan, was sued by a village head [patil] for debt. Chaplin cautioned that this kind of event would lower the dignity of chiefs 'whom we are bound by our engagements to treat as independent and may have the effect of frightening them into a compliance with claims that are not legitimate'.[54] These suits sometimes obstructed the government's revenue policy. The government had replaced the sardars' huks (customary dues collected in the watan lands) with a payment by the government to ease the burden of the ryots and persuade the sardars to improve the wastelands.[55] But, in the Northern Konkan in 1826, a Bombay creditor sued a sardar for debt, attached the huks and demanded the Collector pay part of the debt as the granter of the huks.[56] The government denied the jurisdiction of the King's Court since this case was a matter of revenue.[57]

The King's Court was also used by the 'natives of rank' for various purposes, especially in their family conflicts. This posed a serious problem for the government since such cases involved labyrinthine issues of kinship, joint-property relationships or land titles. Chaplin confessed, for example, that there was no prospect for early adjustment of the family conflict of the Patwardhans. He even admitted that the decisions in the Company's Courts were useless in these disputes, for the European judges were unable to make a proper judgement, and in any event, the parties were unlikely to agree with it. He could do nothing but leave them to solve the dispute by themselves.[58] For the sardars, the King's Court was another option in their forum shopping. An early example includes the case in 1820 of Raja Rutton Singh, a sardar of Malegaon, near Baramati in the Deccan.[59] Singh's father had adopted a son before he was born, but both the father and the adopted son had died, and the son of the adopted son, named Ramchunder, was claiming a share of the family property. Ramchunder employed Frederick Ayrton, the notorious anti-government attorney, and threatened Singh with a suit in the Recorder's Court. Chaplin was concerned that 'any meddling on the part of its inferior agents, amongst the natives of a conquered country, … would be attended with the most mischievous consequences'.[60]

Examining these cases of family conflict allows us to understand the way the sardars used European and Indian agents in their legal manoeuvres. A good example was a prolonged conflict in the Mankeshwurs in the Deccan. The Mankeshwurs were a prominent family under the Peshwa's government. On the accession of Baji Rao II, Sadashew Punt Mankeshwur was appointed as one of his chief officers and eventually became Prime Minister, a position he retained until he died in 1817. As he left no son, his widow adopted a distant relation, Luximon Row.[61] This succession generated fierce controversy with Sadashew's nephew, Mulhar Row, who claimed a share of inheritance as a common property of the joint family. The dispute was first submitted to the panchayat in 1819 and referred to arbitration by the Collector of Poona, H. D. Robertson.[62] But, in March 1820, Mulhar Row retained Frederick Ayrton and threatened the widow with a suit in the Recorder's Court. Robertson was concerned about Ayrton's Indian agent, one Luis Fernandes. Robertson, believing that Mulhar Row 'had the folly' to promise to pay Fernandes a 7% commission of the amount recovered, ordered Fernandes to make out a bill, which exhibited Rs 1500 in total. Robertson said that the bill would save Mulhar Row from 'his foolish bond for percentage' and prevent Fernandes, 'this jackal of the Bombay lawyer', from making any greater demand than was specified in it.[63] But, in turn, Fernandes employed Attorney William Fenwick and served the widow with notice of litigation in the Recorder's Court for the commission amounting to Rs 37,000. Chaplin in disgust reported that this was another attempt of 'the inferior law practitioners in Bombay to establish a footing in cases which appear to me to be absolutely and entirely out of the jurisdiction of the Recorder's Court'.[64] Acting Advocate General George Norton thought that the notice was of no legal effect.[65] In the event, no suit was filed in the court.

Fernandes embodied the proximity of law and violence in early nineteenth-century India. His family was notorious in the Deccan. Before the Third Maratha War, his brother Joseph de Souza was employed in the commissariat department of the Poona subsidiary force. Fernandes was arrested by the government for conspiring with a Pindari chief of Burhanpur to release a state prisoner in the custody of the Peshwa. The brothers also acted as intermediaries of sardars employing and mobilising raiders such as the Arabs and the Bhils.[66] Fernandes was an influential figure in the region—when he was arrested for beating a peon, for example, he was immediately released by 'about 75 Portuguese who severely beat the constable and other police officers'.[67] Such dangerous connections among the sardars, raiders and lawyers must have been recalled by the officials when they noticed the sardars' recourse to the King's Court.[68]

The use of the King's Court by the sardars sometimes became highly political, given the fact that these lawsuits were often directly related to the precolonial privileges of the Indian rulers. The arrest of a sardar, Ramchunder Chowdry, in 1820, for example, caused a sensation in the Deccan. He was detained under a writ of attachment issued in a case for damages of Rs 40,040 in the Recorder's Court. The case had been decided in the panchayat, but the plaintiff, one Balum Bhat Watwey, Peshwa's former military commander[69] and probably Chowdry's under-farmer, was dissatisfied with the decision and petitioned the government to reverse it. When this was rejected, Watway hired the bête noir Frederick Ayrton as his attorney and resorted to the King's Court. Chowdry was arrested but released by paying the security. In his report on the matter, Chaplin commented that the case required special attention to avert 'the acknowledged evils of introducing amongst natives of the interior foreign laws, which are totally at variance with their habits and prejudices'. He demanded that the government 'take an active part in maintaining the integrity of the jurisdiction of its own courts from the encroachments of the Recorder's Court'. Chaplin pointed out that the arrest was illegal on several grounds: Chowdry had never been to Bombay and therefore was not under the jurisdiction of the Recorder's Court; he was a minor and not personally liable to the responsibility of debt; the point in the litigation had been decided in the panchayat, from which no appeal was made; and the sheriff could arrest him only if he was found in his district. Chaplin recommended that, to recover damages for false arrest and imprisonment, the Company's Solicitor should institute a suit against the sheriff in the name of Chowdry.[70]

The news of Chowdry's arrest stirred up the country. Henry Pottinger, the Collector of Ahmednagar, reported that 'a very considerable sensation has been excited amongst all classes of our new subjects and of whom … many are similarly situated with the Chowdry' and warned that, if it was admitted, 'the whole country must inevitably be thrown into a state of confusion and alarm which will put a stop to everything else'.[71] This was due to Chowdry's status as a revenue farmer under the former Maratha empire. Before the British conquest, the sardars were appointed the revenue farmer of their districts by the Peshwa's government and paid a fixed amount of revenue to the Peshwa. They were given judicial and magisterial authority and confiscated revenue defaulters' lands and properties to recover the debt.[72] Chowdry was sued for this behaviour as a revenue farmer. Indeed, similar claims were about to flood into the Company's Court. Pottinger explained that he repeatedly declined to take cognizance of these claims for damages. If the claim against Chowdry was admitted in the King's Court, many of these old and dormant claims amounting to 'crores of rupees' would be instantly brought forth.[73]

In the end, the Chowdry case was concluded when the government requested that the court issue a new order admitting that Chowdry was not under its jurisdiction,[74] to which the court acceded. The government's sense of crisis was strongly expressed in its letter to Calcutta, which was not submitted but kept on the record. This document mandated the Supreme Government to apply to the home authority to define the jurisdiction of the King's Court, in order 'to guard against the great degradation which the natives conceive to result from the arrest of persons of rank'. The Recorder was to be requested to consider 'some sort of process less irritating and repugnant to the feelings of the natives to guard against the danger of violating their prejudices'. The draft letter also referred to a case in which Chimnaji Appa was sued in the Recorder's Court for debt by 'a shopkeeper in Bombay' when the Recorder, Alexander Anstruther, asserted that Chimnaji was amenable to the King's Court and could be arrested. The government warned that even the most powerful sardars such as Chintaman Rao or Appa Desai could have been prosecuted and arrested 'in the midst of their own jageers, if the oppressed party repaired to Bombay and preferred his complaints to any of the practitioners in the King's Court'. The letter concluded that the government's policy towards the sardars would be 'rendered nugatory by the process of a court regulated by the forms prescribed by the laws of England'.[75]

Corruption, Discretion and Regular Government in the Mofussil

As we have seen, while district officials demanded strong measures regarding revenue jurisdiction, the government preferred moderate responses and was averse to an open collision with the Supreme Court. However, the government had to change its attitude when the King's Court's rulings resulted in denying the EIC's revenue and judicial authority *in toto*. By tracing the jurisdictional manoeuvres of a revenue defaulter named Govind Abbajee, one of the most notorious persons in the Northern Konkan during the 1820s, we can see the changing attitude of the government towards the King's Court. Utilising his knowledge, experience and network, Abbajee almost succeeded in outwitting the government.

Abbajee, a Prabhu, was a former head clerk of the Collector's office as translator and interpreter, who was said to have possessed 'an unlimited influence over the Collector'.[76] His relationship with the King's Court started in 1817 when he used it to evade an EIC charge of embezzlement. At that time, a vakeel of the Company's Court at Thana investigated embezzlement cases in the Collector's office and found evidence of corruption among Indian employees including Abbajee. Abbajee then conspired with the vakeel's creditor and filed a suit against him in the Recorder's Court.[77] When the sheriff's officers came to Thana to execute the writ, the EIC's Judge and Magistrate Stephen Babington did not support it because, in his opinion, the case fell outside the jurisdiction of the King's Court.[78] Recorder Alexander Anstruther reprimanded Babington, saying that he would not listen to such doubts about the jurisdiction and that he would be taken into custody if he resisted further.[79] After this initial success for forum shopping, Abbajee continued to use the King's Court to outmanoeuvre the Collector and the Judges in the Northern Konkan for over a decade. He was a bête noir at the centre of a network of those who used the King's Court to evade the collection of revenue arrears.[80]

The cases Abbajee filed indicate that the issue of the King's Court's revenue jurisdiction was intertwined with the problem of the Company's Court's legitimacy in the mofussil. Abbajee filed a plaint against the Northern Konkan Collector J. B. Simson in the Supreme Court in 1826. He claimed that the produce in his grassland was illegally confiscated and sold by the Collector at auction since the Collector had resumed the land in 1823.[81] Simson claimed that the Supreme Court did not have jurisdiction over revenue affairs and vindicated his act by detailing Abbajee's fraudulent measures to take possession of the land. He also explained that selling the crops at auction was a customary way to realise revenue in the region.[82] The government initially approved Simson's acts,[83] but then began considering Abbajee's claims. The focus of the discussion was whether it was lawful for the government to forcibly confiscate the crops before establishing its claim in the Company's Court.[84] Simson believed it was lawful, noting that such measures were allowed by the regulations and that it was customary in the Northern Konkan to prohibit cultivators from removing the crops from the village until they gave security.[85] He emphasised that the Collector had the power to decide on matters of revenue and appeal should be made to the Company's Court, not to the Supreme Court.[86] The Advocate General concurred with this opinion.[87] Nevertheless, the government denied the Collector's claim. The government was concerned about the irregularity of the Collector's confiscation as much as the corruption of Indians. The government's judicial secretary, Charles Norris, explained in his memorandum that Regulation I of 1823 (s.10) stipulated that the Collector could not deprive anyone of lands exempted from assessment without judicial inquiry. The Governor agreed that Simson had to establish the possession of the land in the Company's Court before confiscation and ordered Abbajee's crops be restored.[88]

The Collector repeatedly emphasised 'the fraudulent nature of the transaction and the established unprincipled character of Govind Abbajee' as well as pernicious effects of jurisdictional encroachment of the Supreme Court in the revenue matter. He expressed his concern about how to realise the revenue of the year. He pointed out that the regulations were silent on the rights vested in the Collector to decree arrears. He was doubtful to what extent he was authorised to place the hay land under attachment or to oblige the defendant to give security. He wanted to continue the suit because 'by withdrawing it, the Government will be subjected to heavy costs, and my proceedings will necessarily be looked upon as illegal and unsanctioned, a point of very considerable importance in Salsette, and to be carefully avoided if practicable'.[89] But the Bombay government rejected Simson's argument, reiterating that confiscating the rent-free land without judicial assessment was contrary to the regulations and that Abbajee should be restored the land and compensated.[90] This decision was endorsed by the next Governor John Malcolm.[91]

This transaction underscores the difference between the Collector's local, individual and discretionary approach, on the one hand, and the government's universal, anonymous and systematic approach, on the other, towards the revenue debtors. The Collector's emphasis on the customary legitimacy of his attachment of crops and the bad character of Govind Abbajee indicates that he conceptualised the collection of revenue debt as a series of individual responses to particular arrears. On the other hand, the Governors showed their inclination towards a universalism, in which individualised and localised responses to particular cases were of little importance. A particular corruption of an Indian officer should be redressed within the established system of justice. The systematic and regular enforcement of the regulations was vital in this respect. Thus, the Collector's discretionary attachment contradictory to the regulations was more harmful than good. In other words, the Bombay government conceptualised revenue business as an ordinary or civil matter, which should be regulated by the established system of law. By contrast, Collectors, always under the pressure of revenue maximisation and the threat of revenue debtors' evasion, felt that they were continually dealing with a series of exceptional situations. As a corollary, this difference shows that the government and the district officers took different approaches to deal with the problem of 'native corruption'. They shared the idea of 'universal venality of Indians'.[92] However, while Collectors attempted to deal with this through discretionary measures particular to each case, the government abandoned any such attempt and began incorporating the problem within an anonymous system of regulations. The different priorities of Collectors and Governors led to different attitudes towards the King's Court. The Collector emphasised the practical obstacles caused by the King's Court's intervention. Simson pointed out that his subordinate officers were repeatedly summoned to the court, and during that period, the business of the court was inevitably postponed:

> [Suits] are wilfully or maliciously protracted; on the cases coming to a hearing, the defendants are spoken of no measured strains; the acts of the Government itself are equally liable to unpleasant reflections; and the publick officers attending as witnesses, or otherwise, may hear the acts of their superiors in office in all gradations characterised as violent, or unauthorised, or unjustifiable.[93]

For Governor Malcolm, this exposure by Simson missed the point. Malcolm held that, if the Collector had followed the regulations, Govind Abbajee could not have incurred the damage he claimed, and even if he did, he could have been sued in the zilla court for his fraudulent acquisition of the title of land.[94] In other words, for the Governors, this was not the problem of jurisdictional conflict between the Company's and the King's Court but a matter of the Collector's irregular exercise of discretion. Thus, the government did not oppose the award given in Govind's favour by the prothonotary of the Supreme Court, who had been appointed the arbiter.[95]

However, the government's attitude dramatically changed in 1829, when Abbajee attempted to use the Supreme Court to stop the enforcement of the zilla court's decree against him. Abbajee threatened the Northern Konkan Judge with an action in the Supreme Court not to sell the property under attachment unless a bond of indemnification was taken from the Collector for the full value of the property. This time, Malcolm believed that the Supreme Court's interference did disrupt the regularity of the Company's revenue system—in fact the whole edifice of the judicial system—and strongly opposed it. He sent a letter to the Court of Directors and explained that, if this were allowed, even the Sadr Adalat judges could be prosecuted in the King's Court for their judgements and decrees and consequently the government's authority 'would be annihilated and the judicial and revenue administration of the country would become totally inefficacious'. He added that while the judges of the Company's Court should not be prosecuted by 'any other authority than the regular [sic] constituted court of regular superior jurisdiction', the Supreme Court would be 'a Court of Revision and Appeal over the public servants in the interior'.[96]

Malcolm's letter indicates the locus of government's anxiety: the government feared that the Supreme Court's interference would annihilate the regularity of the Adalat system which was, according to an official's comment, 'a desirable check' on Indians' attempts to defraud the government or to withhold payments of arrear, which underpinned the efficiency of revenue collection.[97] This sense of danger of the system's regularity was the major reason for Governor Malcolm's strong reaction in the Abbajee case and, ultimately, what impelled him to subordinate the power of the King's Court to the EIC's government. In the end, Abbajee failed to make use of the Supreme Court.[98] He also failed to appeal to the Sadr Adalat.[99] But his failure did not originate in the exposure of his specific corruptions. It was because his use of the King's Court threatened the authority and regularity of the Company's revenue and judicial systems. The government's version of universal rule of law in the mofussil was not to be demolished by the King's Court.

Conclusion

The King's Court's revenue intervention in the mofussil posed many problems to the government. The practical hindrance of the summons of district officers as witnesses and Bombay officers as jurors was resented. The sheriff's officers' meddling with local inhabitants disturbed the peace in the locality, and Magistrates who resisted such interference were prosecuted in the King's Court. Amid declining revenue, Collectors were very sensitive to any kind of interference in their revenue business. The revenue debtors' abuse of the King's Court was an annoyance for them, but they did not have effective means to prevent it. The anxiety about the King's Court's revenue interference was a logical conclusion of the district officials' obsession with revenue collection, which justified the use of discretionary power for debt recovery. In other words, these officials dealt with the revenue problems as emergencies. Threatened by material disturbances as well as legal conspiracies, they were always in a state of war.

At first, the district officials' sense of danger was not shared by the Bombay government and its law officers, who were more inclined to maintain regularity of the judicial system. In other words, the problem of revenue debt was conceived as a legal rather than a political issue. The government shared that attitude and could conciliate with the Supreme Court. Both aimed at achieving the regular working of the judicial system, which was less reliant on discretionary interventions of officials in individual cases and more on the established and anonymous system of legal procedures. But, ultimately, the government had to abandon its conciliatory attitude and view the problem in the light of politics and emergency when the examples of uses and 'abuses' of the King's Court were accumulated.

A far more critical situation emerged when the King's Court exercised its jurisdiction over the sardars in the mofussil. These native aristocrats were armed local magnates, whose cooperation and submission was essential for the government to keep the peace. The government had no room for conciliation on this matter. Right from the beginning, the Bombay officials openly criticised the King's Court, ultimately leading to a total revision of their relationship.

Notes

1. British Library [BL], India Office Records [IOR] P/398/71, Bombay Judicial Consultations [BJC] 22 Mar. 1820, 1520, Circular, 18 Dec. 1819. This passage was later adopted in his report. Mountstuart Elphinstone, *Report on the Territories Conquered from the Paishwa Submitted to the Supreme Government of British India* (Calcutta, 1821), 99–100.
2. D. A. Washbrook, 'Law, State and Agrarian Society in Colonial India', *Modern Asian Studies* 15, no. 3 (1981): 649–721; Peter Robb, 'Law and Agrarian Society in India: The Case of Bihar and the Nineteenth-century Tenancy Debate', in Peter Robb, *Peasants, Political Economy, and Law* (New Delhi: Oxford University Press, 2007), 90–123; Neeladri Bhattacharya, *The Great Agrarian Conquest: The Colonial Reshaping of a Rural World* (Ranikhet: Permanent Black, 2018).
3. Ravinder Kumar, *Western India in the Nineteenth Century: A Study in the Social History of Maharashtra* (London: Routledge, 1968); Sumit Guha, *The Agrarian Economy of the Bombay Deccan 1818–1941* (Delhi: Oxford University Press, 1985); Neil Charlesworth, *Peasants and Imperial Rule: Agricultural and Agrarian Society in the Bombay Presidency 1850–1935* (Cambridge: Cambridge University Press, 1985); David Hardiman, *Feeding the Baniya: Peasants and Usurers in Western India* (Delhi: Oxford University Press, 1996); A significant exception is Kenneth Ballhatchet, *Social Policy and Social Change in Western India 1817–1830* (London: Oxford University Press, 1957).
4. André Wink, *Land and Sovereignty in India: Agrarian Society and Politics in Eighteenth-Century Maratha Svarajya* (Cambridge: Cambridge University Press, 1986), chapter 3.
5. *Poona Affairs: Elphinstone's Embassy Part 2 1816–1818*. ed. G. S. Sardesai (Poona Residency Correspondence, vol.8, 1953), 302, the Satara proclamation on 11 February 1818.

6. BL, IOR P/386/18, Bombay Political Consultations [BPC] 31 Jan. 1827, no. 51, M. Elphinstone, minute, 4 Jan. 1827, quoted in Ballhatchet, *Social Policy*, 246.
7. Elphinstone noted that major subjects of litigation were boundary disputes, division of property on the separation of families, inheritance to land ('which is perhaps the greatest source of litigation throughout the whole country') and debts to bankers. Elphinstone, *Report*, 88. For the detail of the working of the court, see Hardiman, *Feeding the Baniya*, 53–56, 106, 187–92.
8. Pamela G. Price, 'The "Popularity" of the Imperial Courts of Law: Three Views of the Anglo-Indian Legal Encounter', in W. J. Mommsen and J. A. De Moor, eds., *European Expansion and Law: The Encounter of European and Indigenous Law in 19th- and 20th-Century Africa and Asia* (Oxford: Oxford University Press, 1992), 179–200.
9. William Chaplin, *A Report Exhibiting a View of the Fiscal and Judicial System of Administration Introduced into the Conquered Territory above the Ghauts under the Authority of the Commissioner in the Dekhan* (Bombay, 1824), 125.
10. Kumar, *Western India*, 153–57; R. De, 'South Asian Legal Traditions', in James D. Wright, ed., *International Encyclopedia of the Social and Behavioural Sciences*, 2nd edition, volume 23 (Amsterdam, 2015), 58–62.
11. *Thana Gazetteer* (1882), 1:306–10.
12. According to Chaplin, the numbers of cases instituted in the Deccan for the years 1819/1820, 1820/1821 and 1821/1822 were 6522, 6370 and 9660 respectively (Chaplin, *Report*, 107–29). The number increased significantly in the late 1820s.

The number of original suits in civil cases in the Company's Court, 1825–1828

	1825	*1826*	*1827*	*1828*	*1829 (first half)*
Deccan					
Instituted	12,405	15,173	24,969	25,041	6092
Decided	13,403	14,779	24,465	25,488	7344
Depending	2991	3383	3886	3439	2187
Old provinces					
Instituted	25,586	24,300	32,178	60,945	10,188
Decided	23,326	26,376	28,811	64,460	11,125
Depending	5608	3532	7878	4357	2380

Source: PP 1831–1832 (735-IV), Appendix, 226, CoD to Gov., 15 Feb. 1832. The fluctuation of the number in 1828 was due to the abolition and resumption of stamp duty. Ibid., 227.

13. BL, IOR P/400/48, BJC 24 Aug. 1831, no. 67, J. A. Dunlop to Gov., 15 Aug. 1831.
14. Guha, *Agrarian Economy*, 17–24.
15. East India Company, *Selection of Papers from the Records at the East-India House Relating to the Revenue, Police, and Civil and Criminal Justice, under the Company's Governments in India*, 4 vols. (London, 1820–26) [SRJ], 4:839–41, St. J. Thackeray to W. Chaplin, 11 Aug. 1822.
16. Elphinstone, *Report*, 9; SRJ, 3:784, Gov. to CoD, 23 Feb. 1822. See also Meera Singh, *British Revenue and Judicial Policies in India: A Case Study of Deccan 1818–1826* (New Delhi: Har-Anand, 1994), 80–83, and Hardiman, *Feeding the Baniya*.
17. Chaplin, *Report*, 174–75.
18. The rest of this paragraph is based on *R. D. Choksey, The Aftermath (1818–1826)* (Bombay: New Book, 1950), 193–95, 197–200, W. Chaplin to Gov., 5 Jan. 1820.
19. Ibid., 193.
20. *Bombay Calendar and Almanac* (Bombay, 1828), Appendix, 47–52.
21. Maharashtra State Archives [MSA], Judicial Department [JD], 1821–1823, 37/45, 1–10, Northern Konkan judge to Gov., 3 July 1821; MSA, JD, 1826, 25/126, 275–82, Northern Konkan judge to Gov. 18 Feb. 1826.
22. MSA, JD, 1821, 18B/21, 109–16, Assistant judge to Gov., 14 Mar. 1821.
23. BL, IOR P/346/24, Bombay Public/General Consultations [BGC] 25 Jan. 1826, no. 18, Gov. to SC, 20 Jan 1826.
24. MSA, JD, 1824, 18/79, 33–44.
25. BL, IOR P/399/25, BJC 8 July 1823, 3046, Sadr Adalat to Gov., 6 June 1823.
26. William Hook Morley, *An Analytical Digest of All the Reported Cases Decided in the Supreme Courts of Judicature in India, in the Courts of the Hon. East India Company, and on Appeal from India, by Her Majesty in Council*, 2 vols. (London, 1849–1850), 2:667, Bombay Supreme Court [SC] Charter, XLIV.
27. Ibid, 2:666, SC Charter XLIII.
28. BL, IOR F/4/1336/52921, 355–7, BGC 4 Jan. 1826, no. 16, R. T. Goodwin, minute, 23 Dec. 1825.
29. MSA, General Department [GD], 1829, 19/196, 333–36, Sadr Adalat to Gov., 12 June 1829; Ibid., 347–48, Sadr Adalat to Gov., 19 June 1829.
30. Frederic Dawtrey Drewitt, *Bombay in the Days of George IV: Memoirs of Sir Edward West, with Hitherto Unpublished Documents*, 2nd edition (London: Longmans, 1935), 223–25; BL, MSS Eur F88/399, 251–332.
31. BL, IOR F/2/9, 24–32, C. Williams Wynn to E. West, 19 Jan. 1827.
32. BL, Mss Eur F88/397, 26–27, Thomas Munro to M. Elphinstone, n.d.

33. BL, IOR P/399/25, BJC 16 July 1823, 3064, W. A. Morgan to Gov., 30 June 1823.
34. BL, IOR P/346/26, BGC 19 Apr. 1826, no. 68, G. Norton to Gov., 17 Apr. 1826.
35. BL, IOR P/399/37, BJC 25 Aug. 1824, 4935–39, V. Hale, Southern Konkan judge, to Gov., 22 June 1824; BL, IOR P/399/37, BJC 15 Sep. 1824, 5264–67, V. Hale to Gov., 1 Sep. 1824; BL, IOR P/399/38, BJC 29 Sep. 1824, 5554–55, E. Grant, Surat criminal judge, to Gov., 10 Sep. 1824.
36. MSA, JD, 1821–23, 37/45, 173–88, J. A. Dunlop to Gov., 11 Apr. 1823.
37. BL, IOR P/398/75, BJC 20 Sep. 1820, 3788–813, enclosure no. 7, H. D. Robertson to W. Chaplin, 5 Sep. 1820.
38. A special volume of 'the sheriff's writ' was compiled in the judicial department: MSA, JD, 1821–23, 44/53.
39. BL IOR/P/398/72, BJC 31 May 1820, 2652–55, H. D. Robertson to W. Chaplin, 13 May 1820. Emphases are original.
40. BL, IOR P/398/75, BJC 20 Sep. 1820, 3788–813, H. D. Robertson to W. Chaplin, 5 Sep. 1820.
41. BL, IOR P/398/74, BJC 9 Aug 1820, 3221–23, W. Chaplin to Gov., 31 July 1820.
42. BL, IOR P/398/78, BJC 13 Dec. 1820, 5268, William Ashburner Morgan to Gov., 1 Dec. 1820.
43. BL, IOR P/346/26, BGC 19 Apr. 1826, no. 72, R. K. Arbuthnot to W. Chaplin, 12 Apr. 1826; BL, IOR P/346/27, BGC 10 May 1826, no. 28, G. Norton to Gov., 26 Apr. 1826 and no. 31, circular, 6 May 1826.
44. For a case relating to the panchayat, see BL, IOR P/398/63, BJC 16 June 1819, 1525, J. W. Pelly to Gov., 14 Apr. 1819; Ibid., Gov. to F. Ayrton, 10 June 1819.
45. BL, IOR P/399/25, BJC 2 July 1823, 2982–85, E. H. Baillie to Gov., 13 June 1823.
46. MSA, JD, 1829, 21/193, 57–75, Alexander Bell, Assistant Judge of the Northern Konkan, to Gov., 22 July 1829.
47. BL, IOR P/399/49, BJC 12 Oct. 1825, no. 18, J. A. Dunlop to W. Chaplin, 26 Sep. 1825, enclosed in W. Chaplin to Gov., 28 Sep. 1825.
48. BL, IOR P/369/9, Bombay Revenue Consultations [BRC] 2 Nov. 1825, no. 58, J. B. Simson to Gov., 24 Oct. 1825; Ibid, no. 59, Gov. to J. B. Simson, 31 Oct. 1825.
49. For another example of one Khanoot Ravoot, see BL, IOR P/369/21, BRC 21 June 1826, nos. 59–61; BL, IOR P/369/29, BRC 6 Dec. 1826, nos. 1–8.
50. BL, IOR P/400/2, BJC 24 Jan. 1827, no. 54, J. B. Simson, to Gov., 15 Jan. 1827; BL, IOR P/400/3, BJC 14 Feb. 1827, no. 29, Alexander Bell, Acting Register of Sadr Adalat, to Gov., 16 Jan. 1827.

51. BL, IOR P/400/3, BJC 28 Feb. 1827, no. 7, E. H. Baillie to Gov., 9 Feb. 1827.
52. BL, IOR P/400/3, BJC 7 Mar. 1827, no. 23, G. Norton to Gov., 14 Feb. 1827.
53. Chaplin, *Report*, 162.
54. Chaplin added that he had just received a complaint of a similar nature from Punt Sucheen (Pant Sachiv), a major jagirdar in the territory of the Raja of Satara, who was under the protection of the British government. BL, IOR P/385/19, BPC 20 Mar. 1822, 1571, W. Chaplin to Gov., 10 Mar. 1822.
55. R. D. Choksey, *Economic Life in the Bombay Konkan 1818–1939* (New York: Asia Publishing House, 1960), 53.
56. BL, IOR P/346/26, BGC 19 Apr. 1826, nos. 31–32, J. B. Simson to Gov., 11 Apr. 1826.
57. Ibid., no. 68, G. Norton to Gov., 17 Apr. 1826; Ibid., no. 69, Gov. to J. B. Simson, 18 Apr. 1826.
58. Chaplin, *Report*, 158. The dispute continued well into the 1840s. Edward W. West, *A Memoir of the States of the Southern Maratha Country* (Bombay: Education Society's Press, 1869), 46–58, 86–100.
59. John Clunes, *Appendix to Itinerary and Directory of Western India* (Bombay: American Mission Press, 1828), 15. He was later entered into the civil list of the second class sardars. BL, IOR P/399/64, BJC 18 Oct. 1826, no. 31, list of sardars.
60. BL, IOR P/398/70, BJC 9 Feb. 1820, 683–86, W. Chaplin to Gov., 26 Jan. 1820. Eventually, Ayrton apologised, and this case was settled. BL, IOR P/398/71, BJC 8 Mar. 1820, 1232, Ollyett Woodhouse to Gov., 2 Mar. 1820.
61. BL, IOR V/27/70/10, 63.
62. Detailed records of this family conflict were compiled in one volume: MSA, JD, 1821–23, 10/10.
63. BL, IOR P/398/72, BJC 5 Apr. 1820, 1599–601, H. D. Robertson to W. Chaplin, 25 Mar. 1820. As to the arbitration, Robertson delegated it to his assistant William J. Lumsden, who decided in favour of Mulhar Row. Luximon Row appealed to the Governor, but it was dismissed in 1822. BL, IOR P/399/16, BJC 21 Aug. 1822, 4942–55.
64. BL, IOR P/399/21, BJC 29 Jan. 1823, 362–64, W. Chaplin to Gov., 10 Jan. 1823.
65. BL, IOR P/399/21, BJC 12 Feb. 1823, 547–50, G. Norton to Gov., 11 Feb. 1823.
66. BL, IOR F/4/501/11941, 1–127, BPL, Gov. to CoD, 22 Aug. 1815 and its enclosures.
67. BL, IOR P/399/26, BJC 27 Aug. 1823, 3535–42, E. H. Baillie to Gov., 13 Aug. 1823.

68. For the Maratha military labour market, see Dirk H. A. Kolff, *Naukars, Rajput and Sepoy: The Ethnohistory of the Military Labour Market in Hindustan 1450–1850* (Cambridge: Cambridge University Press, 1990); Randolf G. S. Cooper, *The Anglo-Maratha Campaign and the Contest for India: The Struggle for Control of the South Asia Military Economy* (Cambridge: Cambridge University Press, 2003).
69. Cf. *Poona Affairs: Close's Embassy 1801–1810*, ed., G. S. Sardesai (Poona Residency Correspondence, vol.7, Bombay, 1940), 455–56, H. Russell to Governor-General, 27 Jan. 1810.
70. BL, IOR P/398/77, BJC 1 Nov. 1820, 4744–48, W. Chaplin to Gov., 26 Oct. 1820.
71. BL, IOR P/398/78, BJC 29 Nov. 1820, 5131, Henry Pottinger to W. Chaplin, 15 Nov. 1820.
72. For revenue farming, see Wink, *Land and Sovereignty*, 339–75.
73. BL, IOR P/398/78, BJC 29 Nov. 1820, 5131, Henry Pottinger to W. Chaplin, 15 Nov. 1820.
74. Ibid., 5132, W. A. Morgan to Gov., 21 Nov. 1820.
75. BL, IOR P/398/78, BJC 29 Nov. 1820, 5139–46, Draft letter to the Supreme Government, 24 Nov. 1820.
76. BL, IOR P/398/45, BJC 6 Aug. 1817, 2813–40, T. M. Keate, Salsette Judge and Magistrate, to Gov., 30 July 1817. The quotation is from BL, IOR P/400/16, BJC 26 Mar. 1828, no. 55, J. B. Simson to E. C. Morgan, 14 Mar. 1828.
77. BL, IOR P/398/44, BJC 18 June 1817, 2262–368, Stephen Babington to Gov., 6 June 1817.
78. BL, IOR, P/398/48, BJC 5 Nov. 1817, 4165–81, S. Babington to Gov., 28 Oct. 1817.
79. Harry Borradaile, *Reports of Civil Cases Adjudged by the Court of Sudder Adawlut for the Presidency of Bombay, Between the Years A.D. 1800 and A.D. 1824*, 2 vols. (Bombay, 1825), 1:364–77; BL, IOR F/4/699/18968, H. G. Macklin to Gov., 7 Nov. 1817, 31 Dec. 1817 and 12 Mar. 1818. See also Morley, *Digest*, vol. 2, 'Jurisdiction', paras 61–62, 74–77.
80. For example, he was acquainted with one of such revenue debtors, one Ramchunder Bawajee, who instituted a suit in the Recorder's Court to overturn the zilla court's sequestration of his property in 1819. BL, IOR P/398/63, BJC 28 July 1819, 1810, Stephen Babington to Gov., 19 July 1819; BL, IOR P/400/47, BJC 17 Aug. 1831, no. 7, L. R. Reid, Principal Collector in the Konkan, to Gov., 9 July 1831.
81. BL, IOR P/369/14, BRC 18 Jan. 1826, no. 28, Govind Abbajee to Gov., 9 Jan. 1826.
82. BL, IOR P/369/14, BRC 25 Jan. 1826, no. 42, J. B. Simson to Gov., 15 Jan. 1826.

83. BL, IOR P/369/15, BRC 15 Feb. 1826, no. 67, G. Norton to Gov., 30 Jan. 1826; Ibid., no. 68, Gov. to J. B. Simson, 10 Feb. 1826.
84. BL, IOR P/400/2, BJC 24 Jan. 1827, no. 66, E. C. Morgan, Company's Solicitor, to Gov., 5 Jan. 1827.
85. Cf. Guha, *Agrarian Economy*, 26–27.
86. BL, IOR P/400/2, BJC 24 Jan. 1827, no. 68, J. B. Simson to E. C. Morgan, 19 Dec. 1826.
87. Ibid., no. 69, G. Norton to E. C. Morgan, 14 Jan. 1827.
88. Ibid., nos. 70, 76, Secretary, memorandum; Ibid., no. 77, Gov. to J. B. Simson, 23 Jan. 1827.
89. BL, IOR P/400/11, BJC 21 Nov. 1827, nos. 41–42, J. B. Simson to Gov., 31 Oct. 1827; BL, IOR P/400/11, BJC 28 Nov. 1828, nos. 24–25, J. B. Simson to Gov., 19 Nov. 1827.
90. Ibid., no. 43, Gov. to J. B. Simson, 12 Nov. 1827; ibid., no. 25, Gov. to J. B. Simson, 27 Nov. 1827.
91. BL, IOR P/400/15, BJC 12 Mar. 1828, no. 63, J. B. Simson to Gov., 30 Jan. 1828; Ibid., no. 64, Gov. to J. B. Simson, 23 Jan. 1827; Ibid., no. 65, John Malcolm, minute subscribed by Commander-in-Chief and R. T. Goodwin, n.d.; Ibid., no. 69, Government resolution, 12 Mar. 1828.
92. Guha, *Agrarian Economy*, 32–38.
93. BL, IOR P/400/16, BJC 26 Mar. 1828, no. 54, J. B. Simson to Gov., 17 Mar. 1828.
94. BL, IOR P/400/15, BJC 12 Mar. 1828, no. 65, J. Malcolm, minute subscribed by Commander-in-Chief and R. T. Goodwin, n.d.
95. Rs 714 was awarded for damages with costs, amounting to Rs 1,331. BL, IOR P/400/47, BJC 17 Aug. 1831, no. 7, L. R. Reid, Principal Collector of the Northern Konkan, to Gov., 9 July 1831.
96. BL, IOR L/PJ/3/918, 137–45, Bombay Judicial Letter [BJL], Gov. to CoD, 29 July 1829, A copy of this letter is in BL, IOR F/4/1339/53186. See also BL, IOR F/4/1339/53186, 53–55, Malcolm, minute, n.d.
97. BL, IOR P/400/48, BJC 24 Aug. 1831, no. 67, J. A. Dunlop to Gov., 15 Aug. 1831.
98. The next Collector filed a suit against Govind Abbajee for a false title in the zilla court, and in July 1828, judgement was given against Abbajee, awarding Rs 17,000 for the government. His petition of appeal was rejected by the Sadr Diwani Adalat because of the lapse of time. BL, IOR P/400/39, BJC 1 Sep. 1830, no. 14, Govind Abbajee to Gov., 22 Aug. 1830; BL, IOR P/400/39, BJC 15 Sep. 1830, no. 16, L. R. Reid to Gov., 3 Sep. 1830.
99. BL, IOR P/400/47, BJC 17 Aug. 1831, no. 7, L. R. Reid to Gov., 9 July 1831.

CHAPTER 4

Indirect Rule Threatened by Raiders, Princes and the King's Court

Introduction

After the conquest of the Deccan, William Chaplin, the Deccan Commissioner, was caught in a dilemma. The semi-military post-war settlement, in which revenue and judicial duties were jointly held by officers, hindered the efficiency of both revenue collection and court proceedings. He explained that the revenue survey was necessary as inequalities of assessment had strained the resources of the country and, so, to ensure that the survey was properly carried out, Collectors should devote their full time to the business of revenue. But, 'at least one half of every week being occupied by business in their criminal and civil courts which compels them some times to neglect their ordinary Revenue duties'. Chaplin recommended the introduction of a separate judiciary in the Deccan.[1] The separation of powers was also preferable since it would make the judiciary more effective. The government's judicial secretary, David Greenhill, noted that, because Collectors were taken up with their revenue activities, the administration of justice was considerably delayed, especially since the judicial functions were often conducted by registers or young employees with little experience.[2] The separation of the executive and the judiciary entailed another important implication: it accelerated the reorganisation of 'sovereign princes' in the newly conquered territories. The government had to determine which chiefs and sardars were to be vested or deprived of sovereign privileges. The

H. Inagaki, *The Rule of Law and Emergency in Colonial India*, Cambridge Imperial and Post-Colonial Studies,
https://doi.org/10.1007/978-3-030-73663-7_4

post-conquest settlement was not a linear process of transition from political/diplomatic relations of allies to domestic relations of subjects and the sovereign. Rather, it entailed a series of reconfigurations of privileges held by major, minor and mobile sovereigns. Some tribes were harshly suppressed; some sardars were given the same status as foreign subsidiary allies now called princely states.[3] This was a rule by abstract categorisation, a key feature of modern statehood,[4] but the British were unable to build a systematic relationship with the sovereign princes, leaving 'residual sovereignty' in the princes' hands.[5] The colonial state only exerted a quasi-sovereignty over these chiefs, and the latter's forum shopping and the resultant jurisdictional jockeying destabilised the British control over these minor sovereigns.[6] In these processes of negotiation over sovereignty, the distinctions between the realms of politics and law were constantly drawn and redrawn.

The most pressing issue concerning this post-conquest settlement was the still-continuing raids and rebellions of the 'wild tribes'. The chaotic situation in the mofussil worsened after the conquest, partly because of the disruption of agrarian relations and resultant economic decline and partly because mercenaries were no longer employed in the same numbers.[7] A critical situation occurred when the Anglo-Burmese War (1824–1826) stimulated rebellions all over India, invoking 'rumours of the Company's collapse'.[8] In Bombay, a major rebellion was provoked in the princely state of Kittur in which British Collector and Political Agent St John Thackeray was killed. The provinces of the Deccan, Konkan and Gujarat were haunted by gang robberies by the Kolis, Ramusis and Bhils. The most notorious were the Bhils in the Deccan Khandesh, the subsistence of whose 50 chiefs and 5000 followers were said to be dependent on plundering.[9] After failing to suppress them by regular troops or to conciliate them with free pardon and pensions, the government embarked on an outright military suppression by employing the Bhils themselves and organising the Bhil Corps.[10] The arrest of robbers was extremely difficult.[11] In the Northern Konkan, during the six years between 1820 and 1825, a total of 483 robberies were reported, and 3163 persons were implicated, but just 406 were arrested.[12] The raids were facilitated by the absence of police in some villages. In the Poona district, for example, 11 out of 49 villages in Pabbul pargana and 131 out of 177 villages in Sewngur pargana had no police establishments.[13] The situation in Gujarat was equally bad. The government villages were troubled by raids and collection of tributes by 'refractory' chiefs (called *girasias* and *mehwasis*) of the Bhils, Kolis and Rajputs who exercised various seigneurial rights and privileges including the power of life and death.[14] Some of them retained large armed forces.[15] Because of the raids, the city of Ahmedabad, and its eastern districts of Dholka, Ranpur, Dhandhuka and Ghoga were 'in a most disturbed state'.[16] Further north, in Mahi Kantha, the Koli raids were so frequent that the government separated the region from Kathiawar in 1821 to enable closer policing. Securities were also taken from the girasia chiefs to ensure that they kept the peace, but their raids and feuds continued.[17]

The Bombay government under Elphinstone and Malcolm believed that indirect rule was the solution to this chaos. The 'natives of rank' should be empowered to exert their internal sovereignty in their territories to organise police to prevent tribal raids. As Thomas Munro, the Governor of Madras, explained to Elphinstone in 1818, the British government in the Deccan should inherit the position of the Peshwa as the head of the confederacy of chiefs.[18] This conception was based on their analysis of the state of sovereignty in precolonial Western India. Before the arrival of the British, sovereignty in the plains in the Deccan and Gujarat was shared by the hill tribes. The tribal chiefs provided the plains powers with watchmen in times of peace and soldiers in times of war. In return, they were given rent-free lands (the village headmen cultivated them), allowed to collect dues (giras) from the plains villages and, in cases of non-payment, raided them. Sovereignty over the villages was thus co-shared by the sardars in the plains and the chiefs in the hills.[19] The raids and rebellions were the tribal chiefs' means of negotiation with the state, which was part of the political structure of Bombay in the 1820s.[20] The government, however, saw such acts as defiance of British rule. Government officials were less concerned about the sardars' open resurrection and more about the decline of the sardars' political and social control which would unleash the raiders.[21] This was because the troubles caused by the wild tribes could 'infest' the British territories. Malcolm explained that the sardars were 'useful, if conciliated, in preserving the local peace, and dangerous to it if outraged or displaced'.[22]

The key to the secure indirect rule was the government's control of the judiciary. Elphinstone was convinced that the government should be the sole arbiter of political relations in the mofussil and that the law courts should not interfere. He was critical of Charles Cornwallis's judicial system in 1793 which 'led to an infinity of lawsuits ...[,] the overthrow of the village corporations, the ruin of the police, and the horrors of dacoity'.[23] It was against that background that the Elphinstone Code of 1827, comprising 33 regulations of civil, criminal, revenue and military branches, was created.[24] These regulations stipulated various exceptions from the civilian administration of law. By specifying exceptions, the government attempted to demarcate the realm of politics under the exclusive control of the government and the realm of law managed by the law courts. In so doing, the government aimed to achieve greater regularity and efficiency in ordinary revenue and judicial business and, at the same time, create a more secure ground for intervention in times of emergency. What emerged from this attempt was not a civil society based on the rule of law, but a conquest society internalising the logic of emergency.

The Realm of Law and the Realm of Politics: Bombay Regulations of 1827

The 1827 Elphinstone Code was characterised by the stipulation of exceptions to general rules. Some were common provisions, as with the Governor's power to suspend all the laws and establish a court-martial in cases of war and rebellion.[25] A Special Court could be established to try 'treason, rebellion, unlawful attempt to alter the established laws, and disturbing the peace of foreign states'.[26] Prisoners could be detained longer than usual if there were 'indispensable reasons'.[27] What was remarkable about the Elphinstone Code, however, was the exemption granted to the chiefs and sardars from the EIC's judiciary for 'reasons of state'.[28] The government tried to protect the sardars' social status and respectability so that they could effectively maintain security as sovereign landholders to deal with emergencies. In this sense, the colonial government constructed a regime of 'sovereign pluralism' to utilise the precolonial layered state of sovereignty, to ensure that British authorities could rely on indigenous elites as collaborators while retaining ultimate power as suzerain to determine the course of politics.[29]

By Regulation XV of 1827, the government vested the chiefs and sardars with policing power in their territories and exempted them from the Company's criminal jurisdiction for police action. These measures were already in force in the Deccan, and the government intended to expand them to the Old Provinces of the Konkan and Gujarat.[30] It targeted the chiefs and sardars in Gujarat who were variously called 'Grasseas, Meweysees, Jageerdars, Enamdars, &ca &ca' and who were 'subject to the Regulations in law but exempt in fact'.[31] This meant that, instead of the Indian police agents sent by the government as in Bengal (the Bombay officials were concerned about their inefficiency),[32] the local chiefs and sardars became responsible for the policing in the mofussil. Deccan

Commissioner William Chaplin recommended to bestow the power to those in charge of surinjam (military jagir) and enam estates in the Deccan (657 in total except those in charge of villages under Sindhia, Holkar and Patwardans) and specifically named 77 major and 27 minor jagirdars.[33] They would deal with 'occasions of necessity, such as the apprehension of public offenders, or the defence of the country against marauders, or an enemy' (s.3). They were expected 'to maintain the public peace throughout his jurisdiction, to apprehend public offenders, to try and to punish offences according to the authority conferred on him by his sunnud' (s.7, c.1).

Crucially important was the Indian rulers' exemption from the British legal process. Collectors and Magistrates in the mofussil expressed their concern about this point during the debate. The Deccan Commissioner Chaplin cautioned that the time had not yet come to make them amenable to the British courts.[34] Otherwise, as the Acting Collector at Broach warned, the 'mere hacking dealers of law' around the cutcherry must fall down the chiefs.[35] Accordingly, the regulation empowered the Governor to put landholders under his immediate authority alone or to determine the particular jurisdiction and procedure to which they were subjected (s.14). Though the sardars could be tried in a Court of Circuit or Special Court that could be convened privately, no one should be excluded whom the landholders wished to be present, and 'any form of courtesy and consideration due to the rank of the accused shall also be observed'(s.18).[36] The fact that the government confirmed the exemption of the sardars from the ordinary process of law was of great significance. They were now formally outside the regular working of the British legal process, and, by excluding them, the government made it clear that the de facto legal pluralism was now de jure. In effect, policing in the mofussil ceased to be a legal issue; it became a political structure falling under the government's sole ambit.

The government intended to further strengthen the authority of chiefs and sardars through a more general exemption from the Company's civil and criminal jurisdiction.[37] In 1825, Chaplin submitted a list of sardars who should be exempted from the ordinary process of the Company's Court. The list totalled 232 persons categorised into three classes. The first class, 22 in all, were wholly exempted from the process of the courts; the second class, totalling 45, were exempted from the ordinary process but 'may be requested to answer demands either by letter or by their wukeels as may be most expedient'; and the third class, with 165 individuals, were subject to the jurisdiction of the Sadr Adalat but exempted from attending the trial in person.[38] Elphinstone also proposed that any civil cases filed against these sardars should be dealt with by a special agent appointed by the government. This agent would be empowered to compound decrees that were already passed, to effectuate the compromise of debts and, 'even in the clearest case of debts', to allow the sardar to keep his house and a portion of his income 'sufficient for his decent maintenance'. The trial should be held not in a public cutcherry but 'should be conducted rather according to the forms of a Durbar than those of a Court of Justice'.[39] Francis Warden, Member of Council, opposed these measures by advocating 'uniformity' and 'efficiency', insisting that the ordinary appeals should go to the Sadr Adalat and not to the government,[40] but this was a minority view. The Judge of the Sadr Adalat, George William Anderson, was appointed as the first Agent for Sirdars in January 1827.[41] The detail of his duty was stipulated in Regulation XXIX of 1827. As recommended, the sardars were placed in three classes, and the list was furnished to the Agent in charge of all civil suits against them. The trial of the first and second classes was solely based on considerations of privilege, custom and usage, and the cases could only be appealed to the Governor. The trial of the third class was also based on custom and usage with some relaxed regulations, but the Sadr Diwani Adalat could hear appeals.[42]

The government supplemented this exemption scheme with another, equally important stipulation in the same Regulation XXIX. Section 6 stated that the Company's civil courts in the Deccan had no jurisdiction over any of the following:

> All claims for damages against persons in authority under the late Government, for abuse of power during that period; All claims against Government on account of enams; All claims against Government on account of jagheers, wurshasuns [religious pensions], pensions, neemnooks [fixed annuities], and other advantages not hereditary; All disputes regarding public rent or revenue payable to Government, and all complaints of exaction by mamlutdars, or district or village officers; All claims on account of village debts, all village boundary disputes, and disputes regarding the use of wells and watercourses.[43]

This meant that the government put the affairs of all service gentry of the former government and all holders of alienated lands (even if they were not on the list of sardars) under its exclusive control, as well as exempting itself from liability in the municipal courts concerning its policies of land and revenue. This particular clause was retained as late as 1876.[44] By this method, the suits against the sardars were categorised to be adjusted outside the court of law. The government via the Agent for Sirdars was to be the sole authority over them. This suspension of regular system of law by the Governor was essentially driven by district officers' political sense of crisis. The next Governor, John Malcolm, carried this system of exemption even further. He appointed the Zilla Judge of Poona, instead of the Sadr Adalat Judge, as the Agent for Sirdars to facilitate the use of records at Poona and introduced a new officer, the Deputy Agent for Sirdars, whose exclusive duty was to deal with suits against the sardars at Poona.[45]

The government's policy of exemption was favourably received by the sardars. They petitioned the government to be included in the lists, resulting in a rapid expansion of names. The initial list of the first class sardars had 20 names, and, 1 year later, 14 new applicants were accepted. The second class list of 57 doubled with an additional 56, and 117 persons were added to the initial 160 names on the third class list. The grand total was 494, up from 237 within a year.[46] The government found the agent's work impressive. Agent John Warden reported in 1832 that the Agent had accommodated 218 out of 308 claims 'without the expense and vexation of regular lawsuits'; 967 claims were preferred to the Deputy Agent who amicably adjusted 810. There were few arrears: between 1827 and 1832, the Agent and the Deputy Agent disposed of 1303 out of 1376 cases.[47] The Bombay government confidently reported this achievement to the Court of Directors (See Tables 4.1 and 4.2). Overall, the Agent seemed to work well. The cases of debt recovery, family disputes and revenue matters were all decided by the Agent with consideration of specific situations of sardars.[48]

The problem was the King's Court. From the start, Elphinstone was concerned about the King's Court's interference in the affairs of sardars. He asked Advocate General George Norton whether the Supreme Court had jurisdiction over the cases under the Agent of Sirdars. His specific concern was that the Agent was perceived as lacking legal authority. Elphinstone even asked the Advocate General about the possibility of conferring the authority of the court of record to the Governor for this purpose.[49] Norton replied that it was illegal, only admissible under the Peshwa's despotic government.[50] Governor Malcolm was also conscious about the necessity to seal off the chiefs and sardars from the influence of the King's Court at Bombay:

Table 4.1 The number of suits disposed of by the Agent for Sirdars, 1827–1832

	1827	*1828*	*1829*	*1830*	*1831*	*1832*	*Total*
Original suits: adjusted without resorting to law proceedings							
Claims	0	11	89	15	77	26	218
Accommodated	0	2	84	17	80	35	218
Remaining	–	–	–	–	–	–	–
Original suits: regular suits							
Claims	23	1	5	1	1	1	32
Disposed of	12	1	3	4	8	1	29
Remaining	–	–	–	–	–	–	3
Appeals from the Deputy Agent							
Appeals	2	10	8	8	15	15	58
Disposed of	0	0	8	2	21	12	43
Remaining	–	–	–	–	–	–	15
Grand total							
Disposed of	12	3	95	23	109	48	290
Remaining	–	–	–	–	–	–	18

Source: BL, IOP L/PJ/3/919, 269, Bombay Judicial Letter [BJL], Gov. to CoD, 6 Feb. 1833

Table 4.2 The number of suits disposed of by the Deputy Agent for Sirdars, 1828–1832

	1828	*1829*	*1830*	*1831*	*1832*	*Total*
Original suits: adjusted without resort to law proceedings						
Claims	64	230	216	188	163	861
Accommodated	14	206	222	232	136	810
Remaining	–	–	–	–	–	51[a]
Original suits: regular suits						
Claims	125	36	24	60	35	280
Disposed of	68	60	30	72	46	276
Remaining	–	–	–	–	–	4
Grand total						
Disposed of	82	266	252	304	182	1086
Remaining	–	–	–	–	–	55

Source: Ibid

[a]All preferred in the last 3 months (Oct.–Dec. 1832)

> It would be attended with an expenditure which the limited income of those chiefs renders them unable to afford, they would live in a society which even in its native branches is altogether uncongenial to their present habits and sentiments, and continually mixing with it would early have one of two effects. They would either be disgusted and discontented, or by forming acquaintance with artful men imbibe imperfect and indistinct ideas of our institutions and courts of law that might eventually involve both them and the Government in trouble and embarrassment.[51]

Elphinstone's and Malcolm's fears were soon to be realised.

Chieftains and the Security in the Mofussil: Bhavnagar and Peinth

The carefully crafted system of judicial exemption was obstructed by the King's Court and the forum shopping by the Indian subjects. One of the most remarkable examples of this was the debt recovery suits against the Thakur of Bhavnagar, a major girasia chief in Kathiawar, Gujarat.[52] As a co-sharer of sovereignty with the Gaikwad and (after the transfer of tribute in 1807) the British, the Thakur had played a crucial role in suppressing the Kati and other raiders in his territories.[53] He had incurred a large amount of debt from his commercial transactions and was sometimes sued by his creditors. As an independent tributary prince, he was exempted from British courts of law. However, as a proprietor of the city of Bhavnagar and neighbouring villages in the Goga pargana, he was also a subject of the British government amenable to the Adalat. Governor Malcolm was concerned about the destabilising effect of civil suits against the Thakur in the Company's Court. In 1827, for example, when a Bania filed a suit against the Thakur in the Company's Court for the recovery of Rs 1,140,000, Malcolm suggested referring the case not to the Adalat but for arbitration.[54]

This already complicated situation was further exacerbated by the Thakur's creditors' forum shopping via the King's Court. In 1827, Advocate General George Norton reported that an agent of Thakur had employed attorney James Patch to file a lawsuit in the Supreme Court. Norton was asked to take a retainer, but, when he perused the case, he discovered 'a system of fraud and conspiracy to abuse the process (by writ of execution on a fictitious judgement) of the Supreme Court in sweeping away some property of the Thakoor in Bombay'. He warned Patch and the case was withdrawn. Norton explained that this attempt was discovered when he was asked to take a retainer for another case, in which a Bombay merchant was planning to sue the Thakur for wrongful seizure of property. Norton declined the offer, as he thought the Thakur did not fall under the jurisdiction of the Supreme Court.[55] These suits against the Thakur were instances of a broader culture of challenging social superiors in the King's Court. As in Bengal, the government was concerned about harassment by the villagers against the Indian revenue intermediaries such as village headmen (patils) or headmen of parganas (deshmukhs).[56] For example, in the Southern Konkan in 1819, a patil was threatened by villagers through a Bombay attorney to desist from exercising what was described as 'unlawful force and injury' against them. The district judge, however, cautioned that 'any such interference with the revenue details of a recently acquired territory in particular must prove mischievous to the public interest and embarrassing to the local functionaries'.[57]

This issue was significant because it was related to security in the mofussil. The government was worried about the dangers inherent in the King's Court hindering the work of the village police. In 1823, the government asked the Court of Directors to make it clear that the hereditary village officials vested with police authority were not under the jurisdiction of the King's Court, expressing its apprehension about 'the inconvenience and distress public and private which must be occasioned if such parties should be summoned to the presidency'.[58] The patils were at the centre of Elphinstone's police system in the mofussil. Their allegiance to the government was vital in times of emergency, lest they should follow the example of the patils in Kittur who ignored orders of the Collector and cooperated with the insurgents.

However, the real danger came not from the villages but from the hills or, more precisely, from the link between the two. The crisis of 1824 significantly increased the government's security anxieties, leading to heightened concerns about the hill tribes. But the King's Court did not care about any distinction between the hills and the plains, since its view was that the court's sovereign jurisdiction covered all the territories and the peoples. Accordingly, in 1825, the sheriff's peons under the authority of the Supreme Court detained Laxdir Dulput Rao III, the Muslim Raja of Peinth in the Deccan Khandesh.[59] The lawsuit had been instituted by a creditor of the Raja for Rs 9000.[60] William S. Boyd, the Second Assistant Collector at Nasik, expressed his worry about the dire consequences of apprehending persons of rank outside the jurisdiction of the King's Court.[61] The Raja claimed that he did not borrow from the supposed creditor nor had he even visited Bombay city.[62] The government was concerned about the security of the Raja's estates, which were situated in thick forests chiefly inhabited by the Kolis.[63] According to John Briggs, the Political Agent for Khandesh who had cooperated with the Raja during the Third Maratha War, the Raja possessed 'considerable influence over the Bhils and Coolies'.[64] Given security challenges in the internal frontier, Elphinstone could not allow the King's Court's interference.

Elphinstone and the government's law officers were determined to protect the Raja from the encroachment of the King's Court. The Company's Solicitor W. A. Morgan pointed out that the arrest was irregular because the Raja was an 'independent sovereign prince' who was not amenable to the Supreme Court. Morgan applied to the Supreme Court to set aside the case, but it was rejected. He advised that the jurisdiction should be contested in the court and the plaintiff prosecuted for perjury.[65] Advocate General George Norton likewise emphasised that the Raja's arrest was 'one of the greatest outrages and abuses of the process of the Court'. He predicted that further abuses of the Supreme Court would occur, as he found that the perjury was done with 'effrontery' and 'a sense of impunity' to do so. He recommended public prosecution of the culprits to prevent further wrongdoing.[66] Elphinstone said that dealing with jurisdiction was a matter of urgency because, if the plaintiff should succeed in his plot in the King's Court, it would induce other creditors of other princes to resort to the same method.[67] Elphinstone's deep concern was based on his belief that the Raja's presence was essential to keep the peace in his hilly territory.[68] After perusing the original sunnuds of the Raja and related documents, he expressed his urgent sense of danger:

> He [Raja of Peinth] seems indeed to be pretty nearly on the same footing that the Dessaee of Kittoor was—His country was restored to him in a great measure on account of the molestation we were likely to experience should we attempt to retain it, and the quiet of the Bheels and Coolies in the neighbourhood seems to depend in a great measure on him anything that might provoke him to rebel is therefore of serious consequence and I think every means should be taken by application to the Court and by prosecuting the sheriff to obtain the immediate relief of the Raja and the punishment of those whose perjury was procured this proceeding against them.[69]

Elphinstone urged that the Raja's right of exemption from the jurisdiction should be proved in the King's Court because, if 'a sovereign prince tributary but not feudatory to the Paishwa' could not be protected, 'there will be no safety for our numerous subordinate chiefs'; but, on the other hand, he also stated that, if there were not good hopes, the proceedings should be dropped, as 'a failure might ultimately be serious even in a political point of view'.[70] Indeed, the prospects for the government were not promising. The Company's Solicitor, E. C. Morgan, could not gather enough evidence to sue the plaintiff and his son for conspiracy and perjury.[71] On receiving this information, Norton opined that the only remaining option was to prove the son's perjury through the testimony of the Raja himself in the Supreme Court.[72] However, the government could not accede to calling on a 'sovereign prince' to attend the court. Eventually, the government dropped all further proceedings.[73]

This case revealed the inability of the government to defy the King's Court in the arena of law. The government was fully determined to deny the King's Court's jurisdiction but failed to do so. The government could and did devise measures to prevent the Company's Court's political interference, such as Regulations XV and XXIX of 1827 or the Agent for Sirdars in the Deccan. The Raja's name was inserted in the lists of the first-class sardars in 1828.[74] But the order of the King's Court was outside the jurisdiction of the government. The government officials' aspiration for institutional and legislative solutions was intensified by this and other similar cases.

Independent Princes Resorted to the King's Court

The political problems posed by the King's Court were not confined to the chiefs and sardars in British India. The independent princes outside British India were also involved in a complex web of practices centred on the court. The problem for the government was that these local rulers began to signal their intentions to 'appeal' to the King's Court to reject their political engagements with the government. In other words, the local rulers started to treat the King's Court as an independent political authority separate from the government. This new dimension pushed the government's sense of crisis to the limit. The princes' resort to the King's Court had grave political implications, since it meant that they were attempting to establish an alternative means of political negotiation that bypassed the Residents appointed by the government. As Michael Fisher shows, maintaining independent means of communication was essential for the Indian rulers to uphold their political authority, and, while the British government imposed the Resident as the sole agent of communication, they tried to evade this arrangement by sending letters directly to the Resident's superiors, such as Governors, Governors-General or even the King in England.[75] In this light, the princes' appeals to the King's Court were a standard political tactic that implied recognition of the King's Court as superior to the government. This threat to political authority was directly related to a more immediate danger of rule in the mofussil. If 1824 was the first major year of crisis, 1827 was the second. A major reason for this was the alliance between the Ramusi raiders led by Umaji Naik and the independent chief of Kolhapur and Satara, both descendants of the founder of the Maratha empire Sivaji Bhonsle and now protected and supervised by British Political Residents.

The Raja of Kolhapur allied himself directly with the raiders to resist the government. This was a return to the traditional political structure of alliance between the plains sardars and the hill tribes. The new Raja, Baba Sahib, who was raised in 1821, was notorious for his bad character. He increased his army, resumed his conflict with the neighbouring Patwardhans and plundered territories of his feudatory jagirdars.[76] Governor Elphinstone described him as 'a great plague'.[77] The government sent its army to Kolhapur in 1825 and concluded a treaty in January 1826.[78] The treaty admitted 'the independence of the said Rajah as a sovereign prince' but bounded him to be advised by the British government on all security matters, to reduce his force and not to raise a force to endanger the tranquillity 'within or without his territories'. The Raja was obliged to suppress raiders and not to molest his subordinate jagirdars whose lands and rights were guaranteed by the British government. If he failed to adhere to these terms, the British government would send the army or police to arrest the raiders in his territory.[79] In response, the dissatisfied Raja turned to the King's Court. The Raja's vakeels informed Elphinstone that the Raja was intending to approach the court, but Elphinstone suspected that they were sent by the Raja to ascertain his attitude on this issue.[80] Soon after this attempt, in September 1827, the Raja allied with the Ramusi chief Umaji Naik and planned a rebellion on a much larger scale.[81] The Ramusis started to levy contributions from villages, often with the connivance of the patils.[82] Eventually, the British troops were sent twice to Kolhapur, and a definitive treaty was concluded in 1829.[83]

The Raja of Satara had acquired a favourable reputation in government circles including Elphinstone.[84] But the government was not satisfied with the Raja's policing of the tribal raiders in his territory. Satara contained the largest number of Ramusis in the Deccan.[85] The raiders plundered goods in the British territories and sold them to Satara's local merchants, with the Raja's subordinate sardars often protecting the bandits.[86] The government perceived that closer supervision of the Raja's subordinate sardars was necessary.[87] The government interfered with the succession of Nimbalkar Naik of Phultun, whose territory was a hub of gang raiders,[88] and criticised the Raja's dealing with Ram Row Duffle as it seemed jeopardising 'the tranquillity and prosperity of the Duffle districts'.[89] The discontented Raja sent several letters to other independent chiefs and sardars, which was contrary to the 'fundamental condition' of his treaty with the British.[90] Indeed, there was a large-scale plot being hatched. In January 1827, it was reported that the Raja was conspiring with Kolhapur, Appa Desai of Nipani, Ichalkaranji, Patwardhan and the Swamee of Sunkeshwur.[91]

It was against this background that the Raja approached the King's Court. It was reported that the Raja was 'very anxious to come to Bombay' and to meet the Chief Justice, although he did not show such eagerness to meet the British Commander-in-Chief or any other Members of the Governor's Council. Malcolm concluded that the Raja intended to provoke a jurisdictional conflict: 'This may arise from two motives, dread of the ill understood and magnified power of the Supreme Court, or more probably from an impression that there are two parties in our administration, and that it may be useful on a notion of the good terms he is with the one, to propitiate the other'.[92] It seems that the use of the name of the King's Court in politics and diplomacy had become fairly common by this time.[93]

The cases of Kolhapur and Satara indicated that the King's Court was seen as an independent political sovereign rather than a branch of the colonial state. The crisis reached its apex in early 1828 when another, far greater threat was posed through the use of the King's Court by Sayaji Rao II, the Gaekwad of Baroda. Baroda was the powerful successor state of the Mughal empire in Gujarat and had been in a subsidiary alliance with the British since the Second Maratha War. The Gaekwad's role in suppressing raiders was crucial because he had the right to receive tribute from many girasia and mehwasi chiefs as the overlord. The peace of Baroda was also vital from a commercial perspective, since the state cut across the opium route from Malwa to the west coast.[94] By the late 1820s, the government realised that the Gaekwad's irregular payment of the giras was the root cause of these raids.[95] The government had deprived Baroda of the power of superintending its tributary chiefs and put them under its direct control.[96] In 1825, the Collector of Khandesh proposed the transfer of the right of distributing giras from the Gaekwad to the Bombay government, 'since the burden and trouble of putting down any risings of such people must always in a great measure fall upon us'.[97] The Gaekwad resisted because the distribution of giras was the mark of his supremacy over the chiefs.[98] This situation was the background against which the government conceived the King's Court's pernicious impact on the security of the territory.

The immediate cause of the Gaekwad's resort to the King's Court was Sayaji's large debt to the local bankers. This amounted to over Rs 133 lakh in 1825 that was supposed to be paid in annual instalments of Rs 15 lakh. This was a serious concern for the government because it involved the bhandari (guarantee) system under which the government underwrote Sayaji's debt payments to the bankers. The enforcement of the Gaekwad's payment of debts was essential for both the maintenance of British power and for peace in the region. Before the arrival of the British, the guarantee was provided by the Arab sardars (or jamadars) who commanded mercenaries. The bhandari was, as Malcolm recognised, a source of their strength and influence as was their military power.[99] It was this arrangement that 'gave to the government the great advantage of settling without war the countries of Guzerat'.[100] It was synonymous with the paramountcy of the British government.[101] From 1801 to 1827, the Bombay government concluded 119 bhandari contracts, of which 65 were redeemed and 54 were still in force.[102] In 1827, the Bombay government imposed upon Sayaji Rao the septennial bhandari settlement, a plan of farming out his districts to the holders of the guaranteed loans in septennial leases. This plan was devised by John Pollard Willoughby, the Assistant Resident at Baroda, with the cooperation of Baroda's Chief Minister Wittal Row Dewanjee. As Michael Fisher points out, the British government often appointed the chief minister to control the internal and external affairs of the Indian princes and provoked their resistance.[103] Sayaji agreed to the scheme with great reluctance and repeatedly complained about it.[104] He sought loans from new bankers not under the government's guarantee and succeeded in borrowing Rs 7 lakh in January 1828.[105]

He also used the King's Court to urge the government to meet his demands, saying that, if not, he would 'appeal' to the King's Court. He sent his notorious Minister Veneram to Bombay to demand two things of the government. One was the reduction of the interest rate of public debts from 7.5 to 4.5%; the other was the removal of internal interference by deposing Chief Minister Wittal Row.[106] The Resident reported that Sayaji expressed an intention that 'he will appeal to Bombay and to England' or, 'if the Governor will not attend to his wishes, he will appeal from government to the Supreme Court'.[107] Malcolm expressed his strong antipathy towards 'a knot of natives at Bombay' who 'by working in the fears, the hopes, and the ignorance of those they delude with false expectations to their ruin' attempted to create a belief that the King's Court's jurisdiction extended beyond its limits.[108] He ordered the reinforcement of troops in Baroda.[109] His sense of danger was strong:

> I have no hesitation in stating it to be my deliberate opinion that as long as an impression exists that there is an authority vested in his Majesty's Court to check and control the exercise of political power by the civil government, it will operate beyond all other cases to disturb the country and destroy its remaining princes and chiefs.[110]

The attempt of Sayaji Rao and Veneram was facilitated by their agents in Bombay. Veneram was said to have received bills drawn by Sayaji personally and jewels worth Rs 5 lakh to take with him to Bombay. He landed at Bassein and communicated with one Munmooindas in Bombay.[111] Also, he visited and sought advice from Cursetjee Manockjee and Amerchund Bedreechund, the two Bombay merchants discussed in Chap. 2.[112] Although Veneram's request was declined by both of them, his attempt suggests that the information about the lawsuits of the Bombay merchants was well known among the chiefs and sardars in Western India. Veneram's Bombay mission heightened tensions in Baroda. The Political Resident, James Williams, reported that the peasants in Baroda had been instigated to prepare complaints against the kamavisdars of the parganas leased under the septennial loan and, when Veneram returned, to deliver their petitions to the Governor.[113] The bankers, who were affiliated with the bhandari of the British government, were also alarmed. False information about Veneram's success was disseminated, and the intimidated bankers issued a public declaration that they would acquiesce to Sayaji Rao.[114] Malcolm, in turn, advocated for strong intervention to preserve the existing system of bhandari.[115] Eventually, Veneram's mission to the King's Court failed. But Sayaji refused to pay his debt. Malcolm was now convinced that the 'System of non-interference then is wholly incompatible with the redemption of a pecuniary obligation where the disposition of the sovereign is sordid ...'.[116] He sequestrated the Gaekwad's territories worth Rs 1,000,000 and leased them to the bankers. Wittal Row was put in charge of the lands. Malcolm later justified the intervention as an act of political emergency:

> This nomination of Wittal Row to the charge of the districts in Guzerat and Kattywar was no doubt most offensive to the feelings and pride of Syajee; but the case was one of emergency; it was produced by his faithlessness; there was no alternative; and the success of the arrangement superseded all other considerations.[117]

The sequestration was completed without any disturbance, except that Sayaji complained against the measure, issued a counter-proclamation ('a manufacture of Bombay, and meant for the London market', said Malcolm), placarded it at Baroda and over his territories and sent it to Calcutta and Benares.[118] The liquidation of debts was completed, and the land was returned in 1832, while Rs 10 lakh remained deposited to the Company.[119]

Conclusion

This chapter argued that, driven by the crisis in the mid-1820s, the government decided to expand its conciliation policy towards the chiefs and sardars. This was deemed essential for effective mofussil governance, especially for policing the 'wild tribes'. Similar problems bedevilled Satara, Kolhapur and Baroda. The chiefs were disaffected by the British government's interference in their internal affairs, particularly in their relationship with their subordinate sardars. The government's intervention was based on its conviction that, to deal with the critical situation in the mofussil, the foreign princes should apply the same policy of conciliation towards their sardars as the government did in British India. In all three cases, the government was concerned about the princes' oppression of their subordinate sardars or their inability to control them and tried to uphold the sardars' sovereignty in their territories. The concern was that the raids and rebellions could easily 'infest' the British territories. As Radhika Singha suggests, the strengthening of British policing of the forest tribes drove the thugs out to the neighbouring Indian states.[120] To deal with the raids, the same policy had to be adopted by the independent chiefs.

In effect, the government was demarcating the boundary between respectable and unrespectable Indian rulers.[121] The government protected and promoted the former to use them for indirect rule in the mofussil. The government articulated that the affairs of sardars were in the realm of state necessity and, concomitantly, outside the realm of law. The post-war settlement in the Deccan was confirmed and expanded to the entire presidency, in which the sardars were regarded as sovereigns in their territories and vested with extraterritoriality. The tribal chiefs in the hills were, on the other hand, to be deprived of the sovereignty in the plains and, if they failed to keep peace, became the object of policing either by the government or by the respectable sardars. They were, with the rest of the population, subjected to the municipal law and placed within the realm of regularity.

Historian Kenneth Ballhatchet points out that Elphinstone had to codify hitherto informal privileges of chiefs in the regulations 'to protect them from the zeal of egalitarian Judges', suggesting that the new administrators would substitute the rule of men with the rule of regulations.[122] The codification of the sardar's exemption indicates that, contrary to Ballhatchet's suggestion, the realm of men would not vanish. The exemption of political discretion from the realm of civil/legal regularity became the essence of colonial governance. The newly conquered territories would remain 'new' during the British Raj because, even after the introduction of regulations, the working of law was buttressed by exemptions of certain state necessities. The division between the realm of law and the realm of politics became the defining characteristic of colonial political structure.[123] As we will see in the next chapter, the King's Court rejected this demarcation, inculcated its version of political order and exercised its jurisdiction over the political affairs of sardars. This was perceived as a threat to the entire system of the EIC's colonial rule.

Notes

1. British Library [BL], India Office Records [IOR] P/399/33, Bombay Judicial Consultations [BJC] 12 May 1824, 2753–62. W. Chaplin to Bombay Government [Gov.], 14 Apr. 1824.
2. BL, IOR P/399/49, BJC 5 Oct. 1825, no. 31, D. Greenhill, memorandum, n.d.

3. For the princely states, see Michael H. Fisher, *Indirect Rule in India: Residents and the Residency System 1764–1858* (New Delhi: Oxford University Press, 1991); Barbara Ramusack, *The Indian Princes and Their States* (Cambridge: Cambridge University Press, 2003).
4. James C. Scott, *Seeing Like a State: How Certain Schemes to Improve the Human Condition Have Failed* (New Haven, CT: Yale University Press, 1998). See also Jon E. Wilson, *The Domination of Strangers: Modern Governance in Eastern India 1780–1835* (Basingstoke: Palgrave Macmillan, 2008).
5. Sudipta Sen, 'Unfinished Conquest: Residual Sovereignty and the Legal Foundations of the British Empire in India', *Law, Culture and the Humanities* 9, no.2 (2012), 227–42. The relevant literature includes Janaki Nair, *Mysore Modern: Rethinking the Region under Princely Rule* (Minneapolis, MN: University of Minnesota Press, 2011); Eric Lewis Beverley, *Hyderabad, British India, and the World: Muslim Networks and Minor Sovereignty, c.1850–1950* (Cambridge: Cambridge University Press, 2015); Bhangya Bhukya, *The Roots of the Periphery: A History of the Gonds of Deccan India* (New Delhi: Oxford University Press, 2017); Tripurdaman Singh, *Imperial Sovereignty and Local Politics: The Bhadauria Rajputs and the Transition from Mughal to British India, 1600–1900* (Cambridge: Cambridge University Press, 2019).
6. Lauren Benton, *A Search for Sovereignty: Law and Geography in European Empires, 1400–1900* (Cambridge: Cambridge University Press, 2010).
7. Radhika Singha, *A Despotism of Law: Crime and Justice in Early Colonial India* (Oxford: Oxford University Press, 1998), 191–92; On the military labour market, see Dirk H. A. Kolff, *Naukars, Rajput and Sepoy: The Ethnohistory of the Military Labour Market in Hindustan 1450–1850* (Cambridge: Cambridge University Press, 1990).
8. Dirk H. A. Kolff, 'Rumours of the Company's Collapse: The Mood of Dasahra 1824 in the Punjab and Hindustan', in Crispin Bates, ed., *Mutiny at the Margins: New Perspectives on the Indian Uprising of 1857: Vol 1, Anticipations and Experiences in the Locality* (New Delhi: SAGE, 2013), 25–42.
9. N. Benjamin and B. B. Mohanty, 'Imperial Solution of a Colonial Problem: Bhils of Khandesh Up to c. 1850', *Modern Asian Studies* 41, no. 2 (2007), 345.
10. A. K. Prasad, *The Bhils of Khandesh: Under the British East India Company (1818–1858)* (Delhi, 1991), 212–41; Ajay Skaria, *Hybrid Histories: Forests, Frontiers and Wildness in Western India* (Oxford: Oxford University Press, 1999), 153–75.
11. Singha, *Despotism of Law*, 194–99.
12. *Thana Gazetteer*, 2:634. The ratio of robbers to arrests were 132:41 for 1820, 193:112 for 1821, 733:73 for 1822, 807:72 for 1823, 204:80 for 1824 and 1094:28 for 1825.

13. R. D. Choksey, *Early British Administration, 1817–1836: Deccan Commissioner's Files and Pre-Mutiny Records on Gujarat* (Poona: Choksey, 1964), 81, R. K. Pringle to H. D. Robertson, 29 Mar. 1824.
14. East India Company, *Selection of Papers from the Records at the East-India House Relating to the Revenue, Police, and Civil and Criminal Justice, under the Company's Governments in India*, 4 vols. (London, 1820–26) [SRJ], 3:677, M. Elphinstone, minute, 15 Aug. 1821; Hiroshi Fukazawa, 'Agrarian Relations: Western India', in Dharma Kumar and Meghnad Desai, eds., *The Cambridge Economic History of India, Volume 2, c.1757–c.1970* (Cambridge: Cambridge University Press, 1983), 190.
15. In Dholka, the chief of Koth had 2000 militia and 150 horses, the chief of Gangad had a constant force of 1000, and the chief of Bhavnagar had 6000–7000 infantry and 500–2500 cavalry. *Ahmedabad Gazetteer* (Bombay, 1879), 147n1; John Clunes, *An Historical Sketch of the Princes of India: Stipendiary, Subsidiary, Protected, Tributary, and Feudatory, with a Sketch of the Origin and Progress of British Power in India* (Edinburgh, 1833), 195.
16. *Ahmedabad Gazetteer*, 196.
17. *Gaikwads of Baroda Maharaja Sayajirao II A. D. 1821 to A. D. 1830 (Selections from the Baroda Residency Records)*, ed. G. B. Pandya (Baroda: Maharaja Sayajirao University of Baroda, 1958), 152–55, Gov. to F. D. Ballantyne, 6 June 1821, F. D. Ballantyne to James Williams, 8 June 1821; Gov. to F. D. Ballantyne, 11 Apr. 1822.
18. Burton Stein, *Thomas Munro: The Origins of the Colonial State and His Visions of Empire* (Oxford: Oxford University Press, 1989), 84, 88, 233–37, 306.
19. Skaria, *Hybrid Histories*, 124–53; André Wink, *Land and Sovereignty in India: Agrarian Society and Politics in Eighteenth-Century Martha Svarajya* (Cambridge: Cambridge University Press, 1986), 189–99; Sumit Guha, *Environment and Ethnicity in India 1200–1991* (Cambridge: Cambridge University Press, 1999), 97, 108–21, 132–33.
20. Bruce Frederick Robinson, 'Adaptation to Colonial Rule by the "Wild Tribes" of the Bombay Deccan 1818–1880: From Political Competition to Social Banditry' (PhD diss., University of Minnesota, 1978); Skaria, *Hybrid Histories*, 131.
21. Cf. Kenneth Ballhatchet, *Social Policy and Social Change in Western India 1817–1830* (London: Oxford University Press, 1957), 88.
22. *The Correspondence of Lord William Cavendish Bentinck, Governor-General of India 1828–1835*, ed. C. H. Philips, 2 vols. (Oxford: Oxford University Press, 1977), 1:27, J. Malcolm to C. Williams Wynn, 19 Apr. 1828.

23. T. E. Colebrooke, *Life of the Honourable Mountstuart Elphinstone*, 2 vols. (London: Murray, 1884), 2:116–17.
24. BL, IOR V/8/24: Bombay Regulations, 1827. The regulations can also be consulted in *Parliamentary Papers.* For example, PP 1829 (201) for 1827, PP 1830 (60) for 1828 and PP 1830 (682) for 1829.
25. Reg. I of 1827, ss.8–11.
26. Reg. XIII of 1827, s.26; Reg. XIV of 1827, ss.12–15.
27. Reg. XII of 1827, s.43, c. 4 and s.50, c.4.
28. The regulation defined the term 'reason of state' as 'the due maintenance of the alliances formed by the British Government with foreign powers, the preservation of tranquillity in the territories of native Princes entitled to its protection, and the security of the British dominions from foreign hostility and from internal commotion'. Reg. XXV of 1827, preamble.
29. Benjamin D. Hopkins, *Ruling the Savage Periphery: Frontier Governance and the Making of the Modern State* (Cambridge, MA: Harvard University Press, 2019).
30. Ballhatchet, *Social Policy*, 169.
31. BL, IOR P/399/56, BJC 1 Mar. 1826, no. 32, M. Elphinstone, minute, n.d.; BL, IOR P/399/62, BJC 5 Aug. 1826, no. 77, Secretary's memorandum, July 1826; Ballhatchet, *Social Policy*, 169–70.
32. See, for example, BL, IOR F/4/1046/28729, 2–3, BJC 19 Jan. 1825, no.46, Thomas Williamson, the Acting Collector of Kaira, to Gov., 5 Jan. 1825.
33. BL, IOR P/399/46, BJC 15 June 1825, no. 15, W. Chaplin to Gov., 28 May 1825.
34. Ibid.
35. BL, IOR F/4/1045/28727, 215–62, the quotation from 258, R. Boyat to Gov., 20 Nov. 1824, BJC 1 Dec. 1824.
36. BL, IOR F/4/1046/28729, 275, BJC 12 July 1826, no. 23, Gov. to Regulation Committee, 6 July 1826.
37. BL, IOR P/399/56, BJC 1 Mar. 1826, nos. 35–36, Secretary, memorandums, n.d.
38. BL, IOR P/399/52, BJC 31 Dec. 1825, no. 1, W. Chaplin to Gov., 25 Nov. 1825. BL, IOR P/399/59, BJC 10 May 1826, no. 61, W. Chaplin to Gov., 8 Apr. 1826, and nos. 62–65; BL, IOR P/399/62, BJC 5 Aug. 1826, no. 75, W. Chaplin to Gov., 8 July 1826. For the original lists, see BL, IOR P/399/64, BJC 18 Oct. 1826, no. 31, list of sardars.
39. BL, IOR P/399/64, BJC 18 Oct. 1826, no. 30, M. Elphinstone, minute, 5 Sep. 1826.
40. Ibid., no. 33, Warden, minute, 26 Sep. 1826.

41. BL, IOR P/400/2, BJC 10 Jan. 1827, no. 87, Gov. to G. W. Anderson, 4 Jan. 1827.
42. Reg. XXIX of 1827, ss.3–5.
43. Reg. XXIX of 1827, s.6.
44. Jamietram Nanabhai and Chimanlal Harilal Stelvad, eds., *Bombay Acts and Regulations with Notes, Decisions, Notifications, &c.* (Bombay: Ripon, 1894), 31.
45. BL, IOR F/4/1035/28544, 45, J. Malcolm, minute, 30 Jan. 1828.
46. 70 names not ascertained were added to the number. BL, IOR F/4/1035/28544, 31, J. Malcolm, minute, 30 Jan. 1828.
47. BL, IOR P/400/61, BJC 23 Jan. 1833, nos. 97–101, John Warden to Gov., 31 Dec. 1832.
48. For example, see BL, IOR P/400/18, BJC 18 June 1828, nos. 8–11, John Warden, Deputy Agent, to Gov., 28 May 1828, *Khooshaldass Damoodhurdass v. Mahomed Hurreef Moonshee*; BL, IOR P/400/18, BJC 18 June 1828, nos. 21–24, John Warden, Deputy Agent, to Gov., 28 May 1828, *Row Gunness Pansey v. Rumma Baee, widow of Gunput Rao Pansey*; BL, IOR P/400/27, BJC 10 June 1829, nos. 37–41, J. A. Dunlop to Gov., 1 June 1829; and BL, IOR P/400/30, BJC 4 Nov. 1829, nos. 1–8, J. A. Dunlop to Gov., 25 Sep. 1829, *Rungoo Wisswanath Nisbit Zukatey v. Bhasker Ram Gokla*.
49. BL, IOR P/399/66, BJC 31 Dec. 1826, no. 7, Gov. to G. Norton, 21 Dec. 1826.
50. BL, IOR P/400/2, BJC 31 Jan. 1827, no. 47, G. Norton to Gov., 6 Jan. 1827.
51. BL, IOR F/4/1035/28544, 9–11, BJC 30 Jan. 1828, J. Malcolm, minute, 16 Jan. 1828.
52. Bhavnagar was a major port city in the region, trading with the Arabs and exporting the Malwa opium. G. D. Sharma, 'Ports of Gujarat in the Nineteenth Century: Trading Networks and Commercial Practices', in Indu Banga, ed., *Ports and Their Hinterlands in India (1700–1950)* (New Delhi: Manohar, 1992), 199–212.
53. Walter Hamilton, *A Geographical, Statistical, and Historical Descriptions of Hindoostan, and the Adjacent Countries* (London, 1820), 673–75; Walter Hamilton, *The East-India Gazetteer*, 2nd edition, 2 vols. (London, 1828), 1:232.
54. BL, IOR P/400/20, BJC 24 Sep. 1828, no. 39, J. Romer, minute, 5 Sep. 1828; ibid., no. 40, J. Malcolm, minute, n.d.
55. BL, IOR P/386/18, Bombay Political Consultations, 14 Feb. 1827, no. 39, G. Norton to Gov., 30 Jan. 1827.
56. For Bengal's cases, see M. P. Jain, *Outlines of Indian Legal and Constitutional History*, 6th edition (New Delhi: LexisNexis, 2006), 81–89.

57. BL, IOR P/398/63, BJC 28 July 1819, 1816–17, J. W. Pelly to Gov., 21 May 1819.
58. BL, IOR L/PJ/3/917, 123, Bombay Judicial Letter [BJL], Gov. to CoD, 25 June 1823.
59. From 1822, the Raja's state was under the agency of Ahmednagar Collector through his Assistant Collector at Nasik. *Selections from the Records of the Bombay Government* [SRBG], new series, 26 (Bombay, 1856), 112, 134, H. E. Goldsmid, report, 21 Sep. 1839.
60. The Raja borrowed Rs 33,000 from a Surat savakar in 1824 to consolidate his debts, amounting to Rs 52,000 in 1827. He owed Rs 12,000 to others, and the total debt was nearly Rs 65,000. Its annual demand far exceeded the revenue of the country. BL, IOR P/399/49, BJC 12 Oct. 1825, no. 16, W. S. Boyd to J. A. Dunlop, 30 June 1825; Maharashtra State Archives [MSA], Judicial Department [JD], 1825, 7/87, 301–19.
61. BL, IOR P/399/46, BJC 6 June 1825, no. 1, W. S. Boyd to J. A. Dunlop, Collector of Ahmednagar, 15 May 1825; MSA, JD, 1825, 7/87, 228–29.
62. BL, IOR P/399/46, BJC 1 June 1825, no. 25, Raja of Peinth to W. S. Boyd, Assistant Collector of Ahmednagar, 15 May 1825; MSA, JD, 1825, 7/87, 219–20.
63. John Clunes, *Appendix to Itinerary and Directory of Western India* (Bombay: American Mission Press, 1828), 29.
64. Deccan Commissioner's Files, 170, J. Briggs to M. Elphinstone, 13 May 1818, quoted in Avind M. Deshpande, *John Briggs in Maharashtra: A Study of District Administration under Early British Rule* (Delhi: Mittal Publications, 1987), 153.
65. BL, IOR P/399/46, BJC 22 June 1825, no. 10, W. A. Morgan to Gov., 4 June 1825, '*Vasy Kunthurdbhoie Rambhae v. Lucksheedhun Dulputrowe*', Affidavit of plaintiff's son, Hindu merchant of Bombay, 6 Apr. 1825; MSA, JD, 1825, 7/87, 233–38.
66. BL, IOR P/399/47, BJC 6 July 1825, no. 39, G. Norton to Gov., 30 June 1825; MSA, JD, 1825, 7/87, 289–91.
67. BL, IOR P/399/49, BJC 12 Oct. 1825, no. 17, Gov. to W. Chaplin, 7 Oct. 1825; MSA, JD, 1825, 7/87, 323.
68. Second Assistant Collector Boyd, Collector Dunlop, and Deccan Commissioner Chaplin had a different view. They emphasised the Raja's maladministration and insisted on the need for direct rule. BL, IOR P/399/49, BJC 12 Oct. 1825, no. 16, J. A. Dunlop to W. Chaplin, 20 Sep. 1825.
69. BL, IOR P/399/46, BJC 22 June 1825, no. 15, M. Elphinstone, minute, n.d.; MSA, JD, 1825, 7/87, 287–88. When the Raja died in 1839 without a male heir, the government admitted the succession of his daughter 'as a matter of expediency'. BL, IOR F/4/1865/79212, 1B, BPL, Gov. to CoD, 26 Sep. 1840.

70. BL, IOR P/399/55, BJC 25 Jan. 1826, no. 28, M. Elphinstone, n.d.; MSA, JD, 1826, 7/108, 156.
71. BL, IOR P/399/63, BJC 16 Aug. 1826, no. 13, Edward Cobb Morgan to G. Norton, 27 July 1826. Edward succeeded his brother William as the Company's Solicitor in 1826.
72. Ibid., no. 14, G. Norton to Gov., 1 Aug. 1826; MSA, JD, 1826, 7/108, 237–40.
73. BL, IOR P/399/63, BJC 16 Aug. 1826, no. 15, Gov. to G. Norton, 11 Aug. 1826.
74. SRBG, ns, 26, 135, H. E. Goldsmid, report, 21 Sep. 1839.
75. Fisher, *Indirect Rule*, 272–82.
76. *Kolhapur Gazetteer* (Bombay, 1886), 238; H. H. Wilson, *The History of British India from 1805 to 1835*, 3 vol. (London, 1848), 3:175–76.
77. M. Elphinstone to C. T. Metcalfe, 1825, quoted in R. D. Choksey, *Mountstuart Elphinstone: The Indian Years 1796–1827* (Bombay: Bhatkal, 1971), 304.
78. *Kolhapur Gazetteer*, 239–40.
79. BL, IOR F/4/1071/29239, Bombay Secret Consultations [BSC], 12 Oct. 1826, nos. 1–6, M. Elphinstone, minute, n.d; *A Collection of Treaties, Engagements and Sanads, Relating to India and Neighbouring Countries.* ed. C.U. Aitchison, 5th edition, 14 vols. (Calcutta, Superintendent Government Printing, 1929–1933), 8:227–29.
80. BL, IOR F/4/1148/30306, 6–16, M. Elphinstone, minute, 4 Jan. 1827.
81. *Raja Pratapsinh of Satara 1818–1839: Select Documents from the Satara Residency Papers, Peshwa Dafter, Poona, and the Elphinstone Papers, India Office Library, London* [*Pratapsinh*], ed. R. D. Choksey (Poona: Bharata Itihasa Samshodhaka Mandala, 1970), 159, Gov. to Hyderabad Resident, 7 Sep. 1827.
82. Alexander Mackintosh, *An Account of the Origin and Present Condition of the Tribe of Ramoossies, Including the Life of the Chief Oomiah Naik* (Bombay, 1833), 140.
83. *Kolhapur Gazetteer*, 238–40; *Treaties, Engagements and Sanads*, ed. Aitchison, 8:229–34.
84. Sumitra Kulkarni, *The Satara Raj (1818–1848): A Study in History, Administration and Culture* (New Delhi: Mittal Publications, 1995), 21.
85. Mackintosh, *Ramoossies*, 6.
86. Ibid., 37.
87. By the treaty of 1819, the Bombay government had guaranteed the possessions of jagirdars in Satara. *Treaties, Engagements and Sanads*, ed. Aitchison, 8:392, article 7. *Pratapsinh*, ed. Choksey, 8.
88. *Pratapsinh*, ed. Choksey, 132–33, J. Briggs to Gov., 1 Jan. 1827.

89. *Pratapsinh*, ed. Choksey, 157, W. Simson to Gov., 16 Apr. 1827; see also *Pratapsinh*, ed. Choksey, 127–28, J. Briggs to Gov., 1 Jan. 1827.
90. It stipulated that the Raja should 'forbear all intercourse with foreign powers, and with all sirdars, jaghiredars, chiefs and ministers' who were not under his authority. *Treaties, Engagements and Sanads*, ed. Aitchison, 8:391–92, article 5 of the 1819 treaty.
91. The Nizam of Hyderabad, the French, the Portuguese, Sindhia, Appa Sahib of Nagpur, the Gaekwad of Baroda and the Pindaris would be invited as well. *Pratapsinh*, ed. Choksey, 137–39, William Simson to M. Elphinstone, 27 Jan. 1827; *Pratapsinh*, ed. Choksey, 140–49, W. Newnham to Gov., 26 Feb. 1827.
92. BL, IOR L/PJ/3/918, 55–58, BJL, Gov. to CoD, 27 Sep. 1828, BJC 27 Sep. 1828, J. Malcolm to Thomas Bradford, 18 July 1828.
93. Malcolm further discovered in 1830 that the Raja's subordinate jagirdar Akulcote instigated a rebellion against the Raja by invoking the name of the King's Court. BL, IOR H/734, 867–74, J. Malcolm to Lionel Smith, 16 Jan. 1830. The Raja's conspiracy itself continued. His attitude hardened through the 1830s, and when another plot was exposed in 1839, he was deposed. *Satara Gazetteer* (Bombay, 1885), 310–11. The detail of the case was printed as *Papers Respecting the Case of the Raja of Sattara* (London, 1840).
94. *Sayajirao II*, ed. Pandya, xii.
95. Skaria, *Hybrid Histories*, chapter 10.
96. *Baroda Gazetteer* (Bombay, 1883), 328–37; *Sayajirao II*, ed. Pandya, 168–69, Baroda Resident to Gov., 30 Oct. 1821.
97. *Sayajirao II*, ed. Pandya, 202–3, J. Briggs to Gov., 30 July 1825.
98. Skaria, *Hybrid Histories*, 156.
99. John Malcolm, *The Government of India* (London, 1833), 7.
100. Malcolm, *Government of India*, 154, Malcolm, minute, n.d.
101. cf. Mani Kamerkar, *British Paramountcy: British-Baroda Relations 1818–1848* (Bombay: Popular Prakashan, 1980), 108–9.
102. BL, IOR R/2/531/294, 404–9, BSC 19 Mar. 1828, no. 5, J. Malcolm, minute, 25 Jan. 1828.
103. Fisher, *Indirect Rule*, 208–27.
104. *Baroda Gazetteer*, 239; Robert Wallace, *The Guicowar, and His Relations with the British Government* (Bombay, 1863), 325–76, 679–80.
105. Kamerkar, *British Paramountcy*, 80.
106. BL, IOR R/2/531/294, 147–51, Baroda Resident, secret diary, 5 Feb. 1828.
107. Ibid., 151.
108. BL, IOR L/PJ/3/918, 55–58, BJL, Gov. to CoD, 27 Sep. 1828, enclosing BJC 27 Sep. 1828, J. Malcolm to T. Bradford, 18 July 1828.

109. BL, IOR R/2/531/294, BSC 5 Mar. 1828, no. 7, 223–24, J. Malcolm, minute, 26 Feb. 1828.
110. BL, IOR P/SEC/BOM/66, BSC 27 Feb. 1828, no. 5, 193–98, J. Malcolm, minute, 25 Feb. 1828.
111. BL, IOR R/2/531/294, 359–66, James Williams to Gov., n.d.
112. Ibid., 619–22, BSC 26 Mar. 1828, no. 2, J. P. Willoughby to Gov., 22 Mar. 1828.
113. Ibid., 359–66, J. Williams to Gov, n.d.
114. Ibid., 409–10, BSC 19 Mar. 1828, no. 5, J. Malcolm, minute, 25 Jan. 1828.
115. Ibid., 413, 427, 429.
116. Ibid., 401.
117. Malcolm, *Government of India*, 23.
118. *The Correspondence of Lord William Cavendish Bentinck, Governor-General of India 1828–1835*, ed. C. H. Philips, 2 vols. (Oxford: Oxford University Press, 1977), 1:35, J. Malcolm to C. Williams-Wynn, 24 May 1828.
119. *Treaties, Engagements and Sanads*, ed. Aitchison, 6:364.
120. Radhika Singha, *A Despotism of Law: Crime and Justice in Early Colonial India* (Oxford: Oxford University Press, 1998), 201.
121. As Lakshmi Subramanian shows, the Bombay government took the same policy (initiated by Alexander Walker) at the sea by distinguishing fair traders and lawless pirates. Lakshmi Subramanian 'Piracy and Legality in the Northward: Colonial Articulation of Law, Custom and Policy in the Late Eighteenth- and Early Nineteenth-Century Bombay Presidency', *Journal of Colonialism and Colonial History* 15, no. 1 (Jan 2014).
122. Ballhatchet, *Social Policy*, 246.
123. Cf. Guha, Ranajit, *Dominance without Hegemony: History and Power in Colonial India* (Cambridge, MA: Harvard University Press, 1997); Samera Esmeir, 'On the Coloniality of Modern Law', *Critical Analysis of Law* 2, no. 1 (2015), 19–41.

CHAPTER 5

Habeas Corpus in Times of Emergency: The Bombay Dispute

Introduction

'[P]aranoia was the hallmark of the colonial imagination', writes historian Rajnarayan Chandavarkar in discussing the Bombay city police in the late nineteenth century.[1] Nothing showed this more clearly than the government headed by John Malcolm in its conflict with the King's Court in the late 1820s. The developments depicted in previous chapters converged and exploded in two cases of habeas corpus in 1828: the case of Moro Ragonath and the case of Bappoo Gunness. In the first case, the King's Court issued a writ to a second-class sardar in Poona. In the second case, a writ was issued to release a revenue defaulter from the gaol. The government overtly intervened in the processes of the King's Court, sparking a strong response from the judges. In these two cases, every dispute discussed in previous chapters—judicial check of the government officers, revenue collection and revenue debts, use and abuse of the civil litigation and the policing of tribes and the rebellions of princes in the mofussil—was raised by the government and the court. Little scholarly attention has been paid to the cases,[2] but they were the single most important political issue for the Bombay government in the late 1820s. Among a total of 64 letters sent out by the Political Department of the Bombay government to the Court of Directors in 1828 and 1829, 59 dealt with the cases. The letters and enclosures amounted to 3000 pages, which were contained in 3 dedicated volumes in the India Office Records.[3] Malcolm

H. Inagaki, *The Rule of Law and Emergency in Colonial India*, Cambridge Imperial and Post-Colonial Studies,
https://doi.org/10.1007/978-3-030-73663-7_5

remarked that 'if there had not been shedding of blood in this war, there had been shedding of ink in abundance'.[4] In the cases, the King's Court and the Bombay government both fully developed their logics of law and emergency.

The Moro Ragonath case jeopardised Governor Malcolm's central policy of preserving the native aristocracy, which was the primary strategy for dealing with the tribal raids in the newly conquered territories. Malcolm was concerned about the fate of sardars. Malcolm's model of government was what he called the 'subah government'. Regarding Malwa and Rajputana in central India, he explained that his object was 'to establish a subah government which in the principles and forms of its administration, should be so constructed as to admit of the co-existence of a native aristocracy with our rule: and to do this, I was satisfied it was indispensable to keep both our regular courts of Adalat and his Majesty's courts of justice at a distance'.[5] In his vision, the judiciary—both the Company's and the King's—had nothing to do with its governance in the newly acquired territories. The chiefs and sardars were to be totally exempted from legal proceedings and placed under the exclusive control of government officials who combined executive, judicial and magisterial powers. The high priority Malcolm gave to the issue of the native aristocracy was indicated in his dispute with the Bengal government on the importance of maintaining nuzzerana (an inheritance tax paid by the subordinate to their superior). The conflict centred on the rent-free lands possessed by the Indian rulers. Bengal officials favoured the resumption of these lands to increase revenue.[6] Malcolm, however, proposed that lands of the heir-less chiefs should not be seized by the government and the revenue realised in the form of nuzzerana. Such a form of taxation, he argued, would limit the 'spirit of discontent and turbulence' and cultivate 'attachment and allegiance' of the chiefs.[7] As this issue of nuzzerana exemplifies, the maintenance of the native aristocracy was at the centre of Malcolm's vision of empire. However, it was endangered by the King's Court.

The habeas corpus cases revealed the ideologies and practices of paternalist Governors such as Malcolm. Eric Stokes in *English Utilitarians and India* (1959) argues that the 1834 charter was a product of an amalgamation between the utilitarianism of Holt Mackenzie, Alexander Ross, James Mill and Macaulay and the paternalism of Elphinstone, Malcolm, Bentinck and Metcalfe.[8] This is an important point. While the role of paternalism tends to be less focused than utilitarianism,[9] we need to pay more attention to these paternalist administrators. Modernity arrived in India not only in the form of utilitarian 'seeing like a state' colonial knowledge. It was also embodied in the pragmatic science of governance developed by the enlightened scholar-administrators such as Elphinstone and Malcolm.[10] Their vision of empire was soaked in the Tory paternalism of Victorian Britain idealising an 'authoritarian, hierarchic, organic, and pluralistic' society,[11] but its distinctive feature in India was a perpetual sense of fear and anxiety in a prolonged state of crisis—what Douglas Peers calls a garrison-state siege mentality imbued with military ideology and preoccupied with 'security, financial solvency, and political legitimacy'.[12] Constant preparedness of the army was essential not only to deal with emergencies but also to convince Indians of the futility of resistance.[13] Malcolm explained that the British empire was 'the empire of opinion':

> [T]here can be no doubt that empire is held solely by opinion; or, in other words, by that respect and awe with which the comparative superiority of our knowledge, justice, and system of rule, have inspired the inhabitants of our own territories; and that confidence in our truth, reliance on our faith, and dread of our armies, which is impressed on every nation in India.[14]

Compared to this logic of emergency, the foundation of the judges' logic of law was self-consciously British in its ethos. The British empire in the early nineteenth century was in a high state of legal pluralism, encompassing a series of conflicts between the executive and the judiciary in colonies such as Canada, Australia, West Africa, the West Indies and India.[15] The judges in these regions criticised the colonial government by arguing that the indigenous population in newly acquired territories should be vested with the status of British subject and placed under the protection of British law immediately after the conquest. The prerogative writ of habeas corpus had a symbolic significance in this respect.[16]

The Logic of Law and the Logic of Emergency Articulated

The habeas corpus case of Moro Ragonath originated in a conflict in a Hindu undivided family, the Dhumderes. Moro Ragonath Dhumdere was a minor in a branch of the family, and Pandoorung Ramchunder Dhumdere was Moro's grand uncle. The Dhumderes had been in charge of the daftar (record office) under the Peshwa's government. Pandoorung was a friend of the Peshwa. He made his grandnephew marry the Peshwa.[17] Both Moro and Pandoorung were on the list of sardars.[18] When his father died, Moro was initially put under the charge of his mother and grandmother, but when both had passed away, he was placed under the protection of Mahadajee Pundit, one of the managers (karkoons) of his estate. Thereafter, he was under the influence of the karkoon and his father-in-law, Dinker Gopall Deo. They claimed that the estate belonged to Moro Ragonath, though Pandoorung insisted that it was not divided.[19] This kind of karkoons' machination was quite familiar to the Bombay officials.[20]

The immediate cause of the legal conflict was Pandoorung's debt incurred in his pilgrimage to Benares up to the year 1816, amounting to Rs 491,525. He demanded that Moro pay it jointly.[21] Going to the pilgrimage to holy cities such as Benares, Allahabad, Jaganath and Gaya and contributing to building temples, ghats and colleges by donation were, as C. A. Bayly points out, important for the Maratha princes and other nobility to claim their princely status.[22] Pandoorung instituted the case in the panchayat in 1820 and got a favourable decision in the following year. Moro appealed to the Zilla Court of Poona and petitioned Chaplin, the Deccan Commissioner, but Chaplin ordered him to pay his share Rs 245,000 with fine of Rs 9800 in 1824.[23] Moro's estates were attached and his karkoons detained. He appealed to the Governor, but the decision was confirmed in 1826.[24] Meanwhile, Pandoorung told the government that Moro's karkoons had appropriated Moro's property. The government inquired about this and, as the karkoons refused to give any account of the estate, appointed Pandoorung as Moro's guardian in 1827.[25] When Moro's karkoons decided to resort to the King's Court instead of appealing to the Privy Council, the family conflict effloresced into one of the biggest political crises of early nineteenth-century India.

Pandoorung was influential yet problematic individual for the government. The government could not ignore his political and social influence, and, after the British conquest, he continued to be appointed as the amanatdar in charge of the record of the Peshwa's secretariat (huzur daftar).[26] He had several inam villages in the Deccan and well understood his power to negotiate with British authorities, frequently petitioning the government to protect his customary rights and privileges. After the Agent for Sirdars was appointed in 1827, for example, Pandoorung immediately requested that his name be placed on the list of sardars.[27] Four months later, he complained that villagers in his inam and jagir lands in Khandesh, Ahmednagar, and Poona were arrested through the Company's Court and demanded the exemption of his subordinates. He explained that the regulation vested the first- and second-class sardars with the original jurisdiction of the inhabitants in their inam and jagir lands. The Collectors were perplexed because there was no such stipulation in the regulations. But the government admitted the claim in the end.[28] The powerful sardar's cooperation was essential for the government's vision of indirect rule.

In July 1828, Governor Malcolm received a letter from the Agent for Sirdars, John A. Dunlop, informing that Moro had been taken from the house of Pandoorung by bailiffs of the Supreme Court. This attachment was based on a writ of capias obtained in a suit instituted by a collaborator of Moro's karkoons.[29] Malcolm believed that the case was 'a trick'. Dunlop expected that 'the judges would not allow any other authority to interfere, ever, with the illegal acts of their officers, reserving to themselves the right of judging …'.[30] Nevertheless, Malcolm was still optimistic at this stage because Chief Justice Edward West was on their side. West agreed that the writ was 'a complete fraud' and the bailiffs had no right to take him away, recommending Malcolm to prosecute them in the Supreme Court.[31] However, West died soon after this correspondence, and the remaining Puisne Judges, Charles Chambers and John Peter Grant, had a far more antagonistic attitude towards the government. The case immediately developed into a critical situation. On 25 August, a writ of habeas corpus was moved in the court and issued on the 29th. The Advocate General, James Dewar, reported that the judges intended to instruct the bailiffs to request the assistance of the military to execute the writ, and, if the request was refused, they would close all the courts of law in Bombay.[32] Pandoorung reportedly lambasted Malcolm, 'in a very crowded durbar', saying that when the rumour of the battalion's mobilisation was circulated, a large number of people gathered around his house to see what was happening and 'his enemies were exulting in his anticipated disgrace'.[33] On 29 September, the alias (second) habeas corpus was issued. Malcolm told Pandoorung via Dunlop that he should not receive it.[34]

This case of Moro Ragonath was accompanied by another case of habeas corpus, in which the government criticised the King's Court's issuing of the writ *within* its jurisdiction on the ground of political expediency. It was issued on 15 July 1828 to the gaoler of Thana in the Northern Konkan to bring the body of one Bappoo Gunness, a revenue defaulter. Bappoo Gunness had been judged guilty in the Company's Court for embezzlement, sentenced to two years' confinement and fined Rs 350.[35] This was a typical use of the King's Court by a revenue defaulter similar to those cases which we saw in Chap. 3. Advocate General Dewar advised Malcolm not to adopt the extreme measure of interfering in the King's Court's process, as the gaoler was under the Company's employment and therefore the case was clearly within the jurisdiction of the Supreme Court.[36] However, because it happened at the same time as the case of Moro Ragonath, the case became crucially important for the government's battle with the King's Court. Malcolm reprimanded Dewar that the case should be considered on political, rather than legal, grounds.[37] Thereafter, the government dealt with the two cases as one.[38]

The government was driven by security concerns emanating from the Indian's misunderstanding about the separation of powers. Malcolm explained it as follows:

> Nothing can be more calculated than such occurrences to weaken the civil government, and to encourage the discontented and seditious … members in our Indian Dominions. The establishment of our power in the Deckan is too recent and its inhabitants too ignorant to enable them to understand those limits, and distinction of authority. The consequence is an impression of division in our internal rule, which is most dangerous to our power.[39]

He explained that Indians regarded the King's Court 'as something great and wonderful, and think … that there is not an action of government, civil, political, or military, that is not subject to its revision or control'.[40] In the court, the government argued that the King's Court had no power to issue a prerogative writ to persons who were outside its ordinary jurisdiction.[41]

The judges denied the government's claim. Chambers argued that the King's Court did have the power to issue a prerogative writ, which was 'unlimited both as to place and person within the territories subject to the Bombay Government', since the court was vested with the power of the King's Bench in Britain to protect the personal and civil liberty of the Indian subjects.[42] Grant elaborated this point by employing a distinction between *potestas jurisdictionis* (the court's judicial power of hearing and determining civil and criminal cases) and *potestas imperii* (the ministerial or mandatorial power of the sovereign to command something to be done). He argued that the latter was not limited by the court's ordinary jurisdiction: 'the limits of the Jurisdiction of any Court to try causes afford no measure of its power to issue the prerogative writs of the Crown, either in respect of the *territory* in which they are to run, of the *persons* to whom they shall be directed, or of the *matters* they may concern and grow out of'.[43] To make this point, the judges relied extensively on the legal authorities of the common law tradition such as Edward Coke and Matthew Hale, the opinions of English judges such as Lord Mansfield and Lord Eldon and the precedents such as the case of *R v. Monisse* in Madras in 1810, in which a sovereign prince was subjected to the court's prosecution.[44] The judges emphasised that they were vested with a sovereign power to command the orders of the King; it was a question of 'the *power of the King in right of his Crown* exercised by his Supreme Judges in this part of his Dominions'.[45] A logical consequence of this argument was that the government officials should obey orders of the King's Court representing the sovereign:

> the Governor of this Presidency, and the council, and the Commander-in-Chief, and all persons in authority are bound to pay obedience to the commands of the Court in execution of its several powers ... so that in any of these persons to refuse obedience was a direct breach of their allegiance to the royal authority and to the sacred person of the King.[46]

In addition to this point of jurisdiction, the judges extensively argued that the case of Moro Ragonath was not a case of emergency. Chambers admitted that 'in times of sedition or public commotion', the general privileges of the subjects should be suspended for the public good, but it did not apply to this case: 'the present case involves no such difficulty, and the principle which we are now considering is of the most general nature'.[47] He criticised the government for creating an 'unnecessary alarm' because the case was 'of no public importance nor of any political consequence .... There are no circumstances of state policy affecting it'.[48] In the same vein, Grant defined the case as an issue of personal rather than political liberty of the Indian subjects:

> It is very true that this is a matter which nearly concerns personal liberty; and I may observe in passing that, although in the British Dominions in India, as in other colonial possessions, the same degree of *political liberty* cannot exist as in the governing country, yet the *personal liberty* of every individual in all the parts of His extensive Dominions, scattered over every clime, and at every variety of distance from the seat of His Government, is equally under the special protection of the King in England, and of His Courts.[49]

This assertion of civil liberties and the denial of political emergency were made possible by the judges' conception of indivisible sovereignty in post-conquest British India. The government saw India as a confederation composed of different countries. The government's Advocate General, James Dewar, told the court that the jurisdiction of the King's Court could not be extended to 'another Kingdom, the Deccan, the Malwa, or other Countries, as separate from each other, and from Bombay, as Russia from Austria'.[50] However, the judges thought that the Deccan was 'the only part of the territory subject to the Bombay Government' and 'a part of the vast fabric of the English Empire, and its inhabitants ... are, as subjects to the Crown of England, entitled to the privileges of Freeman'.[51] Chambers cited the case of Amerchund Bedreechund in which the court displayed a similar distinction and said that, since the conquest of the Deccan in 1817, its inhabitants had been 'the subject of a mixed and limited monarchy' and those who were born after 1817 were Britain's 'natural born subjects'.[52]

The judges' argument was unacceptable for Malcolm, who considered their views dangerous. He proposed that the government protect Pandoorung and resist all further attempts by the King's Court, and, should the judges proceed to enforce its decrees, Malcolm recommended that:

> they must be met at all hazards by the power of Government, the exercise of which will be fully justified, not merely on the grounds of expediency and policy, but on that of self-preservation, a principle which in the rare cases in which it is brought into action, must supersede all others.[53]

For Malcolm, the King's Court's prerogative writs in the mofussil would incur 'the complete subversion of the constitution of all our judicial institutions'.[54] He could not admit a situation in which a peon who brought about the writ to Pandoorung could say 'I can if I choose go and take your Governor prisoner'.[55] On 3 October 1828, the government sent a letter 'directing' the judges to stop proceedings of the cases of Moro Ragonath and Bappoo Gunness, admitting that it was irregular to interfere in the court's process but justifying it from 'exclusive reference to considerations of Civil Government, and of state policy'.[56] The judges were infuriated. Chambers asserted that it was highly irregular for the government to send a public letter in such a dictatorial manner, that the court should always be addressed by everyone in the manner of a humble suitor soliciting protection through counsel or petition and that the government's action was 'highly unconstitutional and criminal'. Grant added that the government did not understand that the writ was not a matter of judges' discretion but a 'writ of right'. The court replied to the government that the letter was received and that the judges could take no notice thereof.[57] On 10 October, the court issued a pluries (third) writ of habeas corpus with a fine of Rs 10,000.[58]

Grant (now left alone due to Chambers' death on 13 October) petitioned the King in Council in November 1828, provoking a further conflict between the government's logic of emergency and the court's logic of law. For Grant, the case of Moro Ragonath was 'a question of private right regarding the personal liberty'. The government's letter on 3 October 1828 was 'the most unconstitutional and criminal attempt' to threaten the court with the civil and military power of the government. It was the government that was causing a public disturbance by diminishing 'respect for the court and confidence in the law, which are the only sure foundations of such peace and obedience'. The government was endangering the British rule not only in the unsettled Deccan but also in the Konkan and Gujarat 'now for many years peacefully submitted to the British rule'. It was dangerous to leave the EIC's provincial courts without control and to place the inhabitants without the protection of habeas corpus.[59] Malcolm criticised Grant for not understanding the crisis in the mofussil. Gujarat was still troubled by the 'predatory tribes of Bheels, Cooleys, and Rajpoots' as well as by the invasions of Muslim and Maratha princes. The writ of habeas corpus was 'little short of a general gaol delivery throughout all the provinces subject to the presidency'. The Supreme Court would set free every criminal; villages and tracts of cultivation would be wasted; outlawry inhabitants would increase; revenue would decline; and 'regularity and public peace and security would be at an end'.[60] To 'preserve and create a native aristocracy', wrote Malcolm, the government conciliated the sardars and introduced a simple code of regulations, but these efforts would be nullified if the King's Court's jurisdiction was extended to the mofussil. Baroda and Satara had made suspicious moves, and Angria and other chiefs solicited the government to protect them when their discontented servants or seditious dependents filed lawsuits against them. The court's jurisdiction, Malcolm warned, would 'seriously weaken the authority and accelerate the downfall of our power in this quarter of India'.[61]

The situation seemed favourable for Grant, however, as he could resist the government with his power to control court procedures.

Throughout the proceedings, the government assumed that it was Moro's karkoons that had instigated the boy to take legal action. Indeed, at an early stage, Malcolm received a letter from Moro Ragonath himself stating that he was happy under the guardianship of Pandoorung and that it was the karkoons who appropriated his property and filed the suit in the Supreme Court.[62] Malcolm believed that the letter was genuine and ordered Advocate General Dewar to submit it to the King's Court.[63] But Dewar replied that, even if the letter was presented to the court, the judge would say that it was written under duress and ignore it. He confessed that there would be no remedy on this matter.[64] Because of procedural power of the judges, the government repeatedly failed to make their argument in the court. In February 1829, Grant finally ordered the attachment of Pandoorung Ramchunder for not making a return to the writ. He directed the Governor and Members of the Council to execute the writ in the King's name. If the government did not obey the order, it would be 'guilty of a great contempt'.[65] The government ignored the order and referred the court to their letter on 3 October 1828.[66]

As a further resistance, Grant declared the closure of the Supreme Court in April 1829 'until the Court receives an assurance that its authority will be respected and its Process obeyed, and rendered effectual by the Government'.[67] The government responded by proclaiming in the *Bombay Courier* that it would make 'every effort in his power to protect their persons and property during this Extraordinary conjuncture'.[68] Dewar expected the inconveniences: criminals would not be arrested and prisoners would remain untried; debtors would escape their creditors; no warrants could issue from the admiralty side of the court; the intestate estates would be wasted as the ecclesiastical side was shut; no one could be brought up to be bailed by habeas corpus. He lamented that 'we are now … in a state without law'.[69]

Another concern of the government was the indigenous information network. The government could not control publications about the court proceedings, let alone personal communications. Malcolm worried about the circulation of the judges' criticisms of the government and banned newspapers from publishing any reports on the proceedings of the cases.[70] But a Gujarati newspaper, *Bombay Samachar*, continued reporting the speech of the judges in 1828 and 1829.[71] Malcolm lamented that native correspondence was faster than the government's and there were many exchanges about the Moro Ragonath case passing unnoticed between the nobility in the Deccan and the Peshwa at Benares.[72] Nor could the government prevent the inflow of metropolitan radical ideas via newspapers and magazines.[73] Frustrated, Malcolm commented that the government 'should be permitted to employ the same weapons for their defence'.[74]

Not having the means to control the judge's discretion in the court, the government sought support from outside of it. This dramatically expanded the arena of conflict. Both the government and the King's Court petitioned higher authorities in Calcutta and London, escalating the habeas corpus cases into one of the most important imperial disputes between the executive and the judiciary in nineteenth-century India.

The Governor's and the Judges' Imperial Networks

Governor Malcolm sought political and legal support from Calcutta, Madras and London. His government reported every detail of the case of Moro Ragonath to the Court of Directors by sending government records and the Advocate General's notes on the court proceedings. Malcolm also appointed his former aide-de-camp, Major Barnwall, as the special agent to England to transmit these papers to the Court of Directors.[75] The government sent letters to Madras and Calcutta requesting assistance of their Advocates General.[76] Malcolm also made numerous private communications with politicians in India and London. He frequently exchanged opinions with Governor S. R. Lushington of Madras and Governor-General William Bentinck of Calcutta, in addition to district officials throughout the Bombay presidency. Bentinck encouraged Malcolm to stand his ground: 'You have taken your line and whether right or wrong, you cannot retreat an inch, without compromising the authority of government and without occasioning great political mischief'.[77] Malcolm exchanged many letters with Tory politicians in London such as the Duke of Wellington and Lord Ellenborough.[78]

The King's Court's resources outside the presidency were limited. In November 1828, Grant sent a petition to the King in Council (the Privy Council), the final tribunal of colonial legal cases, to complain about the government's interference. He appointed Attorney William Fenwick as the agent to London.[79] Grant also petitioned the Board of Control in London, the court's supervising body.[80] He revived the late eighteenth-century conflict between the government and the EIC at home.[81] The Bombay government complained that Grant spoke 'of that Board as a distinct, not a component part of the Indian Government in England'

and tried to impress that 'an assertion of more entire and active sovereignty on the part of the Crown' was only possible by 'a more complete negation of any sovereignty' of the EIC.[82] The problem was that the President of the Board of Control, Lord Ellenborough, was a staunch supporter of the Bombay government. Due to the scarcity of record, the extent of private network of the judge is difficult to trace, but it is known that Grant, via his son William Patrick Grant, sent letters to the chairman of the EIC and the President of the Board of Control when he resigned, while his Indian supporters also sent a letter to Lord Holland.[83] When the court closed, Grant solicited support from the Supreme Government in Calcutta.[84]

The extensive reach of Governor Malcolm's public and private networks decided the course of events. The home authorities were also firmly in support of the Bombay government. In September 1828, immediately after the death of Edward West, Malcolm wrote letters to 'those in authority in England and to all who I supposed were likely to have influence in the nomination' to ensure that the next Chief Justice 'must have temper and judgement ... and above all he must view himself as an aid instead of a check upon the civil government of the country'.[85] Two years later, this lobbying finally bore fruit. Ellenborough, the newly appointed President, appointed Advocate General James Dewar as the next Chief Justice and William Seymour as a Puisne Judge. Ellenborough predicted that 'no more mischief can happen, as he [Grant] will be like a wild elephant led away between two tame ones'.[86] He later added that 'India was won by soldiers and statesmen & we must not allow lawyers to lose it'.[87] This appointment was decisive. In the case of *Moro Ragonath v. Dunlop*, in which Moro's karkoons prosecuted Dunlop (the Agent for Sirdars) for trespass in the Supreme Court,[88] new Chief Justice Dewar judged in favour of the defendant, despite Grant's opposition.[89] Malcolm said that Dewar's appointment was as effective as 'a master stroke'; it was 'like a charm'.[90]

The government was further empowered by the decision of the Privy Council in its favour, which was given in May 1829.[91] The counsels for Grant were Thomas Denman, who was also the counsel for Cursetjee Manockjee and Amerchund Bedreechund, whose cases we saw in Chap. 2, and Edward Hall Anderson, a judge of the Common Pleas. The Company was represented by John Bosanquet, the Company's Standing Counsel, and Robert Spankie, the former Advocate General of Bengal. The Privy Council decided that the Supreme Court could not issue a writ of habeas corpus outside its jurisdiction and that it had no power to release prisoners who were convicted by the Company's Court.[92] After the decision, there were few means left for Judge Grant to resist the government. Malcolm expressed his delight: 'I am discovered to be a great lawyer. God help them'![93]

Petitions from Bombay Merchants and Deccan Sardars

The development of the Bombay cases was anxiously watched by Indians whose future conduct might be significantly affected by the outcome. The sardars in the Deccan had a particular interest in the case, since they would be involved in the same difficulties as Pandoorung Ramchunder. They pressed the government to resolve the issue via a petition signed by 112 'principal inhabitants at Poona':

> The settlement of the country (the Dukhun) was made by the Company's Government. At that time certain terms and Agreements were entered into with all persons of good character, high and low, and Regulations established, for the preservation of Rank and Respectability all which have been enjoyed. Summonses have lately been issued from the King's Court against Pandoorung Ramchunder Dhumdere, which people considered a Breach of these Regulations, it was however well known that the Company's Government shielded us from the evils of this case. But having now that the Court has been suspended in consequence of this affair, doubts have arisen. All people are very apprehensive as to how it will be permanently settled and how their honour and character will be preserved, and protection afforded them. Reflecting on these things we unite in submitting this Petition to Government, and pray that taking the subject into consideration arrangements may be made by which whatever has been enjoyed on the Faith of the Company's Government may be continued in future, and that nothing shall occur to detract from our respectability.[94]

This petition was handed directly to Malcolm by two of the major sardars—Basker Ram Gokla, a relation of the Peshwa's Commander-in-Chief Bappoo Gokla, and Ballajee Punt Nathoo, Elphinstone's chief native servant during the Maratha War. They told him that the agitation had been heightened in all over the Deccan and that they were concerned about 'the evils ... from the extension of the English law' upon their respectability. Malcolm replied that there was no real cause for alarm, reassuring that their interests and honour would continue to be matters of special care for the government. The petition was forwarded to the Court of Directors and the Bengal government.[95] Whether this petition was solicited by Malcolm is not known, but it was clear that the sardars and the government had a shared interest in resisting the King's Court.

By contrast, Indian merchants of Bombay city supported the King's Court. The reform public in Bombay city viewed the political elevation of Dewar to Chief Justiceship with great suspicion and cast a jaundiced eye on all his acts in court.[96] Their feeling was expressed in two Addresses of Thanks printed and circulated on the resignation of Grant as the Puisne Judge in September 1830. The first one was signed by 4400 people and read at a meeting at the courthouse. Introduced by one Jehangheir Nasserwanjee, a Parsi shopkeeper, the statement praised the efforts of Grant, West and Chambers to protect the Indians in the mofussil from the government's false imprisonment, articulating that 'an appellate jurisdiction to the Supreme Court from the judgements of the Provincial Courts [was] the sincere and ardent desire of all the natives who reside under this Presidency'.[97] The second address, expressing that the King's Court administering the British law was beneficial in the mofussil as well as in Bombay city, was read by Bomanjee Hormusjee in a meeting chaired by Jagganath Sunkersett. It was signed by 3000 inhabitants, including the city's biggest merchants such as Jamsetjee Jeejeebhoy, Dhackjee Dadajee and Framjee Cowasjee. It was also signed by Jetmul Anoopchund and Heerachund Bedreechund, the plaintiffs of the Amerchund Bedreechund case. In replying to these addresses, Grant advocated the expansion of the King's Court's jurisdiction in the mofussil.[98]

These addresses show that, while the users of the King's Court included the whole spectrum of society, the Hindu and Parsi merchants in Bombay were most eager for the expansion of the King's Court's jurisdiction in the mofussil. The Hindu merchants were well acquainted with the British law in their commercial transactions.[99] The Parsi community was unique, as Mitra Sharafi shows, in that they were one of the minority groups most actively engaged in British legal culture in colonial society.[100] When the Indians were selected as grand jurors for the first time in Bombay in 1834, for example, Parsis comprised 9 out of 13 Indian members.[101] The addresses further suggest that, in addition to the jury and the press, the expansion of the King's Court's jurisdiction was a major cause through which political radicalism was nurtured in Bombay's commercial communities in the 1820s and the 1830s. Those who signed the addresses—Sunkersett, Hormusjee, Jeejeebhoy, Dadajee and Cowasjee—were directors of the Bombay Native Education Society (later the Elphinstone Institution), which became the incubator of Indian liberal intellectuals in the middle and late nineteenth century.[102] As Mridula Ramanna points out, the Supreme Court had employed the Elphinstonians as interpreters and translators in the early nineteenth century.[103] There was a clear connection between the King's Court, western education and radicalism in early nineteenth-century Bombay.

The government officials were well aware of this. William Newnham, Member of the Council, commented that the second address was 'radical' and the first one 'ultra-radical'. He guessed that the professional lawyers were involved in their drafting and the signatures must have been collected by the same methods used in electioneering in Britain by distributing blank papers on streets and getting as many passers-by as possible to sign.[104] Malcolm concurred, positing his theory of moral contagion passing from Bombay city to the mofussil: the British law and court in the city made people profligate and motivated them to communicate with the discontented persons in the provinces.[105]

The sardars in the Deccan criticised the addresses in a durbar.[106] They worried that the addresses might be considered in Britain to be the genuine voice of all Indians, while they were in fact the opinion of 'a few discontented men, perhaps, some impostors and intriguers, low associates of money usurers, or crafty emissaries of lawyers'. They added that the introduction of English law was contrary to the government's 1818 Satara proclamation and the 1827 Regulations and that their honours and privileges would be easily taken away by 'a low man and bit of paper nobody can read'. The memorandum was signed by four of the first-class sardars, eight of the second class including Pandoorung Ramchunder and Moro Ragonath(!) and other 200 sardars and merchants.[107] The Governor had to issue further notice criticising the addresses.[108]

Thus, the case of Moro Ragonath was a moment of politicisation for the sardars and the Indian merchants in Western India. The sardars in the mofussil strengthened their affiliation with the government, while the merchants in the city identified themselves with the King's Court. In this sense, the Moro Ragonath case drove the government to further prioritise the agrarian politics in the mofussil than the trade and commerce in the presidency town. The government's strong links with the Indian merchants observed in the eighteenth century were fading away, with the government's policy more and more focused on security and revenue collection in the mofussil. The Bombay case embodied this reorganisation of British empire in Western India from a maritime commercial network of merchants to a territorial rule over the vast inner provinces.

Conclusion

The case of Moro Ragonath showed the process by which a local issue in a local province in India became transformed into an imperial agenda in Bombay, Calcutta and London. The government sought support from the home authorities not only utilising the usual departmental letters but also dispatching a special agent to convey all the information and opinions of the government. Tories in London, such as Wellington and Ellenborough, were well informed about the issue thanks to their private correspondence with Malcolm. The intensity of communications between local governments in India was also remarkable in this case. The Bombay government could obtain advice and support from Governors, Members of the Council and Advocates General in Calcutta and Madras through public and private correspondence. The Chief Justice, in addition to his regular communication with the President of the Board of Control, also petitioned the Bengal government and sent a special mission to London to petition the Privy Council. Their connection with the London radicals was especially important in this respect. The hub of such networks was influential Europeans such as Charles Forbes who had been in Bombay and now back in Britain. At the same time, it was clear that the government was in an advantageous position for utilising the established routes of communication, whereas the King's Court had to rely on personal and ad hoc networks. This difference in resources available from outside the presidency brought about a favourable outcome for the government.

The Moro Ragonath case gives us many insights into the nature of Bombay politics in the early nineteenth century. First, forum shopping by the Indians was quite common. Both Pandoorung Ramchunder and the karkoons of Moro Ragonath well understood how to play off the jurisdictional conflict between the government and the King's Court. They allied with the one to criticise the other and employed multiple means to use the conflict to their advantage. The immediately available allies for those resorting to the King's Court were the Bombay attorneys and their subordinates in the mofussil. They could mobilise their relatives and friends to create testimonies and write affidavits. They also used the press to publish the addresses to the Chief Justice. Moro Ragonath's karkoons followed legal practices that were quite common in the Deccan. Second, it was also clear that the appeal structure of the colonial judiciary tended to work in favour of the government. The independent judiciary in India could not realise its independence in the structure, where the final decision was always up to politicians at home rather than the judges in India. Even if the law courts sometimes ruled against the government, the rule of law was structurally limited in the colonies. The power of judicial check was further curtailed in the subsequent debates on charter renewal in Calcutta and London. Because of the scale of the conflict, the governments in Bombay, Calcutta and London saw the need to resolve this jurisdictional anomaly and create a unified and hierarchical order of judicature in India. In that process, the Bombay government's discourse on crisis and danger was given an institutional form.

Notes

1. Rajnarayan Chandavarkar, *Imperial Power and Popular Politics: Class, Resistance and the State in India c. 1850–1950* (Cambridge: Cambridge University Press, 1998), 195.
2. O. P. Bhatnagar, M. P. Jain, and A. G. Noorani outline the cases. M. P. Jain, *Outlines of Indian Legal and Constitutional History*, 6th edition (New Delhi: LexisNexis, 2006), 105–6; O. P. Bhatnagar, 'The Case of Moro Raghunath: A Case Illustrating the Conflict between Judiciary and Executive in India in Early Nineteenth Century', Allahabad High Court (http://www.allahabadhighcourt.in/event/TheCaseofMoroRaghunathOPBhatnagar.pdf, accessed 25 Feb. 2021); A. G. Noorani, *Indian Political Trials 1775–1947* (Oxford: Oxford University Press, 2005), 10–17. See also Jon Wilson, *India Conquered: Britain's Raj and the Chaos of Empire* (London: Simon and Schuster, 2016), 193–200.
3. British Library [BL], India Office Records [IOR] L/PS/6/179–81. Corresponding volumes in the Board's Collection are F/4/1030/28288–28289, F/4/1113/29753A and F/4/1114/29753B–C. In this chapter, I use these compilations instead of Proceedings and Consultations in IOR P. The corresponding volumes in the Maharashtra State Archives are Political Department [PD], 1829/30, 23/347 and 24/348.
4. BL, IOR H/734, 529–30, John Malcolm to S. R. Lushington, Governor of Madras, 21 Oct. 1828.
5. *The Correspondence of Lord William Cavendish Bentinck, Governor-General of India 1828–1835*, ed. C. H. Philips, 2 vols. (Oxford: Oxford

University Press, 1977), 1:55, J. Malcolm to W. Bentinck, 27 July 1828. Malcolm warned that, if both the powers of the Adalat and the King's Court were not speedily restricted, 'their power will soon embrace all India, and be, in my opinion, when so spread, a sufficient cause of the downfall of this empire'. Ibid.

6. *Parliamentary Papers* [PP] 1831–32 (735-III), Appendix, 87, Lord Moira, minute, 21 Sep. 1815. They appointed special commissioners for that purpose in Lower Bengal by Regulation III of 1828. John Rosselli, *Lord William Bentinck: The Making of a Liberal Imperialist 1774–1839* (London: Chatto & Windus, 1974), 262; A. F. Salahuddin Ahmed, *Social Ideas and Social Change in Bengal, 1818–1835*, 2nd edition (Calcutta: RDDHI, 1976), 115–25.
7. PP 1831–32 (735-III), Appendix, 534–35, 538, J. Malcolm, minute, 10 June 1828; BL, IOR P/370/9, BRC 22 Apr. 1829, no. 42, J. Malcolm, minute, 6 Apr. 1829.
8. Eric Stokes, *The English Utilitarians and India* (Oxford: Oxford University Press, 1959), 182–83 and note P, 327.
9. See, for example, Gauri Viswanathan, *Masks of Conquest: Literary Study and British Rule in India* (New York: Columbia University Press, 1989).
10. Martha McLaren, *British India and British Scotland 1780–1830: Carrier Building, Empire Building, and a Scottish School of Thought on Indian Governance* (Akron, OH: University of Akron Press, 2001); Jack Harrington, *Sir John Malcolm and the Creation of British India* (Basingstoke: Palgrave Macmillan, 2010); Neeladri Bhattacharya, *The Great Agrarian Conquest: The Colonial Reshaping of a Rural World* (Ranikhet: Permanent Black, 2018); Shah Mahmoud Hanafi, ed., *Mountstuart Elphinstone in South Asia: Pioneer of British Colonial Rule* (London: Hurst, 2019).
11. David Roberts, *Paternalism in Early Victorian England* (London: Groom Helm, 1979).
12. Douglas M. Peers, *Between Mars and Mammon: Colonial Armies and the Garrison State in India 1819–1835* (London, Tauris, 1995), 8.
13. Peers, *Mars and Mammon*, 38, 45–6, 53–4, 63–5. See also Lynn Zastoupil, *John Stuart Mill and India* (Stanford, CA: Stanford University Press, 1994), 56–74.
14. John Malcolm, *The Political History of India from 1784 to 1823*, 2 vols. (London, 1826), 1:145.
15. John McLaren, *Dewigged, Bothered and Bewildered: British Colonial Judges on Trial 1800–1900* (Toronto: University of Toronto Press, 2011); P. B. Vachha, *Famous Judges, Lawyers and Cases of Bombay: A Judicial History of Bombay During the British Period* (Bombay: N. M. Tripathi, 1962; 2011); Abhinav Chandrachud, *An Independent, Colonial Judiciary:*

A History of the Bombay High Court During the British Raj 1862–1947 (Oxford: Oxford University Press, 2015). See also Mitra Sharafi, 'South Asian Legal History', *Annual Review of Law and Social Science* 11 (2015), 309–36.

16. Paul D. Halliday, *Habeas Corpus: From England to Empire* (Cambridge, MA., Belknap Press of Harvard University Press, 2010); Amanda L. Tyler, *Habeas Corpus in Wartime: From the Tower of London to Guantanamo Bay* (Oxford: Oxford University Press, 2017); Eric M. Freedman, *Making Habeas Work: A Legal History* (New York: New York University Press, 2018).
17. BL, IOR V/27/70/10, 33.
18. Moro was in the third class in the criminal list and the second class in the civil list. Pandoorung was the second-class sardar in criminal and civil lists. BL, IOR, P/399/64, BJC 18 Oct. 1826, no. 29, M. Elphinstone, minute, 5 Sep. 1826.
19. BL, IOR F/4/1030/28289, 325–36, J. A. Dunlop to J. Malcolm, 11 Oct. 1828.
20. For example, Chaplin referred to the karkoons of the Tasgaum branch of the Patwardhans who attempted to 'suppress or destroy the will of their late master and to usurp the management of the estate according to a forged instrument'. William Chaplin, *A Report Exhibiting a View of the Fiscal and Judicial System of Administration Introduced into the Conquered Territory above the Ghauts under the Authority of the Commissioner in the Dekhan* (Bombay, 1824), 160, 164.
21. BL, IOR P/399/35, BJC, 23 June 1824, 3522–81, W. Chaplin to Gov., 9 June 1824.
22. C. A. Bayly, *Rulers, Townsmen and Bazaars: North India in the Age of British Expansion 1770–1870* (Oxford: Oxford University Press, 1997), 137.
23. BL, IOR P/399/35, BJC, 23 June 1824, 3522–81, W. Chaplin to Gov., 9 June 1824.
24. BL, IOR P/399/40, BJC, 1 Dec. 1824, 8518, James Farish, secretary, memorandum on the proceeding of the appeal of Moro Ragonath.
25. BL, IOR F/4/1030/28289, 325–36, J. A. Dunlop to J. Malcolm, 11 Oct. 1828.
26. A. R. Kulkarni, ed., *History in Practice: Historians and Sources of Medieval Deccan-Marathas* (New Delhi: Books and Books, 1993), 127, 154.
27. BL, IOR P/400/14, BJC 16 Jan. 1828, nos. 38–39, Pandoorung Ramchunder to Gov., 7 Nov. 1827.
28. BL, IOR P/400/17, BJC 14 May 1828, nos. 59–60, P. Ramchunder to Gov., 10 Apr. 1828; BL, IOR P/400/17, BJC 11 June 1828, nos. 1–2, S. Marriott to Gov., 23 May 1828; Ibid., no. 49, W. J. Lumsden to Gov., 26 May 1828.

29. BL, IOR H/736, 749–50.
30. BL, IOR L/PJ/3/918, 55–58, BJL, Gov. to CoD, 27 Sep. 1828, J. A. Dunlop to J. Malcolm, 10 July 1828 and J. Malcolm to J. A. Dunlop, 11 July 1828.
31. Ibid., J. Malcolm, note, n.d. (Proceedings dated 10 Sep. 1828) and Edward West to J. Malcolm, 13 July 1828.
32. BL, IOR F/4/1030/28288, 216–19, James Dewar to J. Malcolm, 14 Sep. 1828.
33. Ibid., 233, J. Malcolm to J. Dewar, 18 Sep. 1828.
34. BL, IOR F/4/1030/28288, 254–55, J. Malcolm to J. A. Dunlop, n.d.
35. BL, IOR F/4/1030/28289, 407–32, E. H. Baillie, Northern Concan Judge, to Gov., 13 Sep. 1828, enclosing the court proceedings of 8 May 1828 and J. Dewar's reports dated 2 Oct. 1828.
36. BL, IOR L/PJ/3/918, 55–58, BJL, Gov. to CoD, 27 Sep. 1828, J. Dewar to J. Malcolm, 21 Aug. 1828.
37. Ibid., J. Malcolm to J. Dewar, 3 Sep. 1828; BL, IOR F/4/1030/28288, 240–41, J. Malcolm to J. Dewar, 18 Sep. 1828.
38. In the trial, Bappoo Gunness was defended by the indefatigable James Morley. BL, IOR F/4/1030/28289, 444–50, J. Dewar to Gov., 27 Sep 1828.
39. BL, IOR L/PJ/3/918, 55–58, BJL, Gov. to CoD, 27 Sep. 1828, J. Malcolm, minute, 17 July 1828.
40. Ibid., J. Malcolm to Thomas Bradford, Commander-in-Chief, 18 July 1828.
41. BL, IOR L/PS/6/180, 21–27, *Supreme Court Report*, 15 Sep. 1828, 1–7, J. Dewar.
42. Ibid., 70, 73, *Supreme Court Report*, 29 Sep. 1828, 10, 13, Charles Chambers.
43. Ibid., 84, *Supreme Court Report*, 29 Sep. 1828, 26, John Peter Grant.
44. Ibid.
45. Ibid., 95, *Supreme Court Report*, 29 Sep. 1828, 35, J. P. Grant.
46. Ibid., 100, *Supreme Court Report*, 10 Oct. 1828, 40, J. P. Grant.
47. Ibid., 69, 74, *Supreme Court Report*, 29 Sep. 1828, 9, 14, C. Chambers.
48. Ibid., 97, *Supreme Court Report*, 6 Oct. 1828, 37, C. Chambers.
49. Ibid., 78, *Supreme Court Report*, 29 Sep. 1828, 18, J. P. Grant, emphasis original.
50. Ibid., 66, *Supreme Court Report*, 29 Sep. 1828, 6, J. Dewar.
51. Ibid., 69–70, *Supreme Court Report*, 29 Sep. 1828, 9, 10, C. Chambers.
52. Ibid., 70, *Supreme Court Report*, 29 Sep. 1828, 10, C. Chambers.
53. BL, IOR F/4/1030/28289, 26–27, J. Malcolm, minute, 2 Oct. 1828.
54. Ibid., 37.

55. BL, IOR F/4/1030/28289, 79–80, J. Malcolm, minute, 3 Oct. 1828.
56. BL, IOR L/PS/6/180, 77–79, *Supreme Court Report*, 6 Oct 1828, 17–19. The petition was also printed in John Malcolm, *The Government of India* (London, 1833), Appendix C, 118–20.
57. BL, IOR L/PS/6/180, 96–100, *Supreme Court Report*, 6 Oct 1828, 36–40, C. Chambers and J. P. Grant.
58. BL, IOR F/4/1030/28289, 265–69, J. Dewar to Gov., 10 Oct. 1828.
59. Malcolm, *Government of India*, Appendix C, 115–28, J. P. Grant's petition to the Privy Council, Nov. 1828.
60. Ibid., 136–43, J. Malcolm, minute, 30 Nov. 1828.
61. Ibid., 146–51.
62. BL, IOR F/4/1036/28549(7), J. A. Dunlop to Gov., 26 Nov. 1828, enclosing a letter from Moro Ragonath to the Governor, dated 5th Jemadee ool Awul.
63. Ibid., J. Malcolm, minute, 29 Nov. 1828.
64. BL, IOR L/PS/6/180, 323–26, BPC 21 Jan. 1829, J. Dewar to Gov., 9 Dec. 1828.
65. Ibid., 498–503, BPC 4 Mar. 1829, no. 8, J. Dewar to Gov., 27 Feb. 1829; Ibid., 504–16, SC to Gov., 9 Mar. 1829, BPC 18 Mar. 1829.
66. Ibid., 519–28, BPC 18 Mar. 1829, J. Malcolm, minute, 12 Mar. 1829, and Gov. to SC, 13 Mar. 1829; Ibid., 666–76, BPC 22 Mar. 1829, SC to Gov., 21 Mar. 1829; Ibid., 676–81, BPC 22 Mar 1829, J. Malcolm, minute, n.d., and Gov. to SC, 22 Mar. 1829.
67. *Bombay Courier Extraordinary*, 2 Apr. 1829; BL, IOR L/PS/6/180, 874–79, *Supreme Court Report*, 1 Apr. 1829.
68. *Bombay Courier Extraordinary*, 7 Apr 1829; BL, IOR L/PS/6/180, 706–7, BPL, Gov. to CoD, 8 Apr. 1829, and BL, IOR L/PS/6/180, 880, proclamation.
69. BL, IOR L/PS/6/180, 749–50, 753–54, BPC 8 Apr. 1829, J. Dewar to Gov., 2 Apr. 1829.
70. BL, IOR F/4/1030/28289, 344–54, J. Malcolm, minute, 12 Oct. 1828; Ibid., 375–82, J. Malcolm, minute, 14 Oct. 1828, Government notice, 17 Oct. 1828.
71. Ibid., 399–406, J. Malcolm, minute, 20 Oct. 1828; BL, IOR L/PS/6/180, 319–22, BPC 14 Jan. 1829, W. Clerk, Acting Persian Secretary, to Gov., 6 Jan. 1829.
72. BL, IOR F/4/1030/28289, 84–85, J. Malcolm, minute, 3 Oct. 1828.
73. BL, IOR H/734, 652–3, J. Malcolm to C. T. Metcalfe, 23 June 1829.
74. BL, IOR F/4/1241/40865, 13–26, BGC 28 Oct. 1829, no. 11, J. Malcolm, minute, n.d.
75. BL, IOR F/4/1030/28289, 235–37, J. Malcolm, minute, 8 Oct. 1828. The Judges and Magistrates were instructed not to visit Bombay. Ibid.,

233, 239–40, circular, 10 Oct. 1828. Barnwall had ample knowledge on the harmful effect of legal proceedings on chiefs and sardars as the Political Agent of Kathiawar. He worked under Alexander Walker when Gujarat was first annexed to the British territory. Malcolm, *Government of India*, 77.

76. BL, IOR L/PS/6/180, 339–482, BPC 21 Mar. 1829, Gov. to CoD, 9 Feb. 1829; BL, IOR L/PS/6/180, 794–838, BPC 15 Apr 1829; same one in 992 ff., Gov. to Bengal Government [Ben. Gov.], 15 Apr. 1829.
77. *Bentinck Correspondence*, ed. Philips, 1:93, W. Bentinck to J. Malcolm, 12 Nov. 1828.
78. For example, see BL, IOR H/734, 311–13, J. Malcolm to the Duke of Wellington, 5 Apr. 1829; BL, IOR H/734, 314–16, J. Malcolm to the Earl of Ellenborough, 5 Apr. 1829.
79. BL, IOR F/4/1036/28549(7), SC to Gov., 21 Oct. 1828 and SC to Gov., 3 Nov. 1828.
80. William Hook Morley, *An Analytical Digest of All the Reported Cases Decided in the Supreme Courts of Judicature in India, in the Courts of the Hon. East India Company, and on Appeal from India, by Her Majesty in Council*, 2 vols. (London, 1849–50), 2:662, 683, Supreme Court charter, ss. 38, 71.
81. H. V. Bowen, *The Business of Empire: The East India Company and Imperial Britain 1756–1833* (Cambridge: Cambridge University Press, 2006), 10–11.
82. BL, IOR F/4/1030/28288, 43–44, BPL Gov. to CoD, 20 Oct. 1828.
83. BL, Eur Mss F523/59.
84. BL, IOR L/PS/6/180, 964–88, J. P. Grant to Ben. Gov., 2 Apr. 1829.
85. BL, IOR H/734, 503–5, J. Malcolm to G. Norton, 9 Sep. 1828; *Bentinck Correspondence*, 1:68, J. Malcolm to W. Bentinck, 19 Aug. 1828.
86. John William Kaye, *The Life and Correspondence of Major-General Sir John Malcolm*, 2 vols. (London, 1856), 2:528–30, Ellenborough to J. Malcolm, 21 Feb. 1829.
87. Ellenborough to W. Bentinck, 23 May 1830, quoted in D. N. Panigrahi, *Charles Metcalfe in India: Ideas and Administration 1806–1835* (Delhi: Munshiram Manoharlal, 1968), 170.
88. BL, IOR L/PS/6/181, 135–41, BPC 11 Aug. 1829, R. Mills to Gov., 1 Aug. 1829.
89. Ibid., 499–625.
90. BL, IOR H/734, 419–22, J. Malcolm to Wellington, 7 June 1829; Ibid., 208–9, J. Malcolm to Ellenborough, 12 June 1829.
91. 1 Knapp, 1–59.

92. Ibid., 51–59.
93. BL, IOR H/734, 691, J. Malcolm to S. R. Lushington, 10 Sep. 1829.
94. BL, IOR L/PS/6/180, 1052–65, BPC 25 May 1829, nos. 1–3, petition dated 2 May 1829, and J. Malcolm, minute, 12 May 1829.
95. Ibid.
96. *Asiatic Journal*, new series, 5 (1831), 71.
97. BL, IOR L/PS/6/181, 799–844, BPL, 20 Oct 1830, address and Grant's reply, 10 Sep. 1830.
98. Ibid., 849–71, BPL, 20 Oct 1830, address and Grant's reply, 13 Sep 1830.
99. Lakshmi Subramanian, 'Seths and Sahibs: Negotiated Relationships between Indigenous Capital and the East India Company', in H. V. Bowen, Elizabeth Mancke, and John G. Reid, eds., *Britain's Oceanic Empire: Atlantic and Indian Ocean Worlds c. 1550–1850* (Cambridge: Cambridge University Press, 2012), 311–39; Sheila Smith, 'Fortune and Failure: The Survival of Family Firm in Eighteenth-Century India', *Business History* 35, no. 4 (1993): 44–65.
100. Mitra Sharafi, *Law and Identity in Colonial South Asia: Parsi Legal Culture 1772–1847* (Cambridge: Cambridge University Press, 2014), 8–9; Jesse S. Palsetia, *The Parsis of India: Preservation of Identity in Bombay City* (Leiden: Brill, 2001), chapters 3, 5.
101. Jesse S. Palsetia, 'Mad Dogs and Parsis: The Bombay Dog Riots of 1832', *Journal of the Royal Asiatic Society of Great Britain and Ireland* 11, no. 1 (2001): 28; Dobbin, *Urban leadership in western India*, 24.
102. Christine Dobbin, *Urban Leadership in Western India: Politics and Community in Bombay City 1840–1885* (Oxford: Oxford University Press, 1972), chapters 1–2; Bayly, C. A., *Recovering Liberties: Indian Thought in the Age of Liberalism and Empire* (Cambridge: Cambridge University Press, 2012), 135–37.
103. Mridula Ramanna, 'Social Background of the Educated in Bombay City 1824–58', *Economic and Political Weekly* 14, no. 4 (1989): 203–5, 207–11; Mridula Ramanna, 'Profiles of English Educated Indians: Early Nineteenth Century Bombay City', *Economic and Political Weekly* 27, no. 14 (1992): 716–21, 723–24.
104. BL, IOR L/PS/6/181, 969–80, BPC 29 Sep. 1830, no. 6, William Newnham, minute, 13 Sep. 1830.
105. Ibid., 983–1029, J. Malcolm, minute, 16 Sep. 1830, BPC 29 Sep. 1830, no. 8.
106. It was held on 17 September. Ibid., 923–39.
107. Ibid., BPC 29 Sep. 1830, nos. 21–24, J. Malcolm, minute, 18 Sep. 1830.
108. Ibid., 943–45, Government notice, 27 Sep. 1830.

CHAPTER 6

Bengal, Madras and Imperial Debate on Despotism

Introduction

The East India Company's royal charter was renewed every 20 years. This was the occasion when the whole system of the Indian government was reviewed and revised. The renewal of 1834 was the opportunity for the Bombay government to settle the problem of the King's Court. The logic of emergency was to be firmly established and the chiefs and sardars protected from the encroachment of the King's Court. This chapter assesses the extent to which the Bombay officials' vision of empire was realised in the charter renewal. The reform of the Company's judicial administration, rather than the abolition of the China monopoly, was the central issue of this renewal. The abolition of the monopoly had consensus in Westminster, with the EIC itself admitting that it was unavoidable.[1] Thomas Macaulay gave scant attention to the issue in parliament, noting that 'No voice, I believe, has yet been raised in Parliament to support the monopoly. On that subject, all public men of all parties seem to be agreed'.[2] Instead, the ministers and radicals spent most of the time discussing whether the expansion of the King's Court's jurisdiction would be a blessing or an evil of British colonialism. While the radicals advocated the constitutional check by the King's Court, the government urged the need for uniformity in judicial government.

H. Inagaki, *The Rule of Law and Emergency in Colonial India*, Cambridge Imperial and Post-Colonial Studies,
https://doi.org/10.1007/978-3-030-73663-7_6

The most important outcome of this debate was the establishment of the first all-India Legislative Council, which determined the future form of the rule of law and its exceptions in India. The debate on the Legislative Council institutionalised the Bombay government's paternalist logic of emergency and state necessity in the political structure of Britain's Indian empire. It was conceived to solve the conflict between the government and the King's Court exposed in the Bombay case of Moro Ragonath. The charter limited the power of the King's Court and prescribed its subjugation to the Governor-General's legislature and, by doing so, realised the Bombay officials' aspiration for a more unitary and hierarchical form of authority in India. The following analysis will make it clear that it was not the utilitarians and evangelicals in London such as James Mill, Charles Grant and Macaulay, but the officials in Bombay and Calcutta such as Malcolm, Charles Metcalfe and Bentinck, who demanded and realised this crucial stipulation on the supremacy of the executive over the judiciary.

The process also illustrates the way the constitutional change was brought about by the working of the imperial network. Recent studies on imperial networks have paid more attention to the role of legal professions' criticism of the colonial government.[3] Scholars have also examined processes of constitutional reform in the Atlantic World in which judges and lawyers deployed the language of English liberty to condemn despotic rule in the colonies.[4] The development in Bombay needs to be contextualised in this contemporary development of networked politics of imperial constitutional reform.

The first part of this chapter examines judicial politics in Calcutta and Madras up to the 1820s, which would highlight the historical context against which the charter renewal debate took place. Although Bengal, Madras and Bombay governments had different priorities, especially regarding the status and socio-political role of the Indian aristocracy, they were united in criticising the King's Court's political interference in the mofussil. They shared the sense of danger about the tribal raids and believed that the constitutional check by the judiciary should not hinder the government's power to employ necessary measures in times of emergency. They agreed that the political authority in India should be united in the hands of the EIC and that the King's Court should be subordinate to it. The chapter then examines the London debate on the charter renewal in which the EIC's despotism was superimposed on the King's Court's rule of law.

Bengal: Revenue, Bhadraloks and Zamindars

Scholars have paid sufficient attention to the fact that the Bengal government experienced a series of conflicts with the Supreme Court in the 1770s, which resulted in the Act of 1781. What is not so well known is that the conflict did not cease there, but instead intensified in the 1820s.[5] The first issue was the use of the court by European settlers in the inner territories to evade criminal prosecution in the Company's Court for their violent plantation management. A District Magistrate reported that there were several instances in which the EIC's Magistrates were threatened through the prosecution in the King's Court after merely issuing a warning to European planters gathering armed men. Because of this, the 'Magistrates are really afraid to act against British subjects, except on the strongest grounds'.[6] Another official gave a detailed account in a report titled the 'Conduct of Europeans in India'.[7] The report shows that it was customary for the planters to hold lands in their Indian servants' names to deal with the ryots' various 'resistances' such as breach of contract not performing their duties, getting advances from two different planters, destroying indigo by letting their cattle trespass on the lands and disputing titles or boundaries of estates in the EIC's court.[8] Because of these practices, the planters were virtually exempted from liability in the Company's Court.[9] As Elisabeth Kolsky shows, European settlers' violence of this sort against Indians in the mofussil motivated the Bengal government's codification project.[10] The situation was problematic especially when the government promoted indigo cultivation in response to the financial crisis after the 1824–1826 Burmese war. Security, as well as revenue, was at stake because, as one contemporary pointed out, the impoverished peasants often converted themselves to dacoits.[11]

In the late 1820s, the King's Court at Calcutta started to intervene more overtly in the government's revenue administration in the mofussil. The most disputed case was *Chowdry v. Chowdry* in 1829, in which the Supreme Court decreed partition and re-assessment of a revenue defaulter's land, attached the land and appointed an officer of the court as a receiver (i.e. conservator) of the revenue.[12] This was followed by similar cases.[13] The government was concerned about the collision of authority between Collectors and the Supreme Court over revenue matters. The issue was all the more problematic because the Supreme Court awarded the lands without reference to government records or the EIC's local officers.[14] The judges vindicated their jurisdiction based on the doctrine of 'constructive inhabitancy' allowing those living or having offices in Calcutta to file suits in the King's Court even if the cases originated in the mofussil. Jon E. Wilson points out that these cases reflected the changing pattern of agrarian relationship, particularly the emergence of a bhadralok class living in Calcutta, holding lands in the mofussil and using the King's Court to manage the lands.[15] Reporting the cases to the Court of Directors, the Bengal government explained that 'our main object has been to retain in our own hands the entire control of the revenue arrangements in estates affected by decrees of the Supreme Court, ... we have especially guarded against the drawing of any inference which might imply an acquiescence on the part of government in the jurisdiction exercised by the Supreme Court over estates in the mofussil'.[16]

The larger context to this prolonged conflict was the government's quarrel with Bengali zamindars over revenue assessment and resumption of rent-free lands. The government suspected that the zamindars appropriated rents from the lands that were cultivated after the Permanent Settlement in 1793. In the original settlement, Collectors had to file a lawsuit in the Company's Court to challenge doubtful titles. But Regulation IX of 1825 empowered Collectors to directly examine the titles, and Regulation III of 1828 appointed special commissioners, in place of the ordinary court of law, to receive appeals from the decision of Collectors. This meant that the Bengal government put the affairs of the zamindar's rent-free land under its exclusive control. The zamindars criticised the arbitrariness of these measures by a series of petitions published in the press.[17] These developments led officials such as Holt Mackenzie, the Bengal government's secretary to the Territorial Department in charge of all revenue matters, to believe that 'the theory of a complete separation between the judicial and executive authority, if elsewhere sound, is here misplaced'.[18]

Madras: Police, Princely Debts and Camp Followers

Scholars have shown that the King's Court in Madras was also variously used by Indians in the eighteenth century.[19] Records of the Madras government in the nineteenth century were filled with the issues of jurisdictional conflict commonly observed in other presidencies. The King's Court was used as if it were an appellate court from the EIC's judiciary.[20] The sheriff's execution of writs in the mofussil was disliked by government officials as a cause of disturbance.[21] Summonses of officials from the mofussil to Madras city hindered their ordinary business.[22] Revenue defaulters evaded debt collection by applying for the court's writ of habeas corpus.[23]

The urban policing was, as in Bombay, a focus of the King's Court's criticism of the EIC's despotic rule in Madras. Madras city was famous for its hybrid structure inherited from the precolonial era.[24] The city grew rapidly as a hub of international commerce in the early nineteenth century, and the government tried to tighten control over the city by restricting land transactions and by limiting the influx of the labour force.[25] Against this backdrop, the government attempted to reform the city's police system. William Bentinck's Madras government (1803–1807) appointed a police committee in 1804, and, immediately after the Vellore Mutiny in 1806, the government tried to rehabilitate the police system by abolishing the traditional police force of Poligars, comprising the head officer called Pedda Naik and his subordinate Kavarkars. Pedda Naik received a certain due from the urban residents and in turn compensated for damages caused by thefts and raids in the city.[26] The government tried to Europeanise this police system. Bentinck established the police committee, criticised the corruption of the Poligars, discharged Pedda Naik and appointed a Thanadar to supervise the police.[27] This was approved by the Court of Directors in 1807.[28] The head of this police force was the newly appointed European superintendent of the police Walter Grant.[29] But this reform was severely criticised by Indian residents in the city. They, including Poligars and Dubashes of the city, sent a petition to the government directly criticising the police reform. It appraised the working of the Kavarkars who were well acquainted with the locality and apprehended and sent criminals to the state (circar) with deponents, while the Thanadars failed to guarantee the security of the city and sometimes arrested wrong persons. The petition then started to criticise almost every aspect of the government's administration in the city: the assessment tax, liquor and tobacco tax, undue collection of dues, the salt price and the donation to the temple. It was signed by 1040 residents.[30]

The King's Court strongly supported the petitioners. It was reported that the Poligars solicited support from the King's Court judge Henry Gwillim, who then severely criticised the government's appointing a military man Walter Grant at the top of urban police.[31] This criticism eventually led to the resignation of Grant, who complained that Gwillim's criticism exacerbated the popular contempt for the government's authority and was detrimental to the security of the city.[32] This situation infuriated Governor Bentinck. He commented that 'it is not for us to preach the "Rights of Man" or to submit for the consideration of the multitude, such sentiments as that given by Sir Henry Gwillim, "potior periculosa libertas, quam tutum servitium [dangerous liberty is better than secured servitude]". Much as I admire this sentiment as applicable to Great Britain, the introduction of it here seems to me little short of positive insanity'.[33] But the city inhabitants' criticism did not cease there. Answering Gwillim's charge to the grand jury, the jurors in their presentment criticised the police system headed by the military man as against British law and Indian custom.[34] Bentinck stiffened his attitude and ordered that every journal in the city must be censored before its publication.[35] These developments put the King's Court at the centre of radicalism in the presidency town.[36] The background of the government's sense of crisis was the apprehension that the King's Court exacerbated the security problems in the mofussil. For example, it was suspected that Judge Gwillim had issued a writ of habeas corpus to release a dangerous man named Collooreia, a Brahman, who had been convicted as he instigated a rebellion against the government.[37] The man was a military commander (amirdar) of the Nizam of Hyderabad. He had been hired by the EIC in Seringapatan but dismissed on suspicion of embezzlement and violence. He then moved to Madras to make money and organise an anti-social force.[38] Whether the case was real or not was not recorded, but the home authorities as well as the Madras government accused the King's Court of debasing the reputation of the government in India.[39] The use of the King's Court by such a man was enough for the government to be suspicious of the court's detrimental effect on the security of Madras city.

The King's Court was problematic in the Madras mofussil as well as in the presidency town. By the nineteenth century, the presidency incorporated vast inner territories adjacent to the princely states of Mysore, Nizam and Travancore. As in Bombay, serious disputes were stirred up when the King's Court exercised its jurisdiction over local Indian rulers. Bentinck had been involved in an early example of such cases regarding the Muslim Nawab of Arcot when he was the Governor. When the old Nawab died in 1801, the British confiscated the whole lands by a treaty of alliance and made the new Nawab pensioner.[40] Reflecting this, the Nawab's political authority was always challenged by those who did not admit his succession. He was particularly in a strained state with Hindu military aristocrats in the southern Arcot.[41] The situation was complicated by the fact that he was heavily indebted to bankers due to the successive Carnatic Wars in the eighteenth century. His debts were an object of profitable investment.[42] The government officials, European private traders and the Indian merchants became his creditors and actively supported him in the eighteenth century, but, since the 1770s, they started criticising his rule.[43] They used the Supreme Court at Madras for the recovery of debt. The debt recovery suits meant criticism of the Nawab and the Madras government as his protector; the authority of the EIC was at issue in the suits. Governor Bentinck remarked that '[i]t has been impossible to prevent that part of the family, hostile to the succession from many opportunities which the law affords of bringing action against the Nawab, especially degrading to this public rank and distressing to his personal feeling'.[44] The Nawab claimed that he was not under the municipal law of England and exempted from the jurisdiction of the Company's Court.[45] But Chief Justice Henry Gwillim was insistent on the King's Court's jurisdiction on this independent sovereign prince. Bentinck criticised the court that the Nawab's right of the sovereign should be protected under the British rule, the infringement of which would severely damage 'the public faith of the treaties'.[46]

Equally problematic for the Madras government was that the court was used as an arena in which the political legitimacy of the Nawab was directly tried and determined independently from the government's policy. In a case in 1803, for example, the debate in the court was around the very point that whether the Nawab was an 'independent sovereign prince' or not. The defendant claimed that the Nawab was both independent and sovereign and could be regarded as sending himself as a diplomat to Madras city, and therefore exempted from the court's jurisdiction; the plaintiff insisted that though the Nawab was an independent prince, he was not an independent sovereign prince since he was only admitted by the British and the only sovereign was the Mughal emperor at Delhi.[47] In another case, an important decision was made in 1810 when the Nawab detained one of his adversarial family members in the Chepauk palace. The detained person requested the King's Court to issue a writ of habeas corpus to the Nawab's military commander called Thomas Monisse. Initially, the plaintiff demanded to issue the writ to the Nawab himself, but the court refrained from doing so because of the incident's large political implication. The agent of the Nawab claimed that the court did not have jurisdiction over the family of the Nawab and that the legality of the detainment could only be judged by the Muslim private law. But the judge decided that the court had jurisdiction as the Chepauk palace was within the city.[48]

The Nawab's legitimacy was repeatedly challenged in the courtroom. Also in 1810, the Nawab was sued by a widow of the former Nawab for assault. The Company's Solicitor claimed that the court did not have jurisdiction, but the judge examined several legal documents including the EIC's 1792 and 1801 treaties. Eventually, he admitted the Nawab's status as an independent sovereign prince based on the assumption that he was sending himself as a diplomat,[49] but the government disliked the situation in which politically important issues such as the status of foreign princes could be decided by the court independently from the government. It was true that the government officials were sometimes critical of the Nawab's and his family's abuse of the privilege of legal exemption (especially the Nawab's exercise of his jurisdiction at his court—maḥkama—which often led to the countersuit in the King's Court),[50] but as in Bombay, they were concerned about the fact that they could not monopolise the power to decide on politically important issues free from the court's insistence of the rule of law.

The King's Court's jurisdictional jockeying also caused troubles in the princely states in alliance with the British, showing that the court's working had a diplomatic implication at an all-India level. Grave anxiety was provoked when the King's Court insisted on its jurisdiction over the territory of the powerful Muslim Nizam of Hyderabad in 1818. It originated in a case of bribery that occurred in the British cantonment of Secunderabad in the Nizam's territory. The cantonment was established in 1806 as a result of the subsidiary alliance between the EIC and the Nizam. The goods imported to the Nizam's territory was not taxed, and economic activities of Indian merchants and bankers at General Bazar rapidly expanded, including export from the camp to Hyderabad.[51] As the economy of the camp relied heavily on the Commissariat, its head Indian officer one Srinavas Rao had a large room to pursue economic gain by controlling and eventually monopolising the trade in the camp. He borrowed an entire village near the camp, collected revenue, hired sepoys and strengthened his oppressive rule over the village. He loaned a large sum of money to the Nizam's subordinate military commander (subedar) Raja Rao Ramba, which was a breach of the treaty prohibiting contact between the EIC's servants and the Nizam's subordinate chiefs and sardars.[52] The Nizam complained this to the EIC. Political Resident Henry Russell tried to solve the situation by detaining Rao.[53] The camp followers were under the jurisdiction of the court-martial under the stipulation of the Bengal Regulation XX of 1810.[54] But Srinavas Rao applied for a habeas corpus for the Supreme Court at Madras.[55] It was granted, and he was released from jail. He then embarked on several countersuits in the King's Court accusing the Political Resident's oppression. Governor-General Marquis Hastings lamented that the King's Court's exercise of power 'must be attended either with a violation of the law of nations and the rights of independent sovereign powers, or with the degradation of [EIC's] courts of justice by repeated instances of irremediable failure and contempt'.[56] He continued that, now that Sindia, Holkar, the Raja of Nagpur and others were in alliance with the British, their feelings would be hurt if they find that the Nizam's sovereignty was encroached by the court of law.[57]

There were several such cases, and the government officials were concerned that the cases started to constitute precedents in India. For instance, an EIC's Indian soldier manufactured and circulated false coins in Secunderabad, and when the Bengal government asked its Advocate General about the King's Court's jurisdiction over the issue, he answered that the court did have jurisdiction by referring to such cases as *Smith v. Colonel Gore*[58] and *Sanardanah Poye v. the Company and Colonel Munro*.[59] Political Resident Russel expressed his anxiety that if similar cases were to be tried not in the court-martial but in the King's Court, the EIC would not be able to try the culprit at all.[60] Bengal and Madras governments declared that the court-martial at the camp had jurisdiction over the camp followers.[61] But since the regulations did not directly restrict the King's Court, similar jurisdictional troubles continued thereafter. A similar case happened in the territory of the Raja of Nagpur in central India in which the case of Srinavas Rao was regarded as a precedent. When a man called James Favell was sued by an administrator of an Englishman for debt recovery, the EIC's Advocate General supported the King's Court's jurisdiction over the British in the princely states by referring to *Srinavas Rao v. Resident Russell*.[62] Similar cases continued to happen.[63]

As discussed in the previous two sections, officials in Bengal and Madras had experienced similar inconveniences caused by the King's Court in the same manner as in Bombay. This was a significant background against which these governments fully supported Bombay's jurisdictional jockeying with the King's Court.

The Calcutta Debate on the Legislative Council

To solve these conflicts in Bengal, Madras and above all Bombay, the Bengal government wanted to limit the power of the King's Court in the upcoming charter renewal in 1834.[64] The central figure in this attempt was Charles Theophilus Metcalfe, a Member of the Governor-General's Council in Bengal. He had frequently corresponded with Malcolm during the habeas corpus crisis in Bombay. He could fully sympathise with Malcolm as an enlightened soldier-administrator with ample experience in dealing with predatory tribes as Residents of Delhi (1811–1819, 1825–1827) and Hyderabad (1820–1825).[65] Metcalfe recognised the need to have 'an influential portion of the population attached to our Government by common interests and sympathies'.[66] His sense of danger was fully expressed in a minute written in 1829 that examined several legal cases including *Chowdry v. Chowdry*: 'the sovereign acts of the Government in the disposal of its public Revenue beyond the limits of the Court's local jurisdiction, being once rendered liable to subversion by the fiat of the Court, no security for the Revenue or for the possession of India would remain'.[67] In another minute dedicated to the habeas corpus cases in Bombay, he stated that the 'Legislature cannot have intended that the King's Courts should throw open all the provincial gaols, and release all the prisoners sentenced by the Company's Courts; and it is quite clear that the exercise of such a power would effectually destroy good order in the Company's territories, and render its Courts utterly useless and contemptible'.[68]

The Bengal government discovered the solution in the British political tradition of parliamentary sovereignty—the legislative power of the sovereign monarch should be supreme in its relation with the judiciary.[69] It proposed that the Governor-General should be vested with an all-India legislative power in the form of a Legislative Council, whose laws bind the King's Court, and that, to prevent future conflicts, the members of the Council would include both the King's Court Judges and the Members of the Governor-General's Council. Accordingly, the Bengal government requested Calcutta judges to draft a bill for establishing it.[70] The proposal reflected the government's strong aspiration for what Metcalfe called 'the principle of unity of command'. For example, he suggested combining the post of Commander-in-Chief and the Governor-General, hence unifying the armies of three presidencies into one, and coalescing the civil services of different presidencies.[71] Among such measures, unifying the judiciary into the executive was significant. In 1829, the Bengal government abolished the circuit courts, divided the presidency into 20 small districts and appointed a Commissioner of Revenue and Circuit in each district who was vested with revenue, criminal and police jurisdictions.[72] The government also appointed Collector-Magistrates, a new office that combined the duties of Collectors and Magistrates in the mofussil and strengthened their power of summary justice.[73]

The proposal of the Legislative Council was vehemently criticised by the judges of the Calcutta Supreme Court. They vindicated the court's decisions in cases such as *Chowdry v. Chowdry*. The Chief Justice, Charles Edward Grey, sarcastically stated that 'it may be worthwhile to consider whether it is the Court which sets at naught the Regulations of the Government, or the Government which has forgotten the lawful powers of the Court'.[74] He also claimed that the Legislative Council should be placed under the control of the crown and parliament rather than the EIC.[75] The Puisne Judge, John Franks, positively advocated the plurality of jurisdictions in the mofussil by pointing out that overlapping jurisdictions caused no harm in Britain.[76] Grey concluded that Metcalfe's minute was an attempt to 'make the sovereignty of the King in Parliament only nominal in India, and that there shall be no law there which is not liable to be altered by the executive branch ... the Company and their servants would [be] sovereigns uncontrolled by law'.[77]

On their part, Bengal officials further tried to limit the power of the judges in the council. Bentinck proposed that the Governor-General should have the power to legislate in times of emergency any acts even if the judges thought that 'such law or regulation is not within the powers vested in the Legislative Councils ... any repugnancy or supposed repugnancy notwithstanding'.[78] The judges objected to this proposal as it would confer unrestricted power of emergency legislation to the Governor-General,[79] but the government reiterated that the Governor-General should have the power to pass any laws without consultation with other members or even publishing it when 'in the judgement of the Governor-General, the safety and tranquillity of the British possessions in India, or the public interest' required such measures.[80] The judges grudgingly wrote the bill but deleted all the references to 'emergency' from it.[81] This battle over the word 'emergency' signifies that the judges' concept of Indian society was different from that of the government's. As we have seen in previous chapters, the government officials conceived that Indian society was always in a state of crisis and emergency. For the judges, however, the Indian society was in a state of peace where civil and criminal judicatures should be governed by ordinary courts of law. Because of these fundamentally divergent premises, the government and the judges could not reach a compromise. The settlement of the conflict between the logic of law and the logic of emergency was carried over to the debate in London.

The London Debate on the Imperial Constitution

When the constitution of the Indian Legislative Council was discussed in Calcutta, the metropolitan discussion of the EIC charter was delayed for several years due to political upheavals over the emancipation of the Catholics and the reform of parliament. The delayed London debate can be divided into two periods: an earlier phase of 1830–1831 focused on the Bombay habeas corpus cases and the later period of 1832–1833 on the Legislative Council. Historians often focus only on the latter, especially on Macaulay's celebrated speech in the Commons on 10 July 1833, but I would argue that the former was more important in determining the character of the despotic constitution of Britain's Indian empire. The case of Moro Ragonath was used by Whigs and radicals in parliament to criticise the government in 1830. Henry Brougham criticised that Dewar's appointment as the Chief Justice was the government's attack on 'the independence of the judicial order in India', and James Mackintosh condemned the government's 'scornful negligence' of the administration of justice.[82] Joseph Hume asserted that the government's intervention in the case of Moro Ragonath was 'uncalled for by any exigency', and Daniel O'Connell held that '[a]t any rate, the Governor ought not to be placed, like a dictator, above the Court'.[83] The Bombay government was vindicated by Robert Peel in the Commons, and Ellenborough and the Duke of Wellington in the Lords. Lord Melville, their ally, even articulated that 'the Judges of this country must not show their independence when they went to India; they must be careful not to commit the Governor; they … must not set up their own notions of law'.[84]

The next arena was the Lords and the Commons select committees. In the Lords committee in 1830, Ellenborough and Wellington called Elphinstone and Chaplin, now both at home, as witnesses. They fully explained the problems caused by the King's Court.[85] By contrast, the opposition to the government was feeble. The committee summoned the former Chief Justices, Edward West of Calcutta, Alexander Johnston of Ceylon and Thomas Strange of Madras, but their testimonies were discordant.[86] The arguments in support of the King's Court were further weakened in the inquiry in the Commons' committee in 1831 in which the advocates of the King's Court were virtually absent among the witnesses. In this way, the Bombay government's sense of crisis and its negative opinion of the workings of the King's Court dominated the committees by the end of 1831. The next Commons select committee in January 1832, the first substantial inquiry on the East India affairs, focused on the Legislative Council and the EIC's mofussil governance.[87] The Bombay officials sought to persuade the politicians and the public by printing pamphlets such as Malcolm's *Government of India* (1833). Elphinstone and James Grant Duff encouraged John Clunes, a military officer at Baroda and the anonymous author of *An Account of the Pindaris* (1818), to write and publish *A Historical Sketch of the Princes of India* (1833), which gave a detailed account of the major princes, chiefs and sardars in India.[88]

Moreover, in the committees' inquiry, Bombay's concerns were fully aired by a prominent witness: James Mill. His liberal authoritarianism echoed the Bombay government's fear that the King's Court weakened the authority of the EIC's government in India. Mill was extensively examined in the public and judicial committees and had a definitive impact on the final shape of the Legislative Council. Mill, the examiner of the East India Company, advocated the Bombay government's call for strong and unified authority, arguing that the Supreme Court's resistance against the government was generating 'the habit and contemplation of disobedience'.[89] He cautioned that, if the judges were appointed to the Legislative Council, they 'would overrule the members of council ... and become sole legislators, making the laws which they themselves administer, and ... rendered political organs, rather than what they ought to be exclusively, instruments for the distribution of justice'.[90] He argued that the judiciary should be subordinated to the executive in India:

> The existence of a double authority in the same country of two independent authorities, can never lead to good, must always act unfavourably on the willing obedience of the people, which is the strong arm of the government. It never can be reconciled to common sense, that an authority should exist in any country pretending to be superior to that government to which all must pay obedience, and to which all look up for protection. I think therefore, the existence of courts upon a footing different from the will of the government of the country, is altogether to be avoided....[91]

Mill's argument outweighed other authorities who opposed the Legislative Council such as Peter Auber, T. P. Courtenay and N. B. Edmondstone.[92] The final form of Legislative Council was proposed by the President of the Board of Control, Charles Grant, in parliament in June and July 1833. He bluntly declined Calcutta's original proposal to include the judges in the Legislative Council and said that the Governor-General should be given a 'considerable power ... to restrict the powers of the Supreme Court'.[93] He also proposed to appoint a Law Commission 'to inquire how far it was possible to approach to a more uniform system—how far it was possible to blend the King's Courts and those of the Company, and to amalgamate all systems...'.[94] In the second reading, Thomas Babington Macaulay, the Secretary to the Board of Control, further expressed the ministers' determination to curtail the power of the King's Court by urging 'that the regulations of the Government shall bind the King's Court as they bind all other Courts'.[95] He added that the codification of indigenous laws was necessary to remove the judge-made law.[96] In this way, the charter bill endorsed Bombay government's insistence that the power of the King's Court should be reduced and the British authority in India should be united under the EIC.

The minister's call for strong legislative authority inevitably provoked criticism. Charles Williams Wynn, the former President of the Board of Control, argued that the measure would give the Governor-General 'a vast and unnecessary power'.[97] Radical James Silk Buckingham cautioned that, thereafter, any law or regulation could be passed 'by the unlimited power given to the Legislative Council of India ...; the Trial by Jury, the Liberty of the Press, the Habeas Corpus, and every other constitutional safeguard of liberty, might be suspended or abolished without appeal or without redress'.[98] Tories including Lord Ellenborough(!) joined the opposition from a party-political perspective.[99] However, the interest in the issue was not high in Britain, as it turned out.[100] The bill passed the Commons in an almost empty house.[101]

Conclusion

The Charter Act of 1834 established the supremacy of the EIC over the King's Court. It deprived the King's Court of its legislative function in registering regulations relating to the presidency towns. Though a Law Member was appointed to the Legislative Council, he was more a subordinate legal advisor than a substitute of the King's Court with the power of legislative veto.[102] The Governor-General was empowered to make laws that bound the King's Court as well as the Company's Court, and he was given a free hand in making emergency legislation. In this respect, Malcolm's vision of empire was realised. But, since the key decision-makers involved wider networks of EIC officials and politicians than a handful of Bombay officials, there was also an ironic consequence: Malcolm's concern with the preservation of native aristocracy was given only passing consideration in the charter renewal debate in London. For Macaulay, as for the judges of the King's Court, the territories and peoples of India were already settled, and the tribal raids would pose no problem for British rule:

> I see that we have established order where we found confusion. I see that the petty dynasties which were generated by the corruption of the great Mahometan empire, and which, a century ago, kept all India in constant agitation, have been quelled by one overwhelming power. I see that the predatory tribes who, in the middle of the last century, passed annually over the harvests of India with the destructive rapidity of a hurricane, have quailed before the valour of a braver and sterner race—have been vanquished, scattered, hunted to their strong holds, and either exterminated by the English sword, or compelled to exchange the pursuits of rapine for those of industry.[103]

Mill likewise believed that British direct rule was the only way to prevent raids and rebellions.[104] Consequently, the charter renewal was also a turning point in British attitudes towards the Indian aristocracy. Lord Ellenborough and Charles Grant, the successive Presidents of the Board of Control, had no hesitation in annexing the princely states in cases of maladministration.[105] In 1836 Macaulay objected to the Madras government's draft act of exempting sardars from the ordinary jurisdiction of the Company's Court.[106] To use C. A. Bayly's phrase, the early prudence was being replaced by 'the hard edge of early Victorian dogmatism', and the former princes were being deposed as 'sham kings' and 'drones on the soil'.[107]

Nonetheless, we should not overemphasise discontinuity in the government's policy towards sardars. There were always those officials who favoured either interventionist or non-interventionist policies, and the swing from one to the other was common throughout British rule in India. To understand the nature of British colonial rule, it is equally important to pay attention to the mechanism that strengthened the government's despotism. The establishment of the Legislative Council shows that the political crises in the mofussil were the driving force for the despotic reform of the Indian government. The sense of crisis held by the officials in the turbulent external and internal frontiers was transmitted to the provincial governments, hardened their attitudes and, at a particular juncture such as the charter renewal, resulted in the reform of the structure of colonial rule. This pattern—the sense of crisis at the fringe of empire strengthened the government's logic of emergency and weakened the rule of law—was constantly observable throughout the rest of the nineteenth century, as we shall see in the next chapter.

Notes

1. H. H. Wilson, *The History of British India from 1805 to 1835*, 3 vol. (London, 1848), 3:479–87; C. H. Philips, *The East India Company 1784–1834* (Manchester, 1961), 285–90; Ian Newbould, *Whiggery and Reform 1830–41: The Politics of Government* (Basingstoke: Palgrave Macmillan, 1990), 111–12.
2. Parl. Debs. (series 3) vol. 19, col. 502 (10 July 1833), T. B. Macaulay, speech.
3. Frederick Cooper and Ann Laura Stoler, eds., *Tensions of Empire: Colonial Cultures in a Bourgeois World* (Berkeley, CA: University of California Press, 1997); Zoë Laidlaw, *Colonial Connections 1815–45: Patronage, the Information Revolution and Colonial Government* (Manchester: Manchester university press, 2005); John McLaren, *Dewigged, Bothered and Bewildered: British Colonial Judges on Trial 1800–1900* (Toronto: University of Toronto Press, 2011); Lisa Ford and Tim Rowse, eds., *Between Indigenous and Settler Governance* (London: Routledge, 2013); Alan Lester and Fae Dussart, *Colonization and the Origins of Humanitarian Governance: Protecting Aborigines Across the Nineteenth-Century British Empire* (Cambridge: Cambridge University Press, 2014); Zoë Laidlaw and Alan Lester, eds., *Indigenous Communities and Settler Colonialism: Land Holding, Loss and Survival in an Interconnected World* (London: Palgrave Macmillan, 2015); Kirsten McKenzie, *Imperial Underworld: An Escaped Convict and the Transformation of the British Colonial Order* (Cambridge: Cambridge University Press, 2016).
4. Hannah Weiss Muller, *Subjects and Sovereign: Bonds of Belonging in the Eighteenth-Century British Empire* (New York, NY: Oxford University Press, 2017); Mary Sarah Bilder, *The Transatlantic Constitution: Colonial Legal Culture and the Empire* (Cambridge, MA: Harvard University Press, 2004).
5. Sinha briefly discusses it. Chittaranjan Sinha, *The Indian Civil Judiciary in Making 1800–33* (New Delhi: Munshiram Manoharlal, 1971), 159–86.
6. *Parliamentary Papers* [PP] 1831–32 (734), Appendix, 370.

7. This was attached to the Report of the Commons Select Committee of 1831/32 as General Appendix V. PP 1831–32 (734), Appendix, 343–80.
8. PP 1831–32 (734), Appendix, 352–53.
9. Ibid., 369.
10. Elizabeth Kolsky, *Colonial Justice in British India: White Violence and the Rule of Law* (Cambridge: Cambridge University Press, 2010), chapter 2.
11. A. F. Salahuddin Ahmed, *Social Ideas and Social Change in Bengal 1818–1835*, 2nd edition (Calcutta: RDDHI, 1976), 117–18. White violence was not, however, the main point of jurisdictional conflict between the King's Court and the government in Bengal, for the judges of the King's Court also unanimously supported the government's plan to subject Europeans in the mofussil to the Company's Court. PP 1831 (320E), 112–13, Calcutta Supreme Court [Cal. SC] to Bengal Government [Ben. Gov.], 13 Sep. 1830 (no. 26), enclosure 2.
12. PP 1830 (320E), nos.1–8, 11; Sinha, *Indian Civil Judiciary*, 176–77.
13. British Library [BL], India Office Records [IOR] L/PJ/3/257, 1–29, Bengal Judicial Letter [Ben. JL], Ben. Gov. to CoD, 19 Apr. 1831.
14. BL, IOR L/PJ/3/257, 6, 19–21, Ben. JL, Ben. Gov. to CoD, 19 Apr. 1831.
15. Jon E. Wilson, *The Domination of Strangers: Modern Governance in Eastern India 1780–1835* (Basingstoke: Palgrave Macmillan, 2008), 146–47.
16. BL, IOR L/PJ/3/257, 25–26, Ben. JL, Ben. Gov. to CoD, 19 Apr. 1831.
17. Ahmed, *Social Ideas and Social Change in Bengal*, 118–22; PP 1831–2 (735-III), 222, Mackenzie, evidence, 18 Apr. 1832.
18. PP 1831–32 (734), 136, H. Mackenzie, minute, 1 Oct. 1830.
19. Arjun Appadurai, *Worship and Conflict under Colonial Rule: A South Indian Case* (Cambridge: Cambridge University Press, 1981). Mattison Mines, 'Courts of Laws and Styles of Self in Eighteenth-Century Madras: From Hybrid to Colonial Self', *Modern Asian Studies* 35, no. 1 (2001): 33–74; Niels Brimnes, 'Beyond Colonial Law: Indigenous Litigation and the Contestation of Property in the Mayor's Court in Late Eighteenth-Century Madras', *Modern Asian Studies* 37, no. 3 (2003): 513–50.
20. BL, IOR L/PJ/3/788, 338, Madras Judicial Letter, 4 Jan. 1822, para.44; IOR/L/PJ/3/789, 1–67, Madras Political Letter, 20 Aug. 1822.
21. BL, IOR L/PJ/3/790, Madras Judicial Letter, 4 July 1828, para.28.
22. BL, IOR L/PJ/3/789, 325, Madras Political Letter, 29 Dec. 1826, para.148.
23. BL, IOR P/275/64, 1718–39, Madras Revenue Consultations, 6 May 1803; 'V. Runga Pillay v. EIC (1803)', *The Indian Decisions (Old Series), Being a Verbatim Reprint of the Reports of Cases Decided by the Late*

Supreme Courts and the Sudder Dewanny Adawluts in India, ed. by Lawyers Companion Office (Madras: Venkasawmy Row, 1911–16), 5:80.
24. Susan M. Neild, 'Colonial Urbanism: The Development of Madras City in the Eighteenth and Nineteenth Centuries', *Modern Asian Studies* 13, no. 2 (1979), 217–46.
25. Ravi Ahuja, 'Expropriating the Poor: Urban Land Control and Colonial Administration in Late Eighteenth Century Madras City', *Studies in History* 17, no. 1, n.s. (2001), 81–99; Tirthankar Roy, *An Economic History of Early Modern India* (London: Routledge, 2013), 114–25.
26. David Arnold, *Police Power and Colonial Rule: Madras 1859–1947* (Delhi: Oxford University Press, 1986), 19–20.
27. BL, IOR P/243/11, Madras Public/General Consultations [MGC] 21 Oct. 1806, 6820–58, Police Committee, report, 8 Aug. 1806, and Bentinck's minute; BL, IOR P/243/11, 6898–920, Police Committee, report, 16 Oct. 1806; CPS Dharampal archives, bound volume 10 [Dharampal, vol.10], 33. Historian and Gandhian thinker Dharampal's transcript of the India Office Records can be read online, and I also referred to the page number in the following endnotes. Dharampal Archival Collection (http://cpsindia.org/index.php/dh-archive, accessed 25 Feb. 2021).
28. BL, IOR E/4/900, 461–8, CoD to Madras Gov., 26 Aug. 1807; Dharampal, vol.10, 43.
29. Maya Gupta, *Lord William Bentinck in Madras and the Vellore Mutiny, 1803–7* (New Delhi: Capital, 1986), 98–104.
30. BL, IOR P/243/21, MGC 17 July 1807, 4082–129; Dharampal, vol.10, 183–93. For political implications of petitioning, see Niels Brimnes, *Constructing the Colonial Encounter: Right and Left Hand Castes in Early Colonial South India* (Richmond: Curzon, 1999), 143–46.
31. BL, IOR P/243/21, MGC 21 July 1807, 4173–75, J. Grant to Gov. 14 Mar. 1807; Dharampal, vol. 10, 177.
32. BL, IOR P/243/15, 265–301, esp. 297–300, W. Grant to Bentinck, 4 Jan. 1807; Dharampal, vol. 10, 61–63.
33. BL, IOR P/243/21, MGC 21 July 1807, 4164–72, the quotation at 4169–70, Bentinck, minute, 21 July 1807; Dharampal, vol. 10, 226.
34. BL, IOR H/431, 323–415, July 1807; Dharampal, vol. 10, 211.
35. BL, IOR H/539, 177–84; Dharampal, vol. 10, 243.
36. Eventually, the total transfer from the Poligar to the European police system was made in 1812, but the criticism continued. Madras Police Department, *The History of the Madras Police: Centenary 1859–1959* (Madras: Inspector General of Police, 1959), 111–15.
37. BL, IOR E/4/335, paras. 57–66, Law Department, Madras Gov. to CoD, 6 Mar. 1807; Dharampal, vol. 10, 88–89.

38. BL, IOR P/243/16, MGC 18 Feb. 1807, 686–88, M. Wilkes to W. Grant, n.d.; Dharampal, vol. 10, 171.
39. BL, IOR H/258, 466, George Holford, memorandum, 5 Nov. 1807; Dharampal, vol.10, 158; BL, IOR H/431, 383–5, Charles Grant and Jonathan Parry to the BoC, 7 Nov. 1807.
40. *Treaties, Engagements and Sanads*, ed. Aitchison, 10:58, 60: Treaty of 1801, article 3 and 10.
41. Jim Philips, 'A Successor to the Moguls: The Nawab of the Carnatic and the East India Company, 1763–1785', *International History Review* 7, no. 3 (1985): 364–89, esp. 373.
42. Nicholas B. Dirks, *The Scandal of Empire: India and the Creation of Imperial Britain* (Cambridge, MA: Harvard University Press, 2006), 61–80.
43. Jim Philips, 'A Successor to the Moguls', 384–85.
44. Bentinck to Wellesley, May 1804, quoted in Gupta, *Lord William Bentinck*, 111.
45. Nawab to Bentinck, 12 Jan. 1804, quoted in Ibid.
46. BL, IOR F/4/136/2455, 7–8, Madras Political Letter, 17 Feb. 1802.
47. 'Boojunga Row, son and personal representative of Maleharakistnaijy v. Abdul Mauboodu Cawn Jumshare Jung Bahader (1803)', *The Indian Decisions (Old Series)*, 5:77–80.
48. Thomas Strange, *Notes of Cases in the Court of the Recorder and in the Supreme Court of Judicature at Madras; Commencing in the year 1798, and Ending in the Year 1816*, 3 vols. (Madras, 1816), 2:119–29.
49. Strange, *Notes*, 2:130–42.
50. BL, IOR F/4/1012/27784, Madras Political Letter, 28 Feb. 1826.
51. Shar Manzoor Alam, *Hyderabad-Secunderabad (Twin Cities): A Study in Urban Geography* (Bombay: Allied Publishers, 1965), 7–8; Treaty with the Nizam, 1800, article 14, *Treaties, Engagements and Sanads*, ed. Aitchison, 9:66.
52. BL, IOR P/121/14, Bengal Political Consultations, 17 July 1818, nos.26–27.
53. BL, IOR P/121/19, Bengal Political Consultations, 19 Sep. 1818, no.35, Henry Russell to Madras Gov., 16 Aug. 1818.
54. Article 4, *Treaties, Engagements and Sanads*, ed. Aitchison, 9:39; Eric Lewis Beverley, *Hyderabad, British India, and the World: Muslim Networks and Minor Sovereignty, c.1850–1950* (Cambridge: Cambridge University Press, 2015), 66; T. Jacob, *Cantonments in India: Evolution and Growth* (New Delhi: Reliance Publishing House, 1994), 26–27 and appendix VIII.
55. BL, IOR P/121/54, Bengal Political Consultations, 3 June 1819, no.1, Madras Gov. to Bengal Gov., 29 Apr. 1819.

56. BL, IOR L/PS/5/39, 212–46, Bengal Secret Letter, 13 Nov. 1819., the quotation at 225–26.
57. Ibid., para.47–48 (p.238).
58. In this case, the plaintiff, a merchant and camp follower, complained that he was illegally detained by the EIC for insubordination. The judge admitted the complaint. Strange, *Notes*, 2:142.
59. This case was on compensation for a war booty confiscated by the EIC, which the EIC claimed to be outside the jurisdiction of the King's Court, but the judge admitted it. Strange, *Notes*, 2:372.
60. BL, IOR F/4/773/20923, 1–3, Ben. Gov. to CoD, Bengal Political Letter, 21 Oct. 1820.
61. BL, IOR F/4/773/20923, 46–47, Ben. PC 12 June 1819; IOR V/8/28, Madras Regulation VI, 1821.
62. BL, IOR F/4/1754/71727, 3–25, Madras Secret Consultations 16 Aug. 1819, Samuel Toller to Madras Gov., 2 Aug. 1819.
63. In 1835, for example, a camp follower who was arrested for the charge of counterfeit coin requested the King's Court's writ of habeas corpus, which was admitted, and the man was released, escaping the trial at the court-martial. BL, IOR F/4/1748/71142, India Legislative Letter, 2 May 1836.
64. Another example was observed during the debate of the charter renewal when the Supreme Court at Calcutta maintained that it could take cognizance of a civil suit against the Company in ***Bank of Bengal v. United Company*** in 1831. The Company insisted that the conduct of the sovereign was not amenable to the civil court, but the Court held that the Company was not a sovereign, as 'the sovereign is the King of the United Kingdom'. M. P. Jain, *Outlines of Indian Legal and Constitutional History*, 6th edition (New Delhi: LexisNexis, 2006), 99.
65. C. A. Bayly, 'Metcalfe, Charles Theophilus, Baron Metcalfe (1785–1846)', *ODNB*; online edition, 3 Jan. 2008 [https://doi.org/10.1093/ref:odnb/18617, accessed 25 Feb. 2021]; John William Kaye, *The Life and Correspondence of Charles, Lord Metcalfe*, 2 vols. (London, 1858), 2:433, C. T. Metcalfe, minute, [1818].
66. PP 1831 (734), Appendix, 274, C. T. Metcalfe, minute, 19 Feb. 1829.
67. PP 1831 (320E), 13–15, Bengal Secret Consultations, C. T. Metcalfe, minute, 15 Apr. 1829.
68. Ibid., 25–26, C. T. Metcalfe, minute, 2 May 1829.
69. Ibid., 13, C. T. Metcalfe, minute, 2 May 1829.
70. Ibid., 1–3, Ben. Gov. to Cal. SC, 14 July 1829.
71. D. N. Panigrahi, *Charles Metcalfe in India: Ideas and Administration 1806–1835* (Delhi: Munshiram Manoharlal, 1968), 160–62.

72. This did not work well, and, two years later, the duty of the circuits was transferred to the newly appointed sessions judges; later, the task was further transferred to the district judges of the district and sessions courts. Jain, *Outlines*, 180–82; Eric Stokes, *The English Utilitarians and India* (Oxford: Oxford University Press, 1959), 151–55.
73. Jain, *Outlines*, 182, 187–88; Stokes, *Utilitarians*, 163–65.
74. PP 1831 (320E), 62, Charles Edward Grey, minute, 2 Oct. 1829.
75. Ibid., 58.
76. Ibid., 84, John Franks, minute, 23 Sep. 1829.
77. Ibid., 74–75, C. E. Grey, minute, 2 Oct. 1829.
78. Ibid., 141, Ben. Gov. to Cal. SC, 28 Sep. 1830.
79. Ibid., 150, Cal. SC to Ben. Gov., 7 Oct. 1830.
80. Ibid., 151, Ben. Gov. to Cal. SC, 11 Oct. 1830.
81. Ibid., 155, 157, Cal. SC to Ben. Gov., 13 Oct. 1830.
82. Parl. Debs. (series 2) vol. 22, cols 124–33 (5 Feb. 1830), the quotations at cols. 128, 132.
83. Ibid., cols 1370–93 (8 Mar. 1830), the quotation at cols. 1370, 1374.
84. Ibid., cols 248–64 (9 Feb. 1830), the quotation at col. 260.
85. PP 1830 (646), 163, M. Elphinstone, evidence, 25 Mar. 1830; Ibid., 179, W. Chaplin, evidence, 30 Mar. 1830.
86. Ibid., 79–83, Edward East, evidence, 9 Mar. 1830; Ibid., 120–37, Alexander Johnston, evidence, 19 Mar. 1830; Ibid., 263, Thomas Strange, evidence, 11 May 1830.
87. Public is in PP 1831–32 (735-I) and Judicial in PP 1831–32 (735-IV).
88. John Clunes, *An Historical Sketch of the Princes of India: Stipendiary, Subsidiary, Protected, Tributary, and Feudatory, with a Sketch of the Origin and Progress of British Power in India* (Edinburgh, 1833).
89. PP 1831–32 (735-I), 49–50, J. Mill, evidence, 21 Feb. 1832.
90. Ibid., 46, James Mill, evidence, 21 Feb. 1832.
91. PP 1831–32 (735-IV), 120, J. Mill, evidence, 29 June 1832.
92. PP 1831–32 (735-I).
93. Parl. Debs. (series 3) vol. 18, cols 736–37 (13 June 1833).
94. Ibid., 739.
95. Parl. Debs. (series 3) vol. 19, cols 527–28 (10 July 1833).
96. Ibid., 533.
97. Parl. Debs. (series 3) vol. 19, cols 662–64 (15 July 1833).
98. Parl. Debs. (series 3) vol. 20, cols 26–27 (26 July 1833).
99. Ibid., cols 314–15 (5 Aug. 1833).
100. Cf. H. V. Bowen, *The Business of Empire: The East India Company and Imperial Britain 1756–1833* (Cambridge: Cambridge University Press, 2006), 296.

101. *The Greville Diary, Including Passages Hitherto Withheld from Publication*, ed. Philip Whitwell Wilson, 2 vols. (London: Heinemann, 1927), 2:413, 3 Sep. 1833; *The Holland House Diaries 1831–1840: The Diary of Henry Richard Vassall Fox, Third Lord Holland, with Extracts from the Diary of Dr. John Allen*, ed. Abraham D. Kriegel (London: Routledge, 1977), 463n34.
102. Jain, *Outlines*, 426–27.
103. Parl. Debs. (series 3) vol. 19, cols 521–22 (10 July 1833).
104. PP 1831–32 (735-VI), 6–7, J. Mill, evidence, 16 Feb. 1832, quoted in Thomas R. Metcalf, *The Aftermath of Revolt: India 1857–1870* (Princeton, NJ: Princeton University Press, 1965), 31.
105. C. H. Philips, *The East India Company 1784–1834* (Manchester: Manchester University Press, 1961), 271–74, 279; George D. Bearce, *British Attitudes Towards India 1784–1858* (Oxford: Oxford University Press, 1961), 191.
106. *Lord Macaulay's Legislative Minutes*, ed. by C. D. Dharker (Madras: Oxford University Press, 1946), 237–38, T. B. Macaulay, minute, 7 Mar. 1836.
107. C. A. Bayly, *Indian Society and the Making of the British Empire* (Cambridge: Cambridge University Press, 1998), 135.

CHAPTER 7

Epilogue and Conclusion

Executive and Judiciary After 1834

After Macaulay left the country in 1838, India entered a new era of conquest. The government's attention was fixed on emergencies on the fringes of empire, and the troubles of post-war settlement in the Deccan in the 1820s were repeated throughout the Indian subcontinent in the 1830s and 1840s. The new, aggressive imperialism was fully advocated by Lord Ellenborough, who presided over the Board of Control three times in the 1830s and 1840s. The first manifestation was the Afghan War that lasted from 1838 to 1842. The next target was Sind (1838–1843), the den of predatory tribes who frequently attacked the North-Western frontiers of British India. Charles Napier, who was appointed by Ellenborough as the Chief Commissioner of Sind, proceeded to expunge the chiefs (amirs) and created a semi-military settlement.[1] Then Governor-General Lord Dalhousie (1848–1856) annexed Punjab in the Second Sikh War in 1849 and Pegu in Lower Burma in the Second Burma War in 1852, followed by the annexations of Satara (1849), Nagpur (1854) and Awadh (1856).[2] Meanwhile, Punjab became the arena of paternal rule under Chief Commissioner John Lawrence (1853–1858). He devised a strong bureaucratic hierarchy of district officials combining executive and judicial powers, which became the model of 'Non-Regulation system' in the following years.[3]

H. Inagaki, *The Rule of Law and Emergency in Colonial India*, Cambridge Imperial and Post-Colonial Studies,
https://doi.org/10.1007/978-3-030-73663-7_7

Following this trend and pressed by financial burden of the wars of conquest,[4] the Bombay government wanted to advance its mofussil governance from the stage of conquest to that of consolidation and regularisation. George Arthur (1842–1846), the Governor who supported the Afghan War and the conquest of Sind, targeted the vast alienated lands in the presidency. In 1843, he established the Inam Commission, a special tribunal to examine whether landholders held proper documentation to prove their rightful possession.[5] The Commission was first appointed to investigate tenures in the Southern Maratha Country and extended to the whole presidency in 1852. It eventually 'recovered' Rs 50 lakh, or 40%, out of Rs 122 lakh of inam lands.[6] It was known as the 'great confiscatory Tribunal' led by military men 'not well versed in the principles of law'.[7] Some Bombay officials such as George Clerk,[8] Bartle Frere[9] and James Outram[10] apprehended the excess of aggression against local chiefs and sardars.[11] They were opposed to the lapse of Satara in 1849, for example.[12] Yet even these paternalist officials were more relaxed than those in the 1820s. They could assert that the sardars should be positively remodelled as agents of reform rather than left to their ways. Frere advocated 'the mixture of races'[13] and opined that the sardars should not be cut off from the rest of the world. He recommended that they should learn English and, significantly, travel to Bombay to learn new things.[14] Contrary to Malcolm, then, Frere's empire of opinion did not contradict the chiefs' Anglicisation.[15]

But the governments' conquests were criticised by the judges, and its work of consolidation was hindered by Indians' appropriation of the King's Court. There were many examples to show that the judiciary (the Supreme Courts till 1862 and the High Courts since then) functioned as a check to the government after 1834. Consequently, all the problems observed in the 1820s were repeated in the Indian age of reform.[16] This tendency was manifested in Bombay in the 1840s, when its Chief Justice, Thomas Erskine Perry, once a radical MP in Britain,[17] repeated what the judges did in the 1820s. He insisted that the government officers should assist the execution of writ of the King's Court in the mofussil.[18] He also declared that the Magistrate should attend the court during the trial of all cases committed by him. When the Magistrate said that the Company's regulations forbade him from doing so, Perry replied that he did not care about the regulations because he was administering English law and he would fine the Magistrate Rs 1000 when he was absent next time.[19] He also claimed that the King's Court had jurisdiction over the government's revenue administration.[20] These cases had the same pattern as those of the 1820s. First, the Indians' use of the King's Court led to the King's Court's claim of its extended jurisdiction over formerly limited areas. Second, the judges ruled in favour of the plaintiff in India, but, third, the decisions were overturned by the Privy Council in Britain. This pattern was also followed in cases regarding private law such as the famous Parsi matrimonial case in 1843 (*Perozeboye v. Ardaseer Cursetjee*).[21]

Despite this opposition to the government in the courtroom, though, the ideological outlook of the King's Court was significantly transmuted after 1834. In *Regina v. Shaik Boodin* in 1846, the power of the King's Court to issue a writ of habeas corpus against a native court-martial in the mofussil was disputed. In his long judgement, Perry ruled that the King's Court did not have such power, expressly endorsing the decision of the Privy Council regarding J. P. Grant's petition in 1828. He articulated that English legal decisions could not be applied to the mofussil, where 'race, history, religion, and constitution' were different and, particularly, where the administration should follow the way of oriental despotism, in which distinction between the civil court and the martial court did not exist.[22] Perry abandoned the possibility of applying the same English law in the presidency town and in the mofussil.

The age of reform was abruptly ended by the Revolt of 1857–1858. The Indian government after 1858 was characterised by 'the restoration of the aristocracy' led by Charles Wood, the Secretary of State for India (1859–1866). He resumed a policy of conciliation with a renewed vigour. The minor chiefs (talukdars) who did not join the insurgents were rewarded by the newly created Order of the Star of India.[23] Even those who joined the rebellion in Awadh, the centre of the revolt, were promised to have their lands restored, as they were thought to be 'a useful instrument in restoring order and tranquillity'.[24] The change was also manifested in Bombay. Governor John Elphinstone (1853–1859) was inclined to halt the Inam Commission's work as a 'measure of healing and pacification'.[25] The sardars' privilege of legal exemption was confirmed in the Code of Civil Procedure (Act VIII of 1859, c.12, s.384). The Acting Governor George Clerk (1860–1862) enacted the Ahmedabad Talukdars' Relief Act of 1862 to secure the minor chiefs' estates from attachment or sale for debts, which was later expanded as a general Encumbered Estates Act in 1877.[26] The government under Bartle Frere (1862–1867) introduced a scheme of Inam Commission's 'summary settlement' (Acts II and

VII of 1863) which allowed Collectors to confirm an inam by a summary assessment.[27]

But, as in the 1820s, the governments' policy of conciliation was hindered by the judiciary's interference. The bête noir was Calcutta Chief Justice Barnes Peacock, the Law Member of the Council (1852–1859) and a Member of the Legislative Council (1859–1862).[28] Peacock opposed the government's policy in Bombay city such as the Licence Tax Bill of 1859 and the Arms Act of 1860.[29] He also meddled with the issues of princes and sardars in the mofussil. First, he was opposed to a large grant to the Mysore family made by Charles Wood's home government in 1860. He made a motion in the Legislative Council for papers and correspondence regarding the transaction, which was carried out, legitimating the Legislative Council's power of judicial check to 'procure redress of grievances committed by the executive'.[30] Second, Peacock expressed his view that the Governor-General in Council did not have any power to make grants to alienate lands. Charles Wood and Bartle Frere were infuriated by this 'monstrous' and 'most unjustifiable' denial of 'the sole foundation of all title of landed property'.[31] As a consequence of these oppositions, the government excluded the judges of the King's Court from the Legislative Council in the Indian Councils Act of 1861, which was 'popularly said to be an Act to abolish Sir Barnes Peacock'.[32] In the same Act, the Governor-General's emergency legislation was also strengthened by vesting him with 'a new and extraordinary power of making and promulgating ordinances in cases of emergency on his own responsibility'.[33] The despotism of the Indian government was further consolidated in the late 1860s by Governor-General John Lawrence (1864–1869) and the so-called Punjab school administrators. They tried to model the government of India on their experience in Punjab and other Non-Regulation provinces. They advocated exclusion of local Indian bosses and rigid control by bureaucratic hierarchy from the Governor-General down to district officials in the provinces. The practical expression of this policy was a series of draconian measures infusing militarist perspective into the civil government, such as the Murderous Outrages Act of 1867 or the Frontier Crimes Regulations of 1872, 1887 and 1891.[34]

But, again, the government's logic of emergency was regularly frustrated by the judiciary's intervention, which was illustrated by the process of enactment of the Punjab Criminal Tribes Act (XXVII) of 1871. In 1867, the Punjab Chief Court reviewed two cases in which the government fined and imprisoned tribal raiders for leaving their villages without holding tickets of leave. The court ruled that the government's order to hold tickets was illegal. To take away the effect of this ruling and 'to wage continual warfare' against the tribes, the governments of Punjab and the North-Western Provinces attempted to enact the Criminal Tribes Act.[35] However, they were strongly opposed by the judges of the Punjab Chief Court and the High Court of the North-Western Provinces, who feared that it would jeopardise the personal liberty of the tribal people. William Muir, the Lieutenant Governor of the North-Western Provinces, lamented that the judges' perspective was confined to 'dealing with crime after it has been committed'.[36] The Bombay government was also persistently challenged by the judiciary. In 1870, the Bombay High Court decided that the Acts of local legislatures were not binding Europeans, who could only be punished by indictment in the High Court.[37] The court also continued meddling with political arrangements with the chiefs. In 1871, for example, the Bombay High Court claimed its jurisdiction over the territories that were ceded by the Company to the princely state of Edur (Idar) in Gujarat, 'a mountainous and jungly country, inhabited principally by Bheels'.[38]

In dealing with these jurisdictional conflicts, the government officials developed a new conception of the rule of law, which did not contradict and was even conducive to the government's logic of emergency. At the forefront of this attempt were the two successive Law Members of the Governor-General's Council, Henry Maine (1862–1869) and James Fitzjames Stephen (1869–1872). Maine, as the Law Member of John Lawrence's Council, formulated a more interventionist concept of sovereignty that justified the interference of the British government in the internal affairs of foreign princes. In a famous 1864 minute on Kathiawar, he argued that the Kathiawar states were the 'foreign territory' sharing sovereignty with the British government and enjoying several sovereign rights such as the 'immunity from foreign law', but this was not inconsistent with the right of the British government to interfere 'for the good order of society and the well-being of the people'.[39] In another minute in the year, Maine was asked whether the chiefs of the Central Provinces should be classified as British subjects or as sovereigns. He explained that, if the chiefs were British subjects, the government did not have any power to regulate their position and could not give them any power or privilege not embodied in law. On the other hand, if they were sovereigns, the government could interfere in their internal affairs for the better order of the state or the well-being of the people.[40] In other words, contrary to

Elphinstone and Malcolm in the 1820s, Maine argued that the sovereign status of petty kings could become a legal foundation for the government's right to interfere.

Stephen, the next Law Member under Lord Mayo, further elaborated this line of argument by reconceptualising the legitimacy of the government's political intervention from the perspective of the rule of law. His famous minute of 1872 was an attempt to give a legal foundation to the discretionary government in Punjab. Its primary aim was to retain efficiency and authority of the district officials who represented the government in the eyes of the Indians. He advocated the separation of the district officials' executive and judicial powers. This was because their executive 'vigour' was weakened as they were preoccupied with the technicality and rigidity of judicial works, which eventually resulted in 'converting them into lawyers'.[41] But, while judges with civil jurisdiction should be appointed, Stephen recommended that the district officials should retain criminal jurisdiction—'the most distinctive and most easily and generally recognised mark of sovereign power'.[42] In Stephen's judicial system, the independent judiciary of the King's Court had nothing to do with achieving the rule of law. He admitted that initially, the King's Court was necessary as a check against the officials, the 'irresponsible despots', but that time had gone by when the Company was substituted by the Crown government. Accordingly, the High Courts should be downgraded to a provincial court at the presidency towns as 'exceptional institutions for an exceptional population'; it was necessary 'to give up the notion of checking one part of the Government by another…'.[43] Rather, the government could achieve the rule of law by itself if the law properly defined discretionary power vested in the hands of government officials: 'The notion that there is an opposition in the nature of things between law and executive vigor, rests on a fundamental confusion of ideas and on traditions which are superannuated and ought to be forgotten'.[44] This meant that Stephen justified the government's political intervention in times of peace as well as in war, in the Regulation as well as in the Non-Regulations provinces. Soon after, he instituted this principle in the Code of Criminal Procedure in 1872.[45]

Maine and Stephen reconceptualised the relationship between the government and the law in the mofussil. They denied the King's Court's claim that English rule of law should be introduced (via the presidency towns) in the mofussil; rather, an Indian version of the rule of law should be created by referring to crisis and state necessity in the mofussil. As in the 1820s, the sense of crisis in the mofussil was heightened by the intervention of the judiciary and produced a new type of despotism. Eric Stokes observes that, after the Mutiny, the utilitarians and the paternalists started to diverge from each other, with conflict ensuing between legalists such as Maine and Stephen and administrators such as John and Henry Lawrence.[46] But, from our perspective, their amalgamation was further strengthened by Maine's and Stephen's attempt to legalise the government's political interference in times of peace and war.[47] Their intervention enabled the British government in India to reserve the tribal frontiers as a sphere of 'tradition' but simultaneously make them an object of active intervention from the perspective of imperial policy.[48]

The idea of despotic rule of law climaxed with Tory Governors-General in the late nineteenth century under the aegis of Prime Minister Benjamin Disraeli. Lord Lytton's administration (1876–1880) resumed the war of conquest for the first time since the Mutiny in the Second Afghan War (1878–1880). The devastating famine of 1876–1878 only exacerbated the government's concerns about its authority.[49] The anxiety of authority found its outlet in the Proclamation Durbar in 1877.[50] The government also enacted a series of draconian measures such as the Vernacular Press Act and the Indian Arms Act in 1878.[51] Lord Curzon (1899–1905) inherited this Tory vision of empire. He persuaded Bengali zamindars 'to abstain from drinking too deeply of the wells of justice'.[52] He actively intervened in the internal affairs of the princely states to bring about efficiency.[53] His subordinate, the Lieutenant Governor of Bengal John Woodburn, expressed a typical logic of emergency: 'the union of executive and judicial functions in the District and Sub-Divisional Officers is at present essential', as they should be 'a local head of the district, distinctly and indisputably the central figure, to whom all will turn in times of danger and emergency, and round whom all the forces of law and order will rally'.[54]

The new Toryism was constantly challenged by the judiciary, however, and here we can discern a new development of the late nineteenth century: Indian judges began to criticise it.[55] Bombay led the trend. Bombay lawyers (later Chief Justices) such as Kashinath Trimbak Telang[56] and Badruddin Tyabji[57] criticised Lytton's Tory imperialism and supported the Ilbert Bill of 1883 that empowered Indian judges to try Europeans in the mofussil.[58] In his speech, Telang singled out James Fitzjames Stephen, who was against the Bill,[59] and criticised his jurisprudence as 'the gospel of force' characterised by 'obtrusive antagonism to the doctrines of modern liberalism ... which are embodied in the great Proclamation of 1858'.[60] Indeed, while opinion among the European judges was divided, the Indian judges on the High Courts of Calcutta, Madras and Bombay unanimously defended the Bill.[61] In the 1880s, there was still 'a social war' in Bombay between the government and the judges of the High Court.[62] The relationship between the government's logic of emergency and the court's logic of law was about to enter yet another phase of interaction in the twentieth century.

Conclusion

This book has stressed that the constitutional history should be constructed from below—from the social history of law in India. The study of colonial liberalism focuses on intellectual construction of discourses by, for example, Ram Mohan Roy, but this book's findings show that we need to know more about the practices of Indians which affected the contour of liberal discourse in the colony. This is also true when we consider the ideology of the 'empire of opinion' school administrators. It was not their grounding in the Scottish enlightenment or their political background in Britain but their experiences of colonial governance in India that were the basis of their vision of paternalist imperialism. The case-based approach is also necessary to consider more deeply the construction of liberalism and illiberalism in the colonies.

The emergency perspective of the government officials was not only apparent in obviously political and military issues—the most typical of which was the tribal raids in the hill regions—but also in everyday business of civil and criminal judicatures. The despotic colonial state was not made by a machination of evil councillors in London but emerged out of the struggle of officials in the mofussil grappling with everyday difficulties of governance. The result was the reconceptualisation of the rule of law allowing the executive's free and discretionary interventions in dealing with everyday emergencies.

From this perspective, this book's analysis suggests that the government's interactions with Indian chiefs and sardars—minor and mobile sovereigns—were crucial in determining the framework of British colonialism in India in its fledgeling stage. The colonial state tried to reconstruct political order in the mofussil by selectively securing sovereign privileges of local rulers through treaties, ordinances and sanads, but the government was also bound to adhere to the stipulations, the failure of which would jeopardise the government's political legitimacy. Some of the rulers sought the government's protection, while those who were discontented with the situation relied on other political and legal institutions such as the King's Court. So, as the forum shopping continued, so did the jurisdictional conflicts.[63] This everyday negotiation of sovereignty was at the centre of colonial judicial politics in early nineteenth-century India.

This book has emphasised the need to pay attention to the logic of emergency and the logic of law. In terms of historiography, this means that we should discuss jurisdictional jockeying not as dispute among legal authorities but as political conflicts involving central and local governments. As such, the battle between the executive and the judiciary in Bombay in the 1820s resulted in the establishment of despotic power of 'Governor-General-in-Legislative-Council'. But this did not mean that the judiciary ceased to exist as the institutional check against despotism. Indeed, the very fact that the driving force of change was the legal agency of the Indians in using the court from below meant that the institutional change from above could not eliminate all the anomalies of the King's Court's jurisdictional interference in the mofussil. The consideration of the process reveals several important features of Britain's colonial regime of emergency in India.

Britain's 'dominance without hegemony' in India can be characterised by the colonial state's constant failure in the politics of difference. The government attempted to make a distinction between the social and economic spheres (where the Indians could freely use the court of law) and the political sphere (where the government should preside as a sole arbiter), but, as we saw in this book, attempts of demarcation and categorisation were continuously subverted by the Indians' claim making and forum shopping. Eventually, this led local officials to interpret everything from a political/emergency perspective. The Indians' forum shopping continued in later years, inducing the governments' draconian measures.[64] The agency of the Indians was central to the constitutional history of the British empire in India.

Colonial legal history is a flourishing field of study. Scholars have shed new light on the working of imperial and colonial legal institutions and indigenous practices of appropriation, and more and more studies have started to focus on continuity between precolonial and colonial practices.[65]

At the same time, while it is entirely justified to focus on the fluid and negotiated nature of the working of imperial and colonial law on the spot, it is important not to lose sight of the apparent disparity of power between the colonisers and the colonised in the imperial legal framework. We need to pay attention to the problem of power, and while it is possible to argue that often the agency of the colonised could subvert the intention of the colonisers, it did not mean that they could overcome inequality of power and act as free agents.

The limit of power and agency of Indians should always be borne in mind in the history of colonialism. The story told in this book is, in a sense, about the powerlessness of the colonised against the backdrop of the appellate structure of the British empire. The legal endeavours of the Indian merchants discussed in Chap. 2 ended up with their defeat in the Privy Council in London. The revenue defaulters were often generated first of all by extractive reorganisation of agrarian relationship in the mofussil by the colonial state. The use of the court by major, minor and mobile sovereigns discussed in Chap. 4 was their resistance to the colonial government's attempt to give, take or re-categorise their sovereign privileges admitted in the precolonial era. The final result of the case of Moro Ragonath was also determined in the appellate structure of the empire. And these limited attempts by the colonised resulted in the making of a more despotic colonial regime in the form of the Charter Act of 1834 in the end. The legal history of colonialism was always enveloped in a world of state violence and popular resistance.

This kind of study would be enriched by comparative perspectives. Similar transitions from early modern 'justice-oriented' culture of legal pluralism to modern 'law-oriented' culture of centralised jurisdiction have been observed by scholars of other empires in North America, Latin America and imperial Russia.[66] Historians of international law have revealed the consequent transition from the natural law theories of the laws of nations in the eighteenth century to the positivist and realist views of international law in the nineteenth century.[67] A further comparison focusing on a dialectic between logics of law and emergency would be beneficial for thinking about the historical role of colonial judiciary in different times and places across the globe.

The Governors and lesser officials were primarily concerned about the law and order in the mofussil, with revenue and judicial business subjugated to the ultimate motive of preventing raids and rebellions and preserving the empire. This was especially so in crisis years such as 1824, but the officials had to face numerous smaller commotions in everyday situations as well. This kind of official mindset and policy is analysed by Benjamin D. Hopkins as the 'frontier governmentality'. While most of Hopkins's criteria—indirect rule, sovereign pluralism, imperial objecthood and economic dependency[68]—fit Bombay in the 1820s, this book put more stress on fear and anxiety of the officials in the frontier in the making of such governmentality: I would suggest that it was not the intellectual design of the colonisers but the resistance of the colonised that determined the way the frontier governmentality took effect in historical settings.

The logic of emergency was extruded from the anxiety of Collectors, Judges and Magistrates dealing with everyday situations of difficult colonial governance that could easily be transformed into violent rebellions. This theme of weak colonial states anxious about their very existence was also inherited to later generations. There is a growing body of scholarship discussing 'helpless imperialists', 'empire on the verge of a nervous breakdown', 'empire of the weak' or 'empire of fear' in colonial settings.[69] The fragile and violent regime of emergency constructed in the 1820s and the 1830s discussed in this book was the basis on which later authoritarian governments were framed in colonial and post-colonial India. The military- and emergency-oriented regimes of India, Pakistan and Myanmar succeeded the colonial governmentality and its logic of emergency.[70] Scholars of other parts of the British empire in Asia have also paid attention to this process of normalisation of emergency in, for example, Singapore or Israel.[71] Based on these works, we can envisage comparative legal histories of colonial and post-colonial emergency-oriented regimes. The nature of the anxious and authoritarian colonial state should be further studied.

Notes

1. Matthew A. Cook, *Annexation and the Unhappy Valley: The Historical Anthropology of Sindh's Colonization* (Leiden: Brill, 2015).
2. S. N. Prasad, *Paramountcy under Dalhousie: Being a Thesis on the Policy of Dalhousie Towards the Protected Indian States* (Delhi: Ranjit, 1964).
3. Harold Lee, *Brothers in the Raj: The Lives of John and Henry Lawrence* (Oxford: Oxford University Press, 2002).
4. Neil Charlesworth, *Peasants and Imperial Rule: Agricultural and Agrarian Society in the Bombay Presidency 1850–1935* (Cambridge: Cambridge University Press, 1985), 53.

5. For the origin of the Inam Commission, see Laurence W. Preston, *The Dev of Cincvad: A Lineage and the State in Maharashtra* (Cambridge: Cambridge University Press, 1989), 164–81.
6. Alfred Thomas Etheridge, *Narrative of the Bombay Inam Commission and Supplementary Settlements*, Selections from the Records of the Bombay Government, 132, new series (Poona, 1873).
7. John Kaye and Colonel Malleson, *Kaye's and Malleson's History of the Indian Mutiny of 1857–8*, 6 vols. (London: Longmans, 1909–14), 1:127; A. G. L. Shaw, 'Arthur, Sir George, first baronet (1784–1854)', *ODNB*; online edition, 30 May 2013 [https://doi.org/10.1093/ref:odnb/707, accessed 25 Feb. 2021].
8. The Governor of Bombay, 1848–50.
9. Resident of Satara, 1847–48; the Commissioner for Sind, 1849–59; the Governor of Bombay, 1862–67.
10. The Commissioner for Lower Sind, later combined with Upper Sind, 1839–43; Resident of Satara, 1845–47; Resident of Baroda, 1847–48.
11. George D. Bearce, *British Attitudes Towards India 1784-1858* (Oxford: Oxford University Press, 1961), 191–99; Ainslie T. Embree, 'Napier, Sir Charles James (1782–1853)', *ODNB*; online edition, 3 January 2008 [https://doi.org/10.1093/ref:odnb/19748, accessed 25 Feb. 2021]; R. H. Vetch, 'Outram, Sir James, first baronet (1803–1863)', rev. Ainslie T. Embree, *ODNB*; online edition, 6 Jan. 2011 [https://doi.org/10.1093/ref:odnb/20962, accessed 25 Feb. 2021].
12. *Satara Gazetteer* (Bombay, 1885), 312–14; Barbara Ramusack, *The Indian Princes and Their States* (Cambridge: Cambridge University Press, 2003), 80–87; Sumitra Kulkarni, *The Satara Raj (1818–1848): A Study in History, Administration and Culture* (New Delhi: Mittal Publications, 1995), 31–35.
13. C. A. Bayly, *Recovering Liberties: Indian Thought in the Age of Liberalism and Empire* (Cambridge: Cambridge University Press, 2012), 174–75.
14. John Martineau, *The Life and Correspondence of Sir Bartle Frere*, 2 vols. (London, 1895), 1:476–79, Bartle Frere, address, 4 Sep. 1865.
15. Dharm Pal, *Administration of Sir John Lawrence in India (1864–1869)* (Simla: Minerva, 1952), 113–18.
16. For example, the Madras Supreme Court's authority to issue writs in the princely states was disputed in 1839–1840. British Library [BL], India Office Records [IOR] F/4/1894/80273.
17. Erskine Perry was a founder of the Parliamentary Candidate Society 'to point out proper persons as candidates at the next election' in 1831. The member included Francis Place, Francis Burdett, Jeremy Bentham, Joseph Hume and Daniel O'Connell. See Francis Place, 'Papers relating to the Parliamentary Candidates Society', in *London Radicalism 1830–1843: A*

Selection of the Papers of Francis Place, ed. D. J. Rowe (London: Record Society, 1970), 15–25. [http://www.british-history.ac.uk/london-record-soc/vol5/pp15-25, accessed 25 Feb. 2021].

18. Thomas Erskine Perry, *Cases Illustrative of Oriental Life, and the Application of English Law to India, Decided in H. M. Supreme Court at Bombay* [*Perry O.C.*] (London, 1853), 398–401, *Aga Mahomed Jaffer v. Mahomed Saduck*, 1847.
19. *Friend of India*, 18 Oct. 1849, quoted in Ram Gopal Sanyal, *Reminiscences and Anecdotes of Great Men of India, Both Official and Nonofficial, for the Last One Hundred Years*, 2 vol. (1894–95), 1:105–06.
20. *Perry O.C.*, 360–72, *Ramchund Ursamul v. H. H. Glass*, 1844; *Perry O.C.*, 373–97, *Hurkissondass v. Spooner*, 1847.
21. *Perry O.C.*, 57–72. This case caused some moral panic in the Parsi reformers in Bombay who opposed polygamy. Mitra Sharafi, *Law and Identity in Colonial South Asia: Parsi Legal Culture 1772–1847* (Cambridge: Cambridge University Press, 2014), 171–72. The defendant appealed to the Privy Council and the decision was reversed. M.P. Jain, *Outlines of Indian Legal and Constitutional History*, 6th edition (New Delhi: LexisNexis, 2006), 107–8. The court confirmed the decision next year in *Buchaboye v. Merwangee Nasserwangee* (*Perry O.C.*, 73–75).
22. Nasser Hussain, *The Jurisprudence of Emergency: Colonialism and the Rule of Law* (Ann Arbor: University of Michigan Press, 2003), 86–87; *Perry O.C.*, 434–66.
23. Miles Taylor, 'Queen Victoria and India 1837–61', *Victorian Studies* 46, no. 2 (2004): 271.
24. Thomas R Metcalf, *The Aftermath of Revolt: India 1857–1870* (Princeton, NJ: Princeton University Press, 1965), 137.
25. Speech by Erskine in the Legislative Council, 8 Jun 1861, quoted in Metcalf, *Aftermath*, 238.
26. Charlesworth, *Peasants and Imperial Rule*, 64–65.
27. Charlesworth, *Peasants and Imperial Rule*, 55; see also B. H. Baden-Powell, *The Land Systems of British India*, 3 vols. (Oxford: Clarendon, 1892), 3:304.
28. John Martineau, *The Life and Correspondence of Sir Bartle Frere*, 2 vols. (London, 1895), 1:331, 327, 336–41, 356; Metcalf, *Aftermath*, 182–86, 265; Andrew Sartori, *Liberalism in Empire: An Alternative History* (Berkeley, CA: University of California Press, 2014), chapter 2. The Legislative Council was enlarged by the Charter Act of 1854 and now included the judges of the King's Court as its members.
29. Sanyal, *Reminiscences,* 1:136–37. Martineau, *Life of Frere*, 1:328–31.
30. George Claus Rankin, *Background to Indian Law* (Cambridge: University Press, 1946), 64–65; R. J. Moore, *Sir Charles Wood's Indian Policy 1853–66*

(Manchester: Manchester University Press, 1966), 165–77; BL, IOR V/27/100/2, *Minutes by the Hon Sir Barnes Peacock 1852–1859* (Simla, 1901), 47–54.
31. Martineau, *Life of Frere*, 1:331–32.
32. A. C. Banerjee, *English Law in India* (New Delhi: Abhinav Publications, 1984), 143.
33. H. H. Dodwell, ed., *The Cambridge History of India, Volume VI: The Indian Empire 1858–1918* (Delhi: Cambridge University Press, 1958), 236; Courtenay Ilbert, *The Government of India: Being a Digest of the Statute Law Relating Thereto with Historical Introduction and Illustrative Documents* (Oxford: Clarendon, 1898), 215–16; Ibid., 566, para 26, Wood's despatch, 9 Aug. 1861.
34. Mark Condos, 'Licence to Kill: The Murderous Outrages Act and the Rule of Law in Colonial India 1867–1925', *Modern Asian Studies*, 50, no. 2 (2016): 479–517; Benjamin D. Hopkins, 'The Frontier Crimes Regulation and Frontier Governmentality', *Journal of Asian Studies* 74, no. 2 (2015): 369–89.
35. Sanjay Nigam, 'Disciplining and Policing the "Criminals by Birth", Part 1: The Making of a Colonial Stereotype—The Criminal Tribes and Castes of North India', *Indian Economic and Social History Review* 27, no. 2 (1990): 131–64, the quotation at 145.
36. Andrew J. Major, 'State and Criminal Tribes in Colonial Punjab: Surveillance, Control and Reclamation of the 'Dangerous Classes'', *Modern Asian Studies* 33, no. 3 (1999): 665–68, 686; Nigam, 'Disciplining and Policing, Part 1': 134–50.
37. BL, IOR V/27/100/6, *Minutes by the Hon Sir James Fitzjames Stephen 1869–1872* (Simla, 1898), 118–19, James Fitzjames Stephen, minute, 6 July 1870.
38. Ibid., 140–42, J. F. Stephen, minute, 26 June 1871. For Idar, see *Treaties, Engagements and Sanads*, ed. Aitchison, 7:75–78. The quotation is from John Clunes, *An Historical Sketch of the Princes of India: Stipendiary, Subsidiary, Protected, Tributary, and Feudatory, with a Sketch of the Origin and Progress of British Power in India* (Edinburgh, 1833), 203.
39. BL, IOR V/27/100/3, *Minutes by the Hon Sir H. S. Maine 1862-69 with a Note on Indian Codification dated 17 July 1879* (Calcutta, 1889), 35–38, Proceedings, Foreign Department, Political, A, April 1864, No. 17, Henry Maine, minute, 22 Mar. 1864.
40. Ibid., 40–43, Proceedings, Foreign Department, Political, June 1864, nos. 14–16, H. Maine, minute, 11 May 1864.
41. *Minute by the Hon'ble J. Fitzjames Stephen on the Administration of Justice in British India, Selections from the Records of the Government of India, Home Department, 89* (Calcutta, 1872), 11.

42. Ibid., 33.
43. Ibid., 69, 72.
44. Ibid., 94, 105.
45. Banerjee, *English Law*, 259–60.
46. Eric Stokes, *The English Utilitarians and India* (Oxford: Oxford University Press, 1959), 269–87.
47. Stephen even tried to apply this new mode of the rule of law in Britain in his *Liberty, Equality, Fraternity* (1873) to 'remake England in the image of the Raj' on the brink of Gladstone's introducing mass democracy. Thomas R. Metcalf, *Ideologies of the Raj* (Cambridge: Cambridge University Press, 1995), 56–59.
48. Cf. Hopkins, 'Frontier Crimes Regulation'.
49. David Washbrook, 'Lytton, Edward Robert Bulwer-, first earl of Lytton (1831–1891)', *ODNB*; online edition, 3 Jan 2008 [https://doi.org/10.1093/ref:odnb/17315, accessed 25 Feb. 2021].
50. David Cannadine, *Ornamentalism: How the British Saw Their Empire* (London: Allen Lane, 2001), 46; Bernard S. Cohn, 'Representing Authority in Victorian India', in Eric Hobsbawm and Terence Ranger, eds., *The Invention of Tradition* (Cambridge: Cambridge University Press, 1983), 165–210.
51. Abhinav Chandrachud, *An Independent, Colonial Judiciary: A History of the Bombay High Court During the British Raj 1862–1947* (Oxford: Oxford University Press, 2015), 71–72.
52. *Notable Speeches of Lord Curzon*, ed. C. S. Raghunatha Rao (Madras, 1905), 40, George Nathaniel Curzon, speech, 3 Feb. 1899.
53. Stokes, *Utilitarians*, 310.
54. Quoted in Banerjee, *English Law in India*, 261.
55. For another example of Indian judges similarly in conflict with the British, see Jon Wilson, 'The Temperament of Empire: Law and Conquest in Late Nineteenth Century India', in Gunnel Cederlof and Sanjukta Das Gupta, eds., *Subject, Citizens and Law: Colonial and Independent India* (London, 2017).
56. Chief Justice, 1889–1893.
57. The first Indian barrister in Bombay (1867). A member of the Bombay Legislative Council, 1882–1886.
58. Sandra Den Otter, 'Law, Authority, and Colonial Rule', in Douglas M. Peers and Nandini Gooptu, eds., *India and the British Empire* (Oxford: Oxford University Press, 2012), 184; Chandrachud, *Independent, Colonial Judiciary*, 81, 89.
59. Stephen strongly criticised the Bill from the perspective of inherent superiority of the British, the conquering race. He gave a voice to the nonofficial British in India who feared their decline of influence in the face of rising Indian elites. Metcalf, *Ideologies*, 209–11.

60. Kashinath Trimbak Telang, *Selected Writings and Speeches, Volume 1* (Bombay, 1916), 194.
61. Edwin Hirschmann, *'White Mutiny': The Ilbert Bill Crisis in Indian and Genesis of the Indian National Congress* (New Delhi: Heritage Publishers, 1980), 172–73.
62. Sanyal, *Reminiscences*, 1:102–3. For a similar tension in Calcutta in the 1890s, see Martin J. Wiener, *An Empire on Trial: Race, Murder and Justice under British Rule 1870–1935* (Cambridge: Cambridge University Press, 2009), 149–55, 167–72.
63. Cf. Saliha Belmessous, *Native Claims: Indigenous Law Against Empire 1500–1920* (Oxford, 2012).
64. Aditya Sarkar, *Trouble at the Mill: Factory Law and the Emergence of the Labour Question in Late Nineteenth-Century Bombay* (New Delhi: Oxford University Press, 2018); Rohit De, *A People's Constitution: The Everyday Life of Law in the Indian Republic* (Princeton, NJ: Princeton University Press, 2018).
65. Hamal Foster, Benjamin L. Berger, and A. R. Buck, eds., *Grand Experiment: Law and Legal Culture in British Settler Colonies* (Vancouver: UBC Press, 2008); Mark Hickford, *Lords of the Land: Indigenous Property Rights and the Jurisprudence of Empire* (Oxford, 2011); Nandini Chatterjee, *Negotiating Mughal Law: A Family of Landlords Across Three Indian Empires* (Cambridge: Cambridge University Press: 2020); Nurfadzilah Yahaya, *Fluid Jurisdictions: Colonial Law and Arabs in Southeast Asia* (Ithaka, NY: Cornell University Press, 2020).
66. Daniel J. Hulsebosch, *Constituting Empire: New York and the Transformation of Constitutionalism in the Atlantic World 1664–1830* (Chapel Hill, NC: University of North Carolina Press, 2005); Lisa Ford, *Settler Sovereignty: Jurisdiction and Indigenous People in America and Australia 1788–1836* (Cambridge, MA: Harvard University Press, 2010); Shaunnagh Dorsett and John McLaren, eds., *Legal Histories of Empire: Laws, Engagements and Legacies* (Abington, 2014); Michelle A. McKinley, *Fractional Freedoms: Slavery, Intimacy, and Legal Mobilization in Colonial Lima, 1600-1700* (Cambridge: Cambridge University Press, 2016); Bianca Premo, *The Enlightenment on Trial: Ordinary Litigants and Colonialism in the Spanish Empire* (New York, NY: Oxford University Press, 2017); Stefan B. Kirmse, *The Lawful Empire: Legal Change and Cultural Diversity in Late Tsarist Russia* (Oxford: Oxford University Press), 2020.
67. C. H. Alexandrowicz, *The Law of Nations in Global History*, ed. by David Armitage and Jennifer Pitts (Oxford: Oxford University Press, 2017); Jennifer Pitts, *Boundaries of the International: Law and Empire* (Cambridge, MA: Harvard University Press, 2018).

68. Benjamin D. Hopkins, *Ruling the Savage Periphery: Frontier Governance and the Making of the Modern State* (Cambridge, MA: Harvard University Press, 2019), 6.
69. Maurus Reinkowski and Gregor Thum, eds., *Helpless Imperialists: Imperial Failure, Fear and Radicalization* (Göttingen: Vandenhoeck and Ruprecht, 2013); Harald Fischer-Tiné, ed., *Anxiety, Fear and Panic in Colonial Settings: Empires on the Verge of a Nervous Breakdown* (Basingstoke: Palgrave Macmillan, 2016); J. C. Sharman, *Empire of the Weak: The Real Story of European Expansion and the Creation of the New World Order* (Princeton, NJ: Princeton University Press, 2019); Kim A. Wagner, *Amritsar 1919: An Empire of Fear and the Making of a Massacre* (New Haven, CT: Yale University Press, 2019).
70. Ayesha Jalal, *The State of Martial Rule: The Origin of Pakistan's Political Economy of Defence* (Cambridge: Cambridge University Press, 1990); James Hevia, *The Imperial Security State: British Colonial Knowledge and Empire-Building in Asia* (Cambridge: Cambridge University Press, 2012); Osama Siddique, *Pakistan's Experience with Formal Law: An Alien Justice* (Cambridge: Cambridge University Press, 2013); Shubhankar Dam, *Presidential Legislation in India: The Law and Practice of Ordinances* (Cambridge: Cambridge University Press, 2014); Nick Cheeseman, *Opposing the Rule of Law: How Myanmar's Courts Make Law and Order* (Cambridge: Cambridge University Press, 2019).
71. Jothie Rajah, *Authoritarian Rule of Law: Legislation, Discourse and Legitimacy in Singapore* (Cambridge: Cambridge University Press, 2012); Yoav Mehozay, *Between the Rule of Law and States of Emergency: The Fluid Jurisprudence of the Israeli Regime* (Albany, NY: State University of New York Press, 2016).

Bibliography

Primary Sources

Archives

British Library, London, UK
Asia, Pacific and African Collection
European Manuscripts
Mountstuart Elphinstone Collection: Mss Eur F88
John Peter Grant Collection: Mss Eur F523/59–60
India Office Records
Proceedings and Consultations (P)
Political Department
Secret Department
Public/General Department
Judicial Department
Revenue Department
Board of Control Records
Home Correspondence (F/2)
Board's Collections (F/4)
Home Miscellaneous (H)
John Malcolm Papers: IOR H/733–737
Public and Judicial Department Records (L/PJ)

H. Inagaki, *The Rule of Law and Emergency in Colonial India*, Cambridge Imperial and Post-Colonial Studies,
https://doi.org/10.1007/978-3-030-73663-7

Political and Secret Department Records (L/PS)
Crown Representative's Records, Indian States Residencies (R/2)
Official Publications Series (V)
BL, IOR V/8/24, Bombay Regulations—1827
BL, IOR V/8/25, Bombay Regulations—1828–34
BL, IOR V/27/70/10, Biography of the Principal Marratta Families and Chieftains of the Late Poona State Connected with the British Government. Lithographed, nd.
BL, IOR V/27/100/2, *Minutes by the Hon Sir Barnes Peacock 1852–1859* (Simla, 1901).
BL, IOR V/27/100/3, *Minutes by the Hon Sir Henry Sumner Maine 1862–69, with a Note on Indian Codification dated 17 July 1879* (Calcutta, 1889).
BL, IOR V/27/100/6, *Minutes by the Hon Sir James Fitzjames Stephen 1869–1872* (Simla, 1898).

The National Archives, Kew, UK

TNA, TS 11/122–123: The Hon. Mountstewart Elphinstone and Henry Dundas Robertson v. Heerachund Bedreechund and Jelmeel Anoopchund. Appeal from Supreme Court of Bombay in action to recover value of gold coins taken from Naroo Govind Narroba, a Brahmin. Court: Privy Council

Maharashtra State Archives, Mumbai, India

General Department
Judicial Department
Political Department
Revenue Department

***Dharampal Archival Collection, Centre for Policy Studies* (online)** [http://cpsindia.org/index.php/dh-archive, accessed 25 Feb. 2021]

Newspapers and Periodicals

Bombay Courier
Bombay Gazette
Asiatic Journal
Oriental Herald
Bombay Calendar and Almanac

Parliamentary Papers

PP 1830 (646) Report from the Select Committee of the House of Lords appointed to inquire into the present state of the affairs of the East India Company, and into the trade between Great Britain, the East Indies and China; with the minutes of evidence taken before the committee. 1830.

PP 1831 (320E) Appendix to the report on the affairs of the East India Company. V. On the establishment of legislative councils,—a new system of courts of justice,—and a code of laws, in British India.
PP 1831–32 (734) (735-I–VI) Report from the Select Committee on the Affairs of the East India Company; with minutes of evidence in six parts, and an appendix and index to each.
(735-I. Public, Appendix, Index)
(735-III. Revenue, Appendix, Index)
(735-IV. Judicial, Appendix, Index)
(735-VI. Political or Foreign, Appendix, Index)
Hansard's Parliamentary Debates

Official Publications

Edwardes, S.M., ed., *Gazetteer of Bombay City and Island* [*City gazetteer*], 3 vols. (Bombay, 1909).
Gazetteer of the Bombay Presidency, 27 vol. (Bombay, 1877–1904). [Referred to as, for example, *Thana Gazetteer*]
Volume 4, Ahmedabad (1879)
Volume 7, Baroda (1883)
Volume 13, Thana (1882); Part 2 Thana (1882)
Volume 19 Satara (1885)
Volume 24 Kolhapur (1886)

Published Primary Sources

A Collection of Treaties, Engagements and Sanads, Relating to India and Neighbouring Countries. ed. C.U. Aitchison, 5th edition, 14 vols. (Calcutta, Superintendent Government Printing, 1929–1933).
Borradaile, Harry, *Reports of Civil Cases Adjudged by the Court of Sudder Adawlut for the Presidency of Bombay, Between the Years A.D. 1800 and A.D. 1824*, 2 vols. (Bombay, 1825).
Chaplin, William, *A Report Exhibiting a View of the Fiscal and Judicial System of Administration Introduced into the Conquered Territory above the Ghauts under the Authority of the Commissioner in the Dekhan* (Bombay, 1824).
Clunes, John, *Itinerary and Directory for Western India* (Calcutta, 1828).
Clunes, John, *Appendix to Itinerary and Directory of Western India* (Bombay, 1828).
Clunes, John, *An Historical Sketch of the Princes of India: Stipendiary, Subsidiary, Protected, Tributary, and Feudatory, with a Sketch of the Origin and Progress of British Power in India* (Edinburgh, 1833).

The Correspondence of Lord William Cavendish Bentinck, Governor-General of India 1828–1835, ed. C. H. Philips, 2 vols. (Oxford: Oxford University Press, 1977).

Raja Pratapsinh of Satara 1818–1839: Select Documents from the Satara Residency Papers, Peshwa Dafter, Poona, and the Elphinstone Papers, India Office Library, London, ed. R. D. Choksey (Poona: Bharata Itihasa Samshodhaka Mandala, 1970).

East India Company, *Selection of Papers from the Records at the East-India House Relating to the Revenue, Police, and Civil and Criminal Justice, under the Company's Governments in India*, 4 vols. (London, 1820–26).

East India Company, *Papers Respecting the Case of the Raja of Sattara* (London, 1840).

Elphinstone, Mountstuart, *Report on the Territories Conquered from the Paishwa Submitted to the Supreme Government of British India* (Calcutta, 1821).

Etheridge, Alfred Thomas, *Narrative of the Bombay Inam Commission and Supplementary Settlements*, Selections from the Records of the Bombay Government, 132, new series (Poona, 1873).

Gaikwads of Baroda Maharaja Sayajirao II A. D. 1821 to A. D. 1830 (Selections from the Baroda Residency Records), ed. G. B. Pandya (Baroda: Maharaja Sayajirao University of Baroda, 1958).

Gray, James, *Life in Bombay, and the Neighbouring Out-Stations* (London, 1852).

The Greville Diary, Including Passages Hitherto Withheld from Publication, ed. Philip Whitwell Wilson, 2 vols. (London: Heinemann, 1927).

Hamilton, Walter, *A Geographical, Statistical, and Historical Descriptions of Hindoostan, and the Adjacent Countries* (London, 1820).

Hamilton, Walter, *The East-India Gazetteer*, 2nd edition, 2 vols. (London, 1828).

The Holland House Diaries 1831–1840: The Diary of Henry Richard Vassall Fox, third Lord Holland, with Extracts from the Diary of Dr. John Allen, ed. Abraham D. Kriegel (London: Routledge, 1977).

Ilbert, Courtenay, *The Government of India: Being a Digest of the Statute Law Relating Thereto with Historical Introduction and Illustrative Documents* (Oxford, 1898).

Kaye, John William, *The Life and Correspondence of Major-General Sir John Malcolm*, 2 vols. (London, 1856).

Kaye, John William, *The Life and Correspondence of Charles, Lord Metcalfe*, 2 vols. (London, 1858).

Kaye, John and Malleson, Colonel, *Kaye's and Malleson's History of the Indian Mutiny of 1857–8*, 6 vols. (New impression, London, 1909–14).

Lord Macaulay's Legislative Minutes, ed. C. D. Dharker (Madras: Oxford University Press, 1946).

Mackintosh, Alexander, *An Account of the Origin and Present Condition of the Tribe of Ramoossies, Including the Life of the Chief Oomiah Naik* (Bombay, 1833).

Malcolm, John, *The Government of India* (London, 1833).
Malcolm, John, *The Political History of India from 1784 to 1823*, 2 vols. (London, 1826).
Martineau, John, *The Life and Correspondence of Sir Bartle Frere*, 2 vols. (London, 1895).
Minute by the Hon'ble J. Fitzjames Stephen on the Administration of Justice in British India, Selections from the Records of the Government of India, Home Department, 89 (Calcutta, 1872).
Morley, William Hook, *An Analytical Digest of All the Reported Cases Decided in the Supreme Courts of Judicature in India, in the Courts of the Hon. East India Company, and on Appeal from India, by Her Majesty in Council*, 2 vols. (London, 1849–50).
Nanabhai, Jamietram and Stelvad, Chimanlal Harilal, eds., *Bombay Acts and Regulations with Notes, Decisions, Notifications, &c.* (Bombay, 1894).
Notable Speeches of Lord Curzon, ed. C. S. Raghunatha Rao (Madras, 1905).
Perry, Thomas Erskine, *Cases Illustrative of Oriental Life, and the Application of English Law to India, Decided in H. M. Supreme Court at Bombay* (London, 1853).
Poona Affairs: Close's Embassy 1801–1810, ed., G. S. Sardesai (Poona Residency Correspondence, vol. 7) (Bombay, 1940).
Poona Affairs: Elphinstone's Embassy Part 2 1816–1818. ed. G. S. Sardesai (Poona Residency Correspondence, vol. 13) (Bombay, 1953).
Place, Francis, 'Papers Relating to the Parliamentary Candidates Society', in *London Radicalism 1830–1843: A Selection of the Papers of Francis Place*, ed. D. J. Rowe (London: Record Society, 1970).
Raja Pratapsinh of Satara 1818–1839: Select Documents from the Satara Residency Papers, Peshwa Dafter, Poona, and the Elphinstone Papers, India Office Library, London [*Pratapsinh*], ed. R. D. Choksey (Poona: Bharata Itihasa Samshodhaka Mandala, 1970).
Sanyal, Ram Gopal, *Reminiscences and Anecdotes of Great Men of India, Both Official and Nonofficial, for the Last One Hundred Years*, 2 vol. (Calcutta, 1894–95).
Selections from the Records of the Bombay Government, new series, 26 (Bombay, 1856).
Schmitt, Carl, *Political Theology: Four Chapters on the Concept of Sovereignty*, trans. George Schwab (Chicago, IL: University of Chicago Press, 2005).
Stephen, James Fitzjames, *Liberty, Equality, Fraternity* (London, 1873).
Strange, Thomas, *Notes of Cases in the Court of the Recorder and in the Supreme Court of Judicature at Madras; Commencing in the year 1798, and Ending in the Year 1816*, 3 vols. (Madras, 1816).
Telang, Kashinath Trimbak, *Selected Writings and Speeches*, 2 vols. (Bombay, 1916–31).

Wallace, Robert, *The Guicowar, and his Relations with the British Government* (Bombay, 1863).
West, Edward W., *A Memoir of the States of the Southern Maratha Country* (Bombay, 1869).
Wilson, H. H., *The History of the British India from 1805 to 1835*, 3 vol. (London, 1848).

Secondary Sources

Ahmed, A. F. Salahuddin, *Social Ideas and Social Change in Bengal 1818–1835*, 2nd edition (Calcutta: RDDHI, 1976).
Ahuja Ravi, 'Expropriating the Poor: Urban Land Control and Colonial Administration in Late Eighteenth Century Madras City', *Studies in History* 17, no. 1, n.s. (2001): 81–99.
Alam, Shar Manzoor, *Hyderabad-Secunderabad (Twin Cities): A Study in Urban Geography* (Bombay: Allied Publishers, 1965).
Alexandrowicz, C.H., *The Law of Nations in Global History*, edited by David Armitage and Jennifer Pitts (Oxford: Oxford University Press, 2017).
Appadurai, Arjun, *Worship and Conflict under Colonial Rule: A South Indian Case* (Cambridge: Cambridge University Press, 1981).
Arnold, David, *Police Power and Colonial Rule: Madras 1859–1947* (Delhi: Oxford University Press, 1986).
Baden-Powell, Baden Henry, *The Land Systems of British India*, 3 vols. (Oxford: Clarendon, 1892).
Baker, J. H., *An Introduction to English Legal History*, 4th edition (London: Butterworths, 2007).
Ballhatchet, Kenneth, *Social Policy and Social Change in Western India 1817–1830* (London: Oxford University Press, 1957).
Banerjee, A. C., *English Law in India* (New Delhi: Abhinav Publications, 1984).
Bayly, C. A., 'Bombay's "Intertwined Modernities" 1780–1880', in Michael S. Dodson and Brian A. Hacther, eds., *Trans-Colonial Modernities in South Asia* (London: Routledge, 2012), 231–48.
Bayly, C. A., *Imperial Meridian: The British Empire and the World 1780–1830* (London: Longman, 1989).
Bayly, C. A., *Indian Society and the Making of the British Empire* (Cambridge: Cambridge University Press, 1998).
Bayly, C. A., *Rulers, Townsmen and Bazaars: North India in the Age of British Expansion 1770–1870* (Oxford: Oxford University Press, 1997).
Bayly, C. A., *Recovering Liberties: Indian Thought in the Age of Liberalism and Empire* (Cambridge: Cambridge University Press, 2012).
Bearce, George D., *British Attitudes Towards India 1784-1858* (Oxford: Oxford University Press, 1961).

Belmessous, Saliha, *Native Claims: Indigenous Law Against Empire 1500–1920* (Oxford: Oxford University Press, 2012).

Benjamin, N., and Mohanty, B. B., 'Imperial Solution of a Colonial Problem: Bhils of Khandesh up to c. 1850', *Modern Asian Studies*, 41, 2 (2007), 343–67.

Benton, Lauren, *Law and Colonial Cultures: Legal Regimes in World History 1400–1900* (Cambridge: Cambridge University Press, 2002).

Benton, Lauren, *A Search for Sovereignty: Law and Geography in European Empires 1400–1900* (Cambridge: Cambridge University Press, 2010).

Benton, Lauren and Ross, Richard J., eds., *Legal Pluralism and Empires 1500–1850* (New York: New York University Press, 2013).

Benton, Lauren, and Lisa Ford, *Rage for Order: The British Empire and the Origins of International Law 1800-1850* (Cambridge, MA: Harvard University Press, 2016).

Benton, Lauren, Adam Clulow, and Bain Attwood, eds., *Protection and Empire: A Global History* (New York, NY: Cambridge University Press, 2017).

Beverley, Eric Lewis, *Hyderabad, British India, and the World: Muslim Networks and Minor Sovereignty, c.1850-1950* (Cambridge: Cambridge University Press, 2015).

Bhatnagar, O. P., 'The Case of Moro Raghunath: A Case Illustrating the Conflict Between Judiciary and Executive in India in Early Nineteenth Century', Allahabad High Court [http://www.allahabadhighcourt.in/event/TheCaseofMoroRaghunathOPBhatnagar.pdf, accessed 25 Feb. 2021].

Bhattacharya, Neeladri. *The Great Agrarian Conquest: The Colonial Reshaping of a Rural World* (Ranikhet: Parmanent Black, 2018).

Bhukya, Bhangya, *The Roots of the Periphery: A History of the Gonds of Deccan India* (New Delhi: Oxford University Press, 2017).

Bilder, Mary Sarah. *The Transatlantic Constitution: Colonial Legal Culture and the Empire*. Cambridge, MA: Harvard University Press, 2004.

Birla, Ritu, *Stages of Capital: Law, Culture, Market Governance in Late Colonial India* (Durham, NC: Duke University Press, 2009).

Bowen, H. V., *The Business of Empire: The East India Company and Imperial Britain 1756–1833* (Cambridge: Cambridge University Press, 2006).

Brimnes, Niels, 'Beyond Colonial Law: Indigenous Litigation and the Contestation of Property in the Mayor's Court in Late Eighteenth-Century Madras', *Modern Asian Studies*, 37, 3 (2003): 513–550.

Brimnes, Niels, *Constructing the Colonial Encounter: Right and Left Hand Castes in Early Colonial South India* (Richmond: Curzon, 1999).

Cannadine, David, *Ornamentalism: How the British Saw Their Empire* (London: Allen Lane, 2001).

Chandavarkar, Rajnarayan, *Imperial Power and Popular Politics: Class, Resistance and the State in India c. 1850–1950* (Cambridge: Cambridge University Press, 1998).

Chandrachud, Abhinav, *An Independent, Colonial Judiciary: A History of the Bombay High Court During the British Raj 1862–1947* (Oxford: Oxford University Press, 2015).

Charlesworth, Neil, *Peasants and Imperial Rule: Agricultural and Agrarian Society in the Bombay Presidency 1850–1935* (Cambridge: Cambridge University Press, 1985).

Chatterjee, Indrani, *Gender, Slavery and Law in Colonial India* (Delhi: Oxford University Press, 1998);

Chatterjee, Nandini, *Negotiating Mughal Law: A Family of Landlords Across Three Indian Empires* (Cambridge: Cambridge University Press: 2020).

Chatterjee, Partha, *The Black Hole of Empire: History of a Global Practice of Power* (Princeton, NJ: Princeton University Press, 2012).

Chaudhry, Faisal, 'A Rule of Proprietary Right for British India: From Revenue Settlement to Tenant Right in the Age of Classical Legal Thought', *Modern Asian Studies* 50, 1 (2015): 345–85.

Cheesman, Nick. *Opposing the Rule of Law: How Myanmar's Courts Make Law and Order* (Cambridge: Cambridge University Press, 2015).

Choksey, R. D., *The Aftermath (1818–1826)* (Bombay: New Book, 1950).

Choksey, R. D., *Economic Life in the Bombay Konkan 1818–1939* (New York: Asia Publishing House, 1960).

Choksey, R. D., *Early British Administration, 1817–1836: Deccan Commissioner's Files and Pre-Mutiny Records on Gujarat* (Poona: Choksey, 1964).

Choksey, R. D., *Mountstuart Elphinstone: The Indian Years 1796–1827* (Bombay: Bhatkal, 1971).

Cohn, Bernard S., 'Representing Authority in Victorian India, in Eric Hobsbawm and Terence Ranger, eds., *The Invention of Tradition* (Cambridge, 1983), 165–210.

Colebrooke, T. E., *Life of the Honourable Mountstuart Elphinstone*, 2 vols. (London: Murray, 1884).

Condos, Mark, 'Licence to Kill: The Murderous Outrages Act and the Rule of Law in Colonial India 1867–1925', *Modern Asian Studies* 50, no. 2 (2016): 479–517.

Condos, Mark, *The Insecurity State: Punjab and the Making of Colonial Power in British India* (Cambridge: Cambridge University Press, 2017).

Cook, Matthew A., *Annexation and the Unhappy Valley: The Historical Anthropology of Sindh's Colonization* (Leiden: Brill, 2015).

Cooper, Frederick and Stoler, Ann Laura, eds., *Tensions of Empire: Colonial Cultures in a Bourgeois World* (Berkeley, CA: University of California Press, 1997).

Cooper, Randolf G. S., *The Anglo-Maratha Campaign and the Contest for India: The Struggle for Control of the South Asia Military Economy* (Cambridge: Cambridge University Press, 2003).

Cornish, William, et al. eds., *Oxford History of the Laws of England: Volume XI 1820–1914* (Oxford: Oxford University Press, 2010).

Dam, Shubhankar, *Presidential Legislation in India: The Law and Practice of Ordinances* (Cambridge: Cambridge University Press, 2014).

De, R., 'South Asian Legal Traditions', in James D. Wright, ed., *International Encyclopedia of the Social and Behavioural Science*, 2nd edition, volume 23 (Amsterdam: Pergamon, 2015), 58–62.

De, Rohit. *A People's Constitution: The Everyday Life of Law in the Indian Republic* (Princeton: Princeton University Press, 2018).

Den Otter, Sandra, 'Law, Authority and Colonial Rule', in Douglas M. Peers and Nandini Gooptu, eds., *India and the British Empire* (Oxford: Oxford University Press, 2012).

Desai, Sanjiv P, *The Hand Book of the Bombay Archives* (Bombay: Department of Archives, Government of Maharashtra, 1978).

Deshpande, Avind M., *John Briggs in Maharashtra: A Study of District Administration Under Early British Rule* (Delhi: Mittal Publications, 1987).

Dirks, Nicholas B., 'From Little King to Landlord: Property, Law, and the Gift under the Madras Permanent Settlement', *Comparative Studies in Society and History* 28 (1986): 307–33.

Dirks, Nicholas B., *The Scandal of Empire: India and the Creation of Imperial Britain* (Cambridge, MA: Harvard University Press, 2006).

Divekar, V. D., 'Regional Economy 1757–1857: Western India', in Kumar, Dharna, ed., *Cambridge Economic History of India, Volume 2 c.1757–c1970* (Cambridge: Cambridge University Press, 1983), 332–52.

Dobbin, Christine, *Urban Leadership in Western India: Politics and Community in Bombay City 1840–1885* (Oxford: Oxford University Press, 1972).

Dodwell, H. H., ed., *The Cambridge History of India, Volume VI: The Indian Empire 1858–1918* (Delhi: Cambridge University Press, 1958).

Dorsett, Shaunnagh, and McLaren, John, eds., *Legal Histories of Empire: Laws, Engagements and Legacies* (Abington: Routledge, 2014).

Dossal, Mariam, 'Bombay and the Famine of 1803–6: The Food Supply and Public Order of a Colonial Port City', in Frank Broeze, ed., *Gateways of Asia: Port Cities of Asia in the 13th–20th Centuries* (London: Routledge, 1997).

Dyzenhaus, David, *The Constitution of Law: Legality in a Time of Emergency* (Cambridge: Cambridge University Press, 2006).

Esmeir, Samera, *Juridical Humanity: A Colonial History* (Stanford, CA: Stanford University Press, 2012).

Esmeir, Samera, 'On the Coloniality of Modern Law', *Critical Analysis of Law* 2, no. 1 (2015): 19–41.

Fisher, Michael H., *Indirect Rule in India: Residents and the Residency System 1764–1858* (New Delhi: Oxford University Press, 1991).

Fischer-Tiné, Harald, ed. *Anxieties, Fear and Panic in Colonial Settings: Empires on the Verge of a Nervous Breakdown* (Basingstoke: Palgrave Macmillan, 2016).

Ford, Lisa, *Settler Sovereignty: Jurisdiction and Indigenous People in America and Australia 1788–1836* (Cambridge, MA: Harvard University Press, 2010).

Ford, Lisa and Tim Rowse, eds., *Between Indigenous and Settler Governance* (London: Routledge, 2013).

Foster, Hamal, Berger, Benjamin L., and Buck, A. R., eds., *Grand Experiment: Law and Legal Culture in British Settler Colonies* (Vancouver: UBC Press, 2008).

Fraas, Arthur Mitchell, 'They Have Travailed into a Wrong Latitude': The Laws of England, Indian Settlements and the British Imperial Constitution 1726–1773' (PhD diss., Duke University, 2011).

Freedman, Eric M., *Making Habeas Work: A Legal History* (New York, NY: New York University Press, 2018).

Frykenberg, Robert Eric, *Guntur District 1788–1848: A History of Local Influence and Central Authority in South India* (Oxford: Oxford University Press, 1965).

Fukazawa, Hiroshi, 'Agrarian Relations: Western India', in Dharma Kumar and Meghnad Desai, eds., *The Cambridge Economic History of India, Volume 2, c.1757–c.1970* (Cambridge: Cambridge University Press, 1983), 177–206.

Furber, Holden, *John Company at Work: A Study of European Expansion in India in the Late Eighteenth Century* (Cambridge, MA: Harvard University Press, 1948).

Geertsema, Johan, 'Exception, Bare Life and Colonialism', in Victor V. Ramraj, ed., *Emergencies and the Limits of Legality* (Cambridge: Cambridge University Press, 2008), 337–59.

Ghosh, Durba, *Sex and the Family in Colonial India* (Cambridge: Cambridge University Press, 2006).

Gilmartin, David, Pamela Price, and Arild Engelsen Ruud, eds., *South Asian Sovereignty: The Conundrum of Worldly Power* (Abington: Routledge, 2020).

Guha, Ranajit, *Dominance Without Hegemony: History and Power in Colonial India* (Cambridge, MA: Harvard University Press, 1997).

Guha, Sumit, *The Agrarian Economy of the Bombay Deccan 1818–1941* (Delhi: Oxford University Press, 1985).

Guha, Sumit, 'Wrongs and Rights in the Maratha Country: Antiquity, Custom and Power in Eighteenth-Century India', in Michael R. Anderson and Sumit Guha, eds., *Changing Concepts of Rights and Justice in South Asia* (Delhi, 1998), 14–29.

Guha, Sumit, 'An India Penal Régime: Maharashtra in the Eighteenth Century', *Past and Present* 147 (1995): 101–26.

Guha, Sumit, *Environment and Ethnicity in India 1200–1991* (Cambridge: Cambridge University Press, 1999).

Gune, V. T., *The Judicial System of the Marathas* (Poona: Deccan College Post-Graduate and Research Institute, 1953)

Gupta, Maya, *Lord William Bentinck in Madras and the Vellore Mutiny, 1803–7* (New Delhi: Capital, 1986).
Hall, Catherine, *Macaulay and Son: Architects of Imperial Britain* (New Haven, CT: Yale University Press, 2012).
Halliday, Paul D., *Habeas Corpus: From England to Empire* (Cambridge, MA., Belknap Press of Harvard University Press, 2010).
Hanafi, Shah Mahmoud, ed., *Mountstuart Elphinstone in South Asia: Pioneer of British Colonial Rule* (London: Hurst, 2019).
Hardiman, David, *Feeding the Baniya: Peasants and Usurers in Western India* (Delhi: Oxford University Press, 1996).
Hardwick, Joseph, 'Vestry Politics and the Emergence of a Reform "Public" in Calcutta, 1813–36', *Historical Research* 84, no. 223 (2011): 87–108.
Harrington, Jack, *Sir John Malcolm and the Creation of British India* (Basingstoke: Palgrave Macmillan, 2010).
Hasan, Farhat, *State and Locality in Mughal India: Power Relations in Western India c. 1572–1730* (Cambridge: Cambridge University Press, 2004).
Hawkins, Angus, *Victorian Political Culture: 'Habits of Heart and Mind'* (Oxford: Oxford University Press, 2015).
Hevia, James. *The Imperial Security State: British Colonial Knowledge and Empire-Building in Asia* (Cambridge: Cambridge University Press, 2012).
Hickford, Mark, *Lords of the Land: Indigenous Property Rights and the Jurisprudence of Empire* (Oxford: Oxford University Press, 2011).
Hirschmann, Edwin, *'White Mutiny': The Ilbert Bill Crisis in Indian and Genesis of the Indian National Congress* (New Delhi: Heritage Publishers, 1980).
Hooker, M. B., 'The East India Company and the Crown 1773–1858', in C. H. Alexandrowicz, ed., *Grotian Society Papwer 1968: Studies in the History of the Law of Nations* (The Hague: Martinus Nijhoff, 1970).
Hopkins, Benjamin D., 'The Frontier Crimes Regulation and frontier governmentality', *Journal of Asian Studies* 74, no. 2 (2015): 369–89.
Hopkins, Benjamin D., *Ruling the Savage Periphery: Frontier Governance and the Making of the Modern State* (Cambridge, MA: Harvard University Press, 2019).
Hulsebosch, Daniel J., *Constituting Empire: New York and the Transformation of Constitutionalism in the Atlantic World 1664–1830* (Chapel Hill, NC: University of North Carolina Press, 2005).
Hussain, Nasser, *The Jurisprudence of Emergency: Colonialism and the Rule of Law* (Ann Arbor: University of Michigan Press, 2003).
Inagaki, Haruki, 'Policing the Market: Metropolitan Ideas and Local Contexts in Police Reform in Early Nineteenth-Century Bombay City', in Hiroki Shin, Shinobu Majima and Yusuke Tanaka, eds., *Moving Around: People, Things and Practices in Consumer Culture* (Tokyo: Forum for History of Consumer Culture, 2015), 171–76.

Inagaki, Haruki, 'The Rule of Law and Emergency in Colonial India: The Conflict between the King's Court and the Government in Bombay in the 1820s' (PhD diss., King's College London, 2016).

Inagaki, Haruki, 'Law, Agency and Emergency in British Imperial Politics: Conflict between the Government and the King's Court in Bombay in the 1820s', *East Asian Journal of British History* 5 (2016): 207–24.

Jacob, T., *Cantonments in India: Evolution and Growth* (New Delhi: Reliance Publishing House, 1994).

Jaffe, James, *Ironies of Colonial Governance: Law, Custom and Justice in Colonial India* (Cambridge: Cambridge University Press, 2015).

Jain, M. P., *Outlines of Indian Legal and Constitutional History*, 6th edition (New Delhi: LexisNexis, 2006).

Jalal, Ayesha, *The State of Martial Rule: The Origin of Pakistan's Political Economy of Defence* (Cambridge: Cambridge University Press, 1990).

Kapur, Nandini Sinha, 'The Bhils in the Historic Setting of Western India', in Rudolf C. Heredia and Shereen F. Ratnagar, eds., *Mobile and Marginalised Peoples: Perspective from the Past* (New Delhi: Manohar, 2003), 145-166.

Kamerkar, Mani, *British Paramountcy: British-Baroda Relations 1818–1848* (Bombay: Popular Prakashan, 1980).

Kirmse, Stefan B., *The Lawful Empire: Legal Change and Cultural Diversity in Late Tsarist Russia* (Oxford: Oxford University Press, 2020).

Kolff, Dirk H. A., *Naukars, Rajput and Sepoy: The Ethnohistory of the Military Labour Market in Hindustan 1450–1850* (Cambridge: Cambridge University Press, 1990).

Kolff, Dirk H. A., 'Rumours of the Company's Collapse: The Mood of Dasahra 1824 in the Punjab and Hindustan', in Crispin Bates, ed., *Mutiny at the Margins: New Perspectives on the Indian Uprising of 1857: Vol 1, Anticipations and Experiences in the Locality* (New Delhi: SAGE, 2013), 25–42.

Kolsky, Elizabeth, *Colonial Justice in British India: White Violence and the Rule of Law* (Cambridge: Cambridge University press, 2010).

Kolsky, Elizabeth, 'The Colonial Rule of Law and the Legal Regime of Exception: Frontier "Fanaticism" and State Violence in British India', *American Historical Review* 120, no. 4 (2015): 1218–46.

Kosambi, Meera, 'Commerce, Conquest and the Colonial City: Role of Locational Factors in Rise of Bombay', *Economic and Political Weekly* 20, no. 1 (1985), 32–37.

Kulkarni, A. R., ed., *History in Practice: Historians and Sources of Medieval Deccan-Marathas* (New Delhi: Books and Books, 1993).

Kulkarni, Sumitra, *The Satara Raj (1818–1848): A Study in History, Administration and Culture* (New Delhi: Mittal Publications, 1995).

Kumar, Ravinder, *Western India in the Nineteenth Century: A Study in the Social History of Maharashtra* (London: Routledge, 1968).

Laidlaw, Zoë, *Colonial Connections 1815–45: Patronage, the Information Revolution and Colonial Government* (Manchester: Manchester University Press, 2005).

Laidlaw Zoë, and Alan Lester, eds., *Indigenous Communities and Settler Colonialism: Land Holding, Loss and Survival in an Interconnected World* (London: Palgrave Macmillan, 2015).

Lee, Harold, *Brothers in the Raj: The Lives of John and Henry Lawrence* (Oxford: Oxford University Press, 2002).

Lees, James, *Bureaucratic Culture in Early Colonial India: District Officials, Armed Forces, and Personal Interest Under the East India Company, 1760-1830* (Abington: Routledge, 2020).

Legg, Stephen, and Deana Heath. *South Asian Governmentalities: Michel Foucault and the Question of Postcolonial Orderings* (Cambridge: Cambridge University Press, 2018).

Lemmings, David, *Law and Government in England During the Long Eighteenth Century: From Consent to Command* (Basingstoke: Palgrave Macmillan, 2011).

Lester, Alan and Fae Dussart, *Colonization and the Origins of Humanitarian Governance: Protecting Aborigines Across the Nineteenth-Century British Empire* (Cambridge: Cambridge University Press, 2014).

Lieberman, David, *The Province of Legislation Determined: Legal Theory in Eighteenth-Century Britain* (Cambridge: Cambridge University Press, 1989).

Lloyd, Tim, 'Thuggee, Marginality and the State Effect in Colonial India Circa 1770–1840', *Indian Economic and Social History Review* 45, no. 2, (2008): 201–37.

Lobban, Michael, *The Common Law and English Jurisprudence 1760–1850* (Oxford: Oxford University Press, 1991).

Madras Police Department, *The History of the Madras Police: Centenary 1859–1959* (Madras: Inspector General of Police, 1959).

Major, Andrew J., 'State and Criminal Tribes in Colonial Punjab: Surveillance, Control and Reclamation of the 'Dangerous Classes'', *Modern Asian Studies* 33, no. 3 (1999): 675–88.

Mallampalli, Chandra, *Race, Religion and Law in Colonial India: Trials of an Interracial Family* (Cambridge: Cambridge University Press, 2011).

Mantena, Karuna, *Alibis of Empire: Henry Maine and the Ends of Liberal Imperialism* (Princeton, NJ: Princeton University Press, 2010).

Markovits, Claude, 'Bombay as a Business Centre in the Colonial Period: A Comparison with Calcutta' in Sujata Patel and Alice Thorner, eds., *Bombay: Metaphor for Modern India* (Bombay: Oxford University Press, 1995), 26–46.

Marshall, P. J., 'The Whites of British India, 1780–1830: A Failed Colonial Society?', *International History Review* 12, no. 1 (1990): 26–44.

Marshall, P. J., *The Impeachment of Warren Hastings* (London: Oxford University Press, 1965).

Masselos, Jim, 'Changing Definitions of Bombay: City State to Capital City', in Indu Banga, ed., *Ports and Their Hinterlands in India (1700–1950)* (New Delhi: Manohar, 1992), 271–316.

McKenzie, Kirsten, *Imperial Underworld: An Escaped Convict and the Transformation of the British Colonial Order* (Cambridge: Cambridge University Press, 2016).

McKinley, Michelle A. *Fractional Freedoms: Slavery, Intimacy, and Legal Mobilization in Colonial Lima, 1600-1700* (Cambridge: Cambridge University Press, 2016).

McLaren, Martha, *British India and British Scotland 1780–1830: Carrier Building, Empire Building, and a Scottish School of Thought on Indian Governance* (Akron, OH: University of Akron Press, 2001).

McLaren, John, *Dewigged, Bothered and Bewildered: British Colonial Judges on Trial 1800–1900* (Toront: University of Toronto Press, 2011).

Mehozay, Yoav, *Between the Rule of Law and States of Emergency: The Fluid Jurisprudence of the Israeli Regime* (Albany, NY: State University of New York Press, 2016).

Mehta, Uday Singh, *Liberalism and Empire: A Study in Nineteenth-Century British Liberal Thought* (Chicago, IL: University of Chicago Press, 1999).

Mehrotra, S. R., 'The Poona Sarvajanik Sabha: The Early Phase (1870–1880)', *Indian Economic and Social History Review*, 6, 3 (1969): 293–321.

Metcalf, Thomas R., *The Aftermath of Revolt: India 1857–1870* (Princeton, NJ: Princeton University Press, 1965).

Metcalf, Thomas R., *Ideologies of the Raj* (Cambridge: Cambridge University Press, 1995).

Mines, Mattison, 'Courts of Laws and Styles of Self in Eighteenth-Century Madras: From Hybrid to Colonial Self', *Modern Asian Studies* 35, no. 1 (2001): 33–74.

Moore, R. J., *Sir Charles Wood's Indian Policy 1853–66* (Manchester: Manchester University Press, 1966).

Mootham, Orby, *The East India Company's Sadar Courts 1801–1834* (Bombay: N. M. Tripathi, 1983).

Mukherji, Kumar, 'Aldermen and Attorneys: Mayor's Court, Calcutta', in A. J. R. Russell-Wood, ed., *Local Government in European Overseas Empires 1450–1800* (1950; Aldershot: Routledge, 1999).

Mukherjee, Mithi, *India in the Shadows of Empire: A Legend and Political History 1774–1950* (Oxford: Oxford University Press, 2009).

Muller, Hannah Weiss. *Subjects and Sovereign: Bonds of Belonging in the Eighteenth-Century British Empire* (New York, NY: Oxford University Press, 2017).

Nair, Janaki, *Mysore Modern: Rethinking the Region under Princely Rule* (Mineapolis, MN: University of Minnesota Press, 2011).

Neild, Susan M., 'Colonial Urbanism: The Development of Madras City in the Eighteenth and Nineteenth Centuries', *Modern Asian Studies* 13, no. 2 (1979): 217–46.

Newbigin, Eleanor, *The Hindu Family and the Emergence of Modern India: Law, Citizenship and Community* (Cambridge: Cambridge University Press, 2013).

Newbould, Ian, *Whiggery and Reform 1830–41: The Politics of Government* (Basingstoke: Palgrave Macmillan, 1990).

Nigam, Sanjay, 'Disciplining and Policing the "Criminals by Birth", Part 1: The Making of a Colonial Stereotype—The Criminal Tribes and Castes of North India', *Indian Economic and Social History Review* 27, no. 2 (1990): 131–64.

Nightingale, Pamela, *Trade and Empire in Western India, 1784–1806* (Cambridge: Cambridge University Press, 1970).

Noorani, A. G., *Indian Political Trials 1775–1947* (Oxford: Oxford University Press, 2005).

O'Neill, Daniel, *Edmund Burke and the Conservative Logic of Empire* (Berkeley, CA: University of California Press, 2016).

Pal, Dharm, *Administration of Sir John Lawrence in India (1864–1869)* (Simla: Minerva, 1952).

Palsetia, Jesse S., *The Parsis of India: Preservation of Identity in Bombay City* (Leiden: Brill, 2001).

Palsetia, Jesse S., 'Mad Dogs and Parsis: The Bombay Dog Riots of 1832', *Journal of the Royal Asiatic Society of Great Britain and Ireland* 11, no. 1 (2001): 13–30.

Panigrahi, D. N., *Charles Metcalfe in India: Ideas and Administration 1806–1835* (Delhi: Munshiram Manoharlal, 1968).

Peabody, Norbert, *Hindu Kinship and Polity in Precolonial India* (Cambridge: Cambridge University Press, 2006).

Peers, Douglas M., *Between Mars and Mammon: Colonial Armies and the Garrison State in India 1819–1835* (London: Tauris, 1995).

Philips, C. H., *The East India Company 1784–1834* (Manchester: Manchester University Press, 1961).

Philips, Jim, 'A Successor to the Moguls: The Nawab of the Carnatic and the East India Company, 1763–1785', *International History Review* 7, no. 3 (1985): 364–89.

Pitts, Jennifer, *A Turn to Empire: The Rise of Imperial Liberalism in Britain and France* (Princeton, NJ: Princeton University Press, 2005).

Pitts, Jennifer, *Boundaries of the International: Law and Empire* (Cambridge, MA: Harvard University Press, 2018).

Poole, Thomas, *Reason of State: Law, Prerogative and Empire* (Cambridge: Cambridge University Press, 2015).

Prasad, A. K., *The Bhils of Khandesh: Under the British East India Company (1818–1858)* (Delhi: Konark Publishers, 1991).

Prasad, S. N., *Paramountcy under Dalhousie. Being a Thesis on the Policy of Dalhousie Towards the Protected Indian States* (Delhi: Ranjit, 1964).

Premo, Bianca. *The Enlightenment on Trial: Ordinary Litigants and Colonialism in the Spanish Empire* (New York, NY: Oxford University Press, 2017).

Preston, Laurence W., *The Dev of Cincvad: A Lineage and the State in Maharashtra* (Cambridge: Cambridge University Press, 1989).

Price, Pamela G., 'The "Popularity" of the Imperial Courts of Law: Three Views of the Anglo–Indian Legal Encounter', in W. J. Mommsen and J. A. De Moor, eds., *European Expansion and Law: The Encounter of European and Indigenous Law in 19th- and 20th-Century African and Asia* (Oxford: Oxford University Press, 1992), 179–200.

Price, Pamela, *Kingship and Political Practice in Colonial India* (Cambridge: Cambridge University Press, 1996).

Price, Pamela, *The Writings of Pamela Price: State, Politics, and Cultures in Modern South India: Honour, Authority, and Morality* (New Delhi: Orient Black Swan, 2012).

Priolkar, Anant Kakba, *The Printing Press in India: Its Beginnings and Early Development* (Bombay: Marathi Samshodhana Mandala, 1958).

Rajah, Jothie, *Authoritarian Rule of Law: Legislation, Discourse and Legitimacy in Singapore* (Cambridge: Cambridge University Press, 2012).

Raman, Bhavani, 'Law in Times of Counter-Insurgency', in Balachandran. Aparna, Rashmi Pant, and Bhavani Raman, eds., *Iterations of Law: Legal Histories from India* (New Delhi, Oxford University Press, 2018).

Ramanna, Mridula, 'Profiles of English Educated Indians: Early Nineteenth Century Bombay City', *Economic and Political Weekly* 27, no. 14 (1992): 716–21, 723–24.

Ramanna, Mridula, 'Social Background of the Educated in Bombay City 1824–58', *Economic and Political Weekly* 14, no. 4 (1989): 203–05, 207–11.

Ramusack, Barbara, *The Indian Princes and Their States* (Cambridge: Cambridge University Press, 2003).

Rankin, George Claus, *Background to Indian Law* (Cambridge: Cambridge University Press, 1946).

Reinkowski, Maurus, and Gregor Thum, eds., *Helpless Imperialists: Imperial Failure, Fear and Radicalization* (Göttingen: Vandenhoeck and Ruprecht, 2013).

Roberts, David, *Paternalism in Early Victorian England* (London: Groom Helm, 1979).

Robinson, Bruce Frederick, 'Adaptation to Colonial Rule by the "Wild Tribes" of the Bombay Deccan 1818–1880: From Political Competition to Social Banditry' (PhD diss., University of Minnesota, 1978).

Robb, Peter, *Liberalism, Modernity and the Nation* (Oxford: Oxford University Press, 2007).

Robb, Peter, *Peasants, Political Economy, and Law* (Oxford: Oxford University Press, 2007).

Rosselli, John, *Lord William Bentinck: The Making of a Liberal Imperialist 1774–1839* (London: Chatto & Windus, 1974).

Roy, Tirthankar, 'Indigo and Law in colonial India', *Economic History Review* 64, S1 (2011): 60–75.

Roy, Tirthankar, *An Economic History of Early Modern India* (London: Routledge, 2013).

Saha, Jonathan, *Law, Disorder and the Colonial State: Corruption in Burma c.1900* (Basingstoke: Palgrave Macmillan, 2013).

Sarkar, Aditya, *Trouble at the Mill: Factory Law and the Emergence of the Labour Question in Late Nineteenth-Century Bombay* (New Delhi: Oxford University Press, 2018).

Sarkar, Mahua. *Justice in a Gothic Edifice: The Calcutta High Court and Colonial Rule in Bengal.* Calcutta: Firma KLM Private Limited, 1997.

Sartori, Andrew, 'The British Empire and its Liberal Mission', *Journal of Modern History* 78 (2006): 623–42.

Sartori, Andrew, *Liberalism in Empire: An Alternative History* (Berkeley, 2014).

Scott, James C., *Seeing Like a State: How Certain Schemes to Improve the Human Condition Have Failed* (New Haven, CT: Yale University Press, 1998).

Sen, Sudipta, 'Unfinished Conquest: Residual Sovereignty and the Legal Foundations of the British Empire in India', *Law, Culture and the Humanities* 9, no.2 (2012): 227–42.

Sharafi, Mitra, *Law and Identity in Colonial South Asia: Parsi Legal Culture 1772–1847* (Cambridge: Cambridge University Press, 2014).

Sharafi, Mitra, 'South Asian Legal History', *Annual Review of Law and Social Science* 11 (2015): 309–36.

Sharma, G. D., 'Ports of Gujarat in the Nineteenth Century: Trading Networks and Commercial Practices', in Indu Banga, ed., *Ports and Their Hinterlands in India (1700–1950)* (New Delhi: Manohar, 1992), 199–212.

Sharman, J. C., *Empire of the Weak: The Real Story of European Expansion and the Creation of the New World Order* (Princeton, NJ: Princeton University Press, 2019).

Sherman, Taylor C., *State Violence and Punishment in India* (Abington: Routledge, 2010).

Siddique, Osama, *Pakistan's Experience with Formal Law: An Alien Justice* (Cambridge: Cambridge University Press, 2013).

Siddiqui, Asiya. *Bombay's People 1860–98: Insolvents in the City* (New Delhi: Oxford University Press, 2017).

Singh, Meera, *British Revenue and Judicial Policies in India: A Case Study of Deccan 1818–1826* (New Delhi: Har-Anand, 1994).

Singh, Tripurdaman, *Imperial Sovereignty and Local Politics: The Bhadauria Rajputs and the Transition from Mughal to British India, 1600–1900* (Cambridge: Cambridge University Press, 2019).

Singha, Radhika, *A Despotism of Law: Crime and Justice in Early Colonial India* (Oxford: Oxford University Press, 1998).

Sinha, Chittaranjan, *The Indian Civil Judiciary in Making 1800–33* (New Delhi: Munshiram Manoharlal, 1971).

Sinha, Nitin, 'Mobility, Control and Criminality in Early Colonial India 1760s–1850s', *Indian Economic and Social History Review* 45, no. 1 (2008): 1–33.

Skaria, Ajay, *Hybrid Histories: Forests, Frontiers and Wildness in Western India* (Oxford: Oxford University Press, 1999).

Smith, K. J. M., *James Fitzjames Stephen: Portrait of a Victorian Rationalist* (Cambridge: Cambridge University Press, 1988).

Smith, Sheila, 'Fortune and Failure: The Survival of Family Firm in Eighteenth-Century India', *Business History* 35, no. 4 (1993), 44–65.

Sood, Gagan D. S., 'Sovereign Justice in Precolonial Maritime Asia: The Case of Mayor's Court of Bombay 1726–1798', *Itinerario* 37, no. 2 (2013): 46–72.

Sreenivas, Mytheli, *Wives, Widows and Concubines: The Conjugal Family Ideal in Colonial India* (Bloonmington, IN: Indiana University Press, 2008).

Stephens, Julia, 'The Phantom Wahhabi: The Liberalism and the Muslim Fanatic in Mid-Victorian India', *Modern Asian Studies* 47, no.1 (2013): 22–52.

Stein, Burton, *Thomas Munro: The Origins of the Colonial State and His Visions of Empire* (Oxford: Oxford University Press, 1989).

Stern, Philip J., 'Rethinking Institutional Transformations in the Making of Modern Empire: The East India Company in Madras', *Journal of Colonialism and Colonial History* 9, no. 2 (2008).

Stern, Philip J., *The Company-State: Corporate Sovereignty and the Early Modern Foundations of the British Empire in India* (New York: Oxford University Press, 2011).

Stokes, Eric, *The English Utilitarians and India* (Oxford: Oxford University Press, 1959).

Sturman, Rachel L., *The Government of Social Life in Colonial India: Liberalism, Religious Law and Women's Rights* (Cambridge: Cambridge University Press, 2013).

Subramanian, Lakshmi, 'A Trial in Transition: Courts, Merchants and Identities in Western India Circa 1800', *Indian Economic and Social History Review* 41, no. 3 (2004): 269–92.

Subramanian, Lakshmi, *Indigenous Capital and Imperial Expansion: Bombay, Surat and the West Coast* (Delhi: Oxford University Press, 1996).

Subramanian, Lakshmi, 'Seths and Sahibs: Negotiated Relationships between Indigenous Capital and the East India Company', in H. V. Bowen, Elizabeth

Mancke, and John G. Reid, eds., *Britain's Oceanic Empire: Atlantic and Indian Ocean Worlds c. 1550–1850* (Cambridge: Cambridge University Press, 2012), 311–39.

Subramanian, Lakshmi, 'Piracy and Legality in the Northward: Colonial Articulation of Law, Custom and Policy in the Late Eighteenth- and Early Nineteenth-Century Bombay Presidency', *Journal of Colonialism and Colonial History* 15, no. 1 (Jan 2014).

Tamanaha, Brian Z., *On the Rule of Law: History, Politics, Theory* (Cambridge: Cambridge University Press, 2004).

Taylor, Miles, 'Queen Victoria and India 1837–61', *Victorian Studies* 46, no. 2 (2004): 264–74.

Travers, Robert, *Ideology and Empire in Eighteenth Century India: The British in Bengal* (Cambridge: Cambridge University Press, 2007).

Tyler, Amanda L., *Habeas Corpus in Wartime: From the Tower of London to Guantanamo Bay* (Oxford: Oxford University Press, 2017).

Vachha, P. B., *Famous Judges, Lawyers and Cases of Bombay: A Judicial History of Bombay During the British Period* (Bombay: N. M. Tripathi, 1962; 2011).

Viswanathan, Gauri, *Masks of Conquest: Literary Study and British Rule in India* (New York: Columbia University Press, 1989).

Wagner, Kim A., *Thuggee: Banditry and the British in Early Nineteenth-Century India* (Basingstoke: Palgrave Macmillan, 2007).

Wagner, Kim A., *Amritsar 1919: An Empire of Fear and the Making of a Massacre* (New Haven, CT: Yale University Press, 2019).

Washbrook, David, *The Emergence of Provincial Politics: The Madras Presidency 1870–1920* (Cambridge: Cambridge University Press, 1976).

Washbrook, D. A., 'Law, State and Agrarian Society in Colonial India', *Modern Asian Studies* 15, no. 3 (1981): 649–721.

Washbrook, David, 'Economic Depression and the Making of "Traditional" Society in Colonial India 1820–1855', *Transactions of the Royal Historical Society*, Sixth Series, 3 (1993): 237–63.

Washbrook, D. A., 'India 1818–1860: The Two Faces of Colonialism', in Andrew Porter, ed., *The Oxford History of the British Empire Volume III: The Nineteenth Century* (Oxford: Oxford University Press, 1999), 395–421.

Whelan, Frederick G., 'Burke on India', in David Dwan and Christopher Insole, eds., *Cambridge Companion to Edmund Burke* (Cambridge, 2012), 172–76.

Wiener, Martin J. *An Empire on Trial: Race, Murder and Justice under British Rule 1870–1935* (Cambridge: Cambridge University Press, 2009).

Wilson, Jon E., *The Domination of Strangers: Modern Governance in Eastern India 1780–1835* (Basingstoke: Palgrave Macmillan, 2008).

Wilson, Jon, 'The Silence of Empire: Imperialism and India', in David Craig and James Thompson, eds., *Languages of Politics in Nineteenth-Century Britain* (Basingstoke: Palgrave Macmillan, 2013), 218–41.

Wilson, Jon, *India Conquered: Britain's Raj and the Chaos of Empire* (London: Simon and Schuster, 2016).

Wilson, Jon, 'The Temperament of Empire: Law and Conquest in Late Nineteenth Century India', in Gunnel Cederlof and Sanjukta Das Gupta, eds., *Subject, Citizens and Law: Colonial and Independent India* (London: Routledge, 2017).

Wink, André, *Land and Sovereignty in India: Agrarian Society and Politics in Eighteenth-Century Martha Svarajya* (Cambridge: Cambridge University Press, 1986).

Yahaya, Nurfadzilah, *Fluid Jurisdictions: Colonial Law and Arabs in Southeast Asia* (Ithaka, NY: Cornell University Press, 2020).

Zastoupil, Lynn, *John Stuart Mill and India* (Stanford, CA: Stanford University Press, 1994).

Zastoupil, Lynn, *Rammohun Roy and the Making of Victorian Britain* (Basingstoke: Palgrave Macmillan, 2010).

Index[1]

[1] Note: Page numbers followed by 'n' refer to notes.

H. Inagaki, *The Rule of Law and Emergency in Colonial India*, Cambridge Imperial and Post-Colonial Studies,
https://doi.org/10.1007/978-3-030-73663-7

The manufacturer's authorised representative in the EU is Springer Nature Customer Service Centre GmbH, Europaplatz 3, 69115 Heidelberg, Germany. If you have any concerns regarding our products, please contact ProductSafety@springernature.com

Printed and bound by CPI Group (UK) Ltd, Croydon, CR0 4YY
30/09/2026
02225450-0003